柬埔寨王国刑法典

夏 勇　尉立坤 **译**

中国·武汉

图书在版编目(CIP)数据

柬埔寨王国刑法典/夏勇,尉立坤译. —武汉:华中科技大学出版社,2023.4
 ISBN 978-7-5680-9082-7

Ⅰ.①柬… Ⅱ.①夏… ②尉… Ⅲ.①刑法-法典-柬埔寨 Ⅳ.①D933.54

中国国家版本馆 CIP 数据核字(2023)第 047363 号

柬埔寨王国刑法典 夏 勇 尉立坤 译
Jianpuzhai Wangguo Xingfadian

策划编辑:郭善珊
责任编辑:张 丛
封面设计:沈仙卫
责任校对:李 弋
责任监印:朱 玢
出版发行:华中科技大学出版社(中国•武汉)　电话:(027)81321913
　　　　　武汉市东湖新技术开发区华工科技园　邮编:430223
录　　排:华中科技大学出版社美编室
印　　刷:湖北新华印务有限公司
开　　本:880mm×1230mm　1/16
印　　张:16.5
字　　数:328 千字
版　　次:2023 年 4 月第 1 版第 1 次印刷
定　　价:68.00 元

本书若有印装质量问题,请向出版社营销中心调换
全国免费服务热线:400-6679-118　竭诚为您服务
版权所有　侵权必究

译者序

柬埔寨刑法简介

一

柬埔寨(Cambodia),全称柬埔寨王国(The Kingdom of Cambodia),地处东南亚,位于中南半岛西南,东部及东南部与越南接壤,东北部与老挝交界,西部及西北部与泰国毗邻,南部面向泰国湾,国土面积约 18 万平方公里,总人口约 1700 万。柬埔寨行政区划包括 24 省和首都金边市。柬埔寨古称高棉,历史悠久,公元 1 世纪就建立了统一王国,9 至 14 世纪的吴哥王朝为鼎盛时期,创造了辉煌的吴哥文明,13 世纪中叶起至 1434 年因泰国的素可泰王朝入侵而衰落。16 和 17 世纪,柬埔寨曾先后成功抵御西班牙和荷兰两国势力的介入,之后发生内战,同时不断遭受邻国入侵。1863年,柬埔寨寻求法国保护,成为殖民地。1940年,柬埔寨被日本占领,1945年日本投降,柬埔寨再次受法国统治。经过柬埔寨人民的长期斗争,在诺罗敦·西哈努克亲王的不懈努力下,柬埔寨终于在1953年11月9日获得完全独立,建立了柬埔寨王国。20世纪70年代开始,柬埔寨经历了不断的战乱、政权更迭及对峙。1991年10月柬埔寨问题国际会议在巴黎召开并签署《柬埔寨冲突全面政治解决协定》。经过一年多过渡,在联合国驻柬埔寨临时权力机构的组织和监督下,柬埔寨举行大选,产生制宪会议(1993年5月),通过新宪法,恢复君主立宪制,制宪会议转为国民议会(1993年9月),重新成立柬埔寨王国政府,联合国维和部队全部撤离(1993年11月)。总体上,柬埔寨终于逐渐进入和平重建民族和解历史新时期。经过近20多年的恢复建设,柬埔寨经济社会获得良好发展,2016年7月,世界银行宣布柬埔寨正式脱离最不发达行列,成为中等偏下收入国家。

二

柬埔寨刑法的发展沿革与其国家历史相对应。在1863年成为法国"保护国"之前,柬埔寨主要实行包括刑法在内的习惯法。法国殖民时期,柬埔寨刑法逐步向成文法发展。1810年《法国刑法典》不仅得以在柬埔寨实施,而且还直接成为1929年柬埔寨刑法典的蓝本。独立后的柬埔寨仍然沿用1929年刑法典,主要部分保持不变,仅1959年有些许修正。1979年越南入侵,建立亲越政权,开始颁布一些刑事法律规范。1980年2号法令规定对叛国、间谍、谋杀、盗取私有财产等重罪的处罚。其中,对叛国、反人类、奸杀等犯罪,可以适用死刑。1986年27号法令主要规定刑事司法程序,其中第6部分规定了妨碍或者违反程序构成犯罪的法律后果——有的依照刑法予以处罚,有的依照该法令规定的刑罚论处。不过,越南扶持的政权及法律并未得到国际社会广泛承认。

1992年,联合国驻柬埔寨临时权力机构制定了《关于柬埔寨在过渡时期适用的司法和刑法及程序的规定》,其中第4、5、6三个部分即为"刑法",规定犯罪与刑罚的相关内容,为过渡时期的柬埔寨社会编织了刑事法网,起到临时刑法典作用,被称为"联合国驻柬埔寨临时权力机构刑法",也被称为"过渡刑法"。

"过渡刑法"第4部分规定重罪罪名及刑罚,主要有:(1)谋杀罪,可处以10至20年监禁。(2)其他蓄意杀人罪,可处以8至15年监禁。(3)强奸罪,可处以5至10年监禁或者10至15年监禁。(4)抢劫罪,可处以3至10年监禁。(5)非法拘禁罪,可处以3至5年监禁或者10年监禁。(6)有组织犯罪,可处以3至15年监禁。(7)公职人员贪污罪,可处以3至10年监禁,并处贪污财产价值2倍的罚金。(8)公职人员敲诈勒索罪,可处以3至7年监禁,并处敲诈勒索财产价值2倍的罚金。(9)非法交易买卖毒品罪,可处以5至15年监禁,等等。

"过渡刑法"第5部分规定轻罪罪名及刑罚,主要有:(1)疏失致死罪,可处以1至3年监禁。(2)暴力侵犯人身罪,根据程度不同,可处以1至5年监禁、6个月至2年监禁、2个月至1年监禁,使用武器的监禁期翻倍。(3)强制猥亵罪,可处以1至3年监禁,伴有暴力、诈骗、威胁的,或者利用职务便利的,或者被害人不满16岁的,刑期翻倍,以卖淫为目的或者利用未成年人卖淫的,处以2至6年监禁。(4)盗窃罪,处以6个月至5年监禁。(5)涉及文化财产的轻罪,处以6个月至10年监禁。(6)诈骗罪,处以1至5年监禁。(7)侵占罪,处以1至5年监禁。(8)伪造公章、钞票、公文、邮票和商标罪,处以5至15年监禁。(9)伪造或者有意使用私人商业或者银行文件罪,处以5年监禁或者100万至1000万瑞尔的罚金。(10)收买或者隐匿赃物罪,处以1至5年监禁。(11)蓄意损毁罪,根据程度不同处以1至3年监禁或者2个月至1年监禁。(12)纵火罪,处以1至3年监禁,对他人住所纵火,刑期翻倍。(13)胁迫证人罪,处以1至2年监禁。(14)伪证罪,处以1至2年监禁。(15)贿赂罪,处以1至3年监禁。(16)煽动犯罪罪,处以1至5年监禁,等等。

"过渡刑法"第6部分规定刑罚原则和制度,包括刑罚平等、废除死刑、未成年人减轻情节和免除处罚、共同犯罪、缓刑、假释、罚金缴纳,等等。

除了《关于柬埔寨在过渡时期适用的司法和刑法及程序的规定》,临时权力机构还制定了一些特别刑法文件,以打击特定领域的刑事犯罪。例如,(1)1996年1月26日通过的《禁止赌博法》规定,非经政府允许,柬埔寨境内所有赌博活动均属违法;任何参与赌博者,处以1万至5万瑞尔的罚金或者处以1周至1个月监禁,屡教不改者,处以5万至50万瑞尔的罚金,并处

1个月至1年监禁;开设、拥有或者管理赌场、赌馆或者充当赌博代理人,处以500万至2000万瑞尔的罚金,并处1年至5年监禁,屡教不改者,处以最高金额和刑期;未经政府批准,为牟利而生产、进口赌具或者赌博设备,处以50万至500万瑞尔的罚金,并处1个月至1年监禁,屡教不改者,处以最高金额和刑期;未经批准开设赌场或者赌馆的政府官员或者代理人,处以1年至5年监禁。(2)1996年2月29日通过的《打击拐骗、买卖和剥削人口法》规定,拐骗、买卖人口或者卖淫罪,处以10至15年监禁,被害人是不满15岁未成年人,处以15至20年监禁;组织卖淫罪,处以5至10年监禁,重复犯罪者加倍处罚,如果被害人为不满15岁未成年人、使用暴力或者威胁、组织被害人到国外卖淫或者向外国人卖淫、行为人与被害人具有亲密关系,处以10至20年监禁;淫乱罪和组织淫乱者,处以1至5年监禁,并处500万至3000万瑞尔的罚金,重复犯罪者加倍处罚,与未满15岁未成年人发生淫乱行为者,处以10至20年监禁。(3)1997年1月24日通过的《毒品控制法》严厉禁止麻醉植物的种植和毒品的生产、使用、销售、走私,界定了麻醉、精神物质的分类及法律性质,规定了查处方式和刑罚后果,对相关洗钱活动的预防和查处,等等。

"过渡刑法"适用过程中,柬埔寨王国有关部门积极起草正式刑法典,为过渡时期的结束做准备。2000年9月,柬埔寨王国司法部下设刑法起草委员会在法国顾问帮助下完成最初草案。同时,前司法部顾问毛巴斯也在1956年刑法基础上完成修正草案。两个文本融合形成统一草案。2003年将草案呈送内阁会议,未获认可。起草委员会继而拟定草案第2稿,但政府于2005年暂停批准该草案。直到2009年6月19日,内阁会议讨论并通过刑法典草案并于10月1日提交议会。10月12日,草案获得通过,11月17日又在参议院获得通过。11月30日,《柬埔寨王国刑法典》正式发布并于2010年12月生效。2018年2月27日,柬埔寨王国立法机构发布了刑法典修正案,增加第437条之一"侮辱国王罪"。

现行柬埔寨刑法的渊源,除了刑法典,还有宪法、国民议会和参议院表决通过并由国王签署批准的国际条约和公约、有效的单行刑事法律和其他法律中的刑事规定,以及必要时由行政部门发布的规定仅能处以罚金的轻微犯罪的规范性文件。其中《ECCC法》[①]亦可视为柬埔寨刑法的重要渊源。

根据《ECCC法》,特别法庭有权审判所有被指控在1975年4月17日至1979年1月6日期间犯有下列罪行的被告人:(1)1956年柬埔寨刑法典规定的凶杀、酷刑、宗教迫害的犯罪。对这些罪行,1956年刑法典规定的时效可延长20年。修改后的《ECCC法》将此时效变更为30年。(2)1948年《防止及惩治灭绝种族罪公约》所界定的灭绝种族罪。该罪不存在诉讼时效。(3)危害人类罪。该罪不存在诉讼时效。(4)严重违反1949年8月12日《日内瓦公约》的犯罪。(5)违反《关于在发生

---

① 全称《柬埔寨法院设立特别法庭以起诉民主柬埔寨时期所犯罪行的法律》(Law on the Establishment of Extraordinary Chambers in The Courts of Cambodia for the Prosecution of Crimes Committed During the Period of Democratic Kampuchea)。——译者注

武装冲突时保护文化财产的海牙公约》的犯罪。（6）违反1961年《维也纳外交关系公约》的犯罪。

三

《柬埔寨王国刑法典》共有6编50章672条。① 从各编的功能区分来看，第1编是总则性条文，第2编至第4编是分则性条文，第5编和第6编属于附则性条文。

第1编"一般规定"包括三个部分共14章182条。第1部分"刑法"有3章23条，主要规定刑法的一般准则、时间效力和空间效力。第2部分"刑事责任"有4章19条，主要是一般规定、责任减免、未成年人刑事责任、法人刑事责任。第3部分"刑罚"有7章140条，主要规定刑种、加重和减轻情节、量刑原则、并发犯罪、刑罚执行、未成年人刑罚适用、法人的刑罚。

第2编"侵犯人身的犯罪"包括三个部分共15章170条。第1部分规定几种国际公认的大规模严重危害人身的犯罪及刑罚，包括灭绝种族罪、危害人类罪和战争罪，共有3章16条。第2部分规定针对特定个体的侵犯人身犯罪及刑罚，包括杀人罪、侵犯人身完整性的犯罪、性侵罪、非法剥夺自由的犯罪、亵渎人格尊严的犯罪、侵犯个人自由的犯罪，共有6章122条。第3部分规定侵害未成年人和亲属的犯罪及刑罚，包括遗弃未成年人的犯罪、遗弃亲属的犯罪、干扰对未成年人监护的犯罪、侵

---

① 不含2009年刑法修正案增加的第437条之二。——译者注

犯亲属关系的犯罪、伤害未成年人的犯罪以及其他侵害亲属的犯罪，共有 6 章 32 条。

第 3 编"侵犯财产的犯罪"包括两个部分共 6 章 80 条。第 1 部分规定诈取财产的犯罪及刑罚，包括窃取及相关犯罪、诈骗及相关犯罪、违反诚信及相关犯罪、衍生的财产犯罪，共有 4 章 57 条。第 2 部分规定毁损财产的犯罪及刑罚，包括破坏、污损和损坏财产的犯罪、与信息技术有关的犯罪，共有 2 章 23 条。

第 4 编"危害国家的犯罪"包括四个部分共 13 章 235 条。[①]第 1 部分规定侵犯重要国家机构的犯罪及刑罚，包括侵犯国王的犯罪、危害国家安全的犯罪、危害公共安全的犯罪、危害国家权力的犯罪、侵犯国教的犯罪，共有 5 章 84 条。[②]第 2 部分规定侵犯司法的犯罪及刑罚，包括危害司法制度的犯罪、侵犯司法程序的犯罪、有关羁押的犯罪、不服从某些司法判决的犯罪，共有 4 章 69 条。第 3 部分规定侵害行政管理的犯罪及刑罚，包括公共代表侵害行政管理的犯罪、个人侵犯行政管理的犯罪，共有 2 章 40 条。第 4 部分规定了损害公众信心的犯罪及刑罚，包括伪造罪、伪造政府机关文件的犯罪，共有 2 章 42 条。

第 5 编"衔接性规定"仅 1 章 3 条，主要规定刑法典与其他刑事立法之间的适用关系。

第 6 编"生效规定"仅 1 章 2 条，主要规定刑法典的生效适用及其与此前刑事立法之间的效力关系。

---

① 不含 2009 年刑法修正案增加的第 437 条之二。——译者注
② 不含 2009 年刑法修正案增加的第 437 条之二。——译者注

四

从《柬埔寨王国刑法典》内容来看，主要有以下几个特点：

1. 较为严格和充分的罪刑法定主义

《柬埔寨王国刑法典》第3条明确规定"法定主义原则"："只有在发生之时构成犯罪的行为才能被定罪。只有在犯罪之时合法适当的刑罚才能被适用。"这显然就是"法无明文不为罪和法无明文不处罚"的罪刑法定原则。该原则在刑法典条文中得到较为充分的体现。

（1）清楚规定犯罪概念的内涵与外延。《柬埔寨王国刑法典》第2条第1款："本法规定，犯罪是由自然人或者法人实施的引起社会混乱的特定行为。"也就是说，《柬埔寨王国刑法典》所称犯罪，必须是"本法规定"的行为，而"引起社会混乱"明显是对犯罪实质的规定。联系起来看，这是一个形式与实质相结合的犯罪概念。其内在关系是：一方面，不能"引起社会混乱"的行为，"本法"不会将其"规定"为犯罪——体现的是犯罪实质对立法的制约；另一方面，只有"本法规定"的"引起社会混乱"的行为才是犯罪，才能予以追究和处罚——体现的是法律形式对司法的制约。这正是罪刑法定的基本意蕴。

总之，"本法"只将"特定行为"规定为犯罪，那些虽然"引起社会混乱"却在"本法"中无明文规定的行为，不是犯罪。同时，法定原则并未局限于"本法"，而是通过第5编的衔接性规定以及第1编第1条等规定，将"法定"的范围延伸到所有的"其他有效刑事法律和刑事条款规定的犯罪"。

（2）犯罪分类的标准同样是实质与形式相结合。《柬埔寨王国刑法典》第2条第2款规定："根据严重程度，犯罪可以分为重罪、轻罪和轻微罪。"这里的"根据严重程度"显然是实质标准，但只是立法标准而非司法标准。司法者不能根据抽象观念把握犯罪严重程度和区分重罪、轻罪和轻微罪。从法定原则出发，《柬埔寨王国刑法典》为司法提供了把握犯罪类别的形式标准。第46条"重罪的定义"规定"重罪是可以被判处以下最高监禁刑期的犯罪：（一）终身监禁；（二）五年以上三十年以下监禁。罚金刑可以与监禁刑并处。"第47条"轻罪的定义"规定"轻罪是可以被判处六天以上五年以下监禁刑期的犯罪。罚金刑可以与监禁刑并处。"第48条"轻微罪的定义"规定"轻微罪是下列犯罪：（一）可以被判处六天以下监禁刑期的犯罪。罚金刑可以与监禁刑并处。（二）只能处以罚金的犯罪。"刑事司法只能通过法定的刑罚后果判断犯罪是重罪、轻罪还是轻微罪。

（3）分则性条文明确规定具体犯罪及相应刑罚。分则性条文以明确的罪名及描述将犯罪概念具体化，且不存在"兜底"条款，对犯罪表现出较严格的"法定"要求。分则性条文在每个罪名之后明确规定具体刑罚后果及轻重情节，不仅是对刑罚的"法定"要求，而且也为犯罪分类提供了"法定"具体标准。

此外，总则性条文还有一些直接体现"法定"的条款，例如，第42条"依照法律和法规性文件的明文规定，法人的机构或者代表人以法人的名义实施犯罪的，法人可以承担刑事责任，但国家除外。"第5条"在刑事领域，应当严格解释法律。法官既不能扩大其适用范围,也不能类推解释。"第 10 条"规定了较重刑罚的新条款仅适用于新条款生效后实施的行为。"第 54 条"只有被起诉的重罪、轻罪或者轻微罪明确规定了附加刑,才能予以宣告。"

2. 个人权利与国家权力两极保护的罪名体系

《柬埔寨王国刑法典》第 2、3、4 编的分则性条文筑造起罪名体系的基本结构。第 2 编"侵犯人身的犯罪"和第 3 编"侵犯财产的犯罪"都是侵害权利法益的犯罪,即分别是侵害个人的人身权利和财产权利的犯罪,与此对应,对这两编规定的犯罪进行惩处,旨在保护个人的人身权利和财产权利。第 4 编"危害国家的犯罪"是侵害权力法益的犯罪,即对国家执掌的公权力的犯罪,与此对应,对该编规定的犯罪进行惩处,旨在保护国家权力。这样一来,《柬埔寨王国刑法典》设置的三大类犯罪便一分为二,形成个人权利与国家权力的两极保护。在此基础上从不同角度再对个人权利与国家权力细分,生发出一系列具体犯罪组成的罪名体系。

具体而言,"侵犯人身的犯罪"因人身权利的细分,区分为侵犯一般对象人身权利的犯罪与侵犯特殊对象人身权利的犯罪。特殊对象即是未成年人和亲属,此外便是一般对象。就对象而言,又有群体与个体之分。所谓群体即是国家、民族、种族或者宗教团体。无论何种对象,犯罪所侵犯的人身权利内容还可细分为生命权利、身体完整性(身体健康和健全)权利、性自主权利、身体自由权利、人格尊严权利、隐私权利、名誉和荣誉权利等,侵犯这些不同内容的人身权利,便会形成不同罪名。"侵犯财产的犯罪"虽然也有一些显现对财产权利内容进行区分的罪名,例如,妨碍投标自由罪侵犯的是财产处分权利,挪用查封或者担保品罪侵犯的是财产占有权利,蓄意损坏财产罪侵犯的是财产所有权利,但是,侵犯财产的犯罪分类角度并非财产所有、占有、使用、收益、处分等财产权利内容,而是对这些权利内容进行侵犯的行为方式。也就是说,"侵犯财产的犯罪"主要是因侵犯行为的方式来设置罪名的,而不论侵犯的财产权利内容是什么。

"危害国家的犯罪"以双重角度的结合设置罪名。这两个角度分别是:其一,国家权力内容的区分;其二,侵犯国家权力危害后果的区分。"危害国家的犯罪"有四个大类:① 侵犯重要国家机构的犯罪;② 侵犯司法的犯罪;③ 侵犯行政管理的犯罪;④ 损害公众信心的犯罪。其中,第 2 类和第 3 类犯罪是按照国家权力内容的不同来区分的,分别侵犯的是国家司法权力和国家行政权力。第 1 类和第 4 类犯罪则是按照侵犯国家权力的危害后果来区分的,分别威胁到国家政权的存在和国家权力运行的民众基础。

将柬埔寨刑法的罪名体系与我国刑法典分则罪类加以对照,不难发现,许多相当于我国刑法中"秩序"类犯罪的罪名,在柬埔寨刑法中被分别归入了侵犯个人权利的犯罪与侵犯国家权力的犯罪。

我国刑法典分则的十大类犯罪,专门针对个人权利的有两章,即第 4 章"侵犯公民人身权利、民主权利罪"和第 5 章"侵犯财产罪";专门针对国家权力的有五章,即第 1 章"危害国家安全罪"、第 7 章"危害国防利益罪"、第 8 章"贪污贿赂罪"、第 9 章

"渎职罪"、第 10 章"军人违反职责罪";其余三章是专门针对"秩序"的犯罪,即第 2 章"危害公共安全罪"、第 3 章"破坏社会主义市场经济秩序罪"、第 6 章"妨害社会管理秩序罪"。专门规定"秩序"类犯罪是因为:一方面,这类犯罪侵犯的法益往往具有多样性、综合性、不确定性,很难将其侵犯的法益定位于个人权利或者国家权力。具体而言,同一个犯罪(例如爆炸罪),既可能侵犯个人权利也可能侵犯国家权力(例如在商场里实施爆炸或者对公安派出所实施爆炸),既可能侵犯人身权利也可能侵犯财产权利(例如对野外景点的游客实施爆炸或者对企业仓库实施爆炸),既可能同时侵犯人身权利、财产权利和国家权力(例如在政务便民大厅制造爆炸),也可能只侵犯其中的一种法益(仅对游客爆炸或者仅对仓库爆炸或者仅对派出所爆炸)。另一方面,这类犯罪在不确定地侵犯到人身权利、财产权利、国家权力的同时,必定侵犯到了"秩序","市场经济秩序"和"社会管理秩序",自不待言,"公共安全"也是秩序——安全是公众生活秩序和工作秩序最低限度的正常状态和基本要求。我国刑法正是从保护法益的确定性着眼,规定了侵犯"秩序"犯罪类别。

比较起来,《柬埔寨王国刑法典》并不把"秩序"法益作为犯罪大类的归属依据,而是将实际存在的"秩序"类犯罪分别归入侵犯个人权利的犯罪与侵犯国家权力的犯罪。例如,将劫持交通工具罪(危害公共安全)作为剥夺个人自由的犯罪,将损害尸体完整性罪(妨害管理秩序)、容留卖淫活动或者提供卖淫场所的犯罪(妨害管理秩序)作为亵渎人格尊严的犯罪,从而将这些犯罪归入了"侵犯人身的犯罪"。再例如,将不当投标罪或者妨碍投标自由罪等(破坏经济秩序)作为"类似诈骗的犯罪",将擅自进入或者停留于自动数据处理系统罪、擅自输入、删除或者修改数据罪等"与信息技术有关的犯罪"(妨害管理秩序)以及收赃罪(妨害管理秩序)、洗钱罪(破坏经济秩序)等,都纳入"侵犯财产的犯罪"。又例如,将生产或者贩运武器、爆炸物和弹药和未经批准持有或者运输武器等犯罪(危害公共安全)、拒不执行司法判决、隐藏证据、破坏现场、拒不出庭、为犯罪人提供帮助、伪证、脱逃、伪造公文等犯罪(妨害管理秩序)、伪造法定流通货币、流通伪造的货币和钞票、储存伪造的货币或者钞票、非法持有制造货币或者钞票的设备、伪造柬埔寨王国债券、伪造外国债券、使用伪造的债券等犯罪(破坏经济秩序)作为"危害国家的犯罪"。

3. 轻重有度和惩防并举的刑罚制度

《柬埔寨王国刑法典》规定的刑罚制度主要体现为总则性条文中的刑罚种类、替代措施、一般量刑情节、刑罚执行制度以及分则性条文中的具体法定刑和量刑情节。这些规定具体细密,范围清晰,轻重分明,总体宽缓。

(1)刑罚种类。与当代大多数国家一样,《柬埔寨王国刑法典》将自由刑和财产刑作为基本的刑罚种类,没有生命刑。如前所述,越南扶持的政权曾通过法令对某些严重犯罪适用死刑,但未获得国际社会的广泛承认,也未获得之后主权独立的柬埔寨政府的承认。《柬埔寨王国刑法典》没有规定死刑。据报道,2019年柬埔寨首相洪森慰问孤儿时表示,性侵或强奸子女、孙子或侄子的罪犯是禽兽不如的"魔鬼",应受最严厉惩罚,希望通过修改宪法,对强奸犯判处死刑。①但面对各界异议,洪森首相及时澄清:柬埔寨还是不适合死刑。"柬埔寨自古以来都没有动用死刑。""若动用死刑,一旦误判就不可挽回。因此,不必要修改宪法对强奸自己子女或孙子的罪犯处以死刑。"应当通过宣传教育和加强执行法律来杜绝强奸儿童事件。②

《柬埔寨王国刑法典》规定的主刑只有两种:监禁刑和罚金刑。监禁刑包括终身监禁和监禁。终身监禁是最重刑罚,仅适用于部分重罪。第 44 条第 1 款规定,"如果犯罪的刑罚是监禁,法律应当设定可以判处的最短和最长刑期。"即监禁刑期由上限与下限共同设定。犯罪种类不同,上限和下限也不同:重罪可以判处 5 年以上 30 年以下监禁;轻罪可以判处 6 天以上 5 年以下监禁;轻微罪可以判处 6 天以下监禁,或者只处以罚金。可见,一方面,虽然没有死刑,但针对重罪的生刑不轻,不仅有终身监禁,而且监禁刑期的上限较高。轻罪监禁刑期的上限也不低。另一方面,轻罪监禁刑期的下限与轻微罪监禁刑期的上限相衔接,以数天为限。刑法典第 44 条第 2 款规定:"如果犯罪的刑罚是罚金,法律应当设定可以判处的最小和最大数额。"不过,关于罚金数额的上限与下限,总则性

---

① Ben Sokhean, *Hun Sen mulls death penalty for child rapists*, Khmer Times(Mar. 11,2019), https://www.khmertimeskh.com/50585534/hun-sen-mulls-death-penalty-for-child-rapists/

② Nat Sopheap, *Hun Sen Decides Against Death Penalty for Incest Child Rape*, Vodkhmer.news(Mar. 11,2019), https://vodenglish.news/hun-sen-decides-against-death-penalty-for-child-rape/

条文并没有直接作出一般性规定,而是在分则性条文中针对特定犯罪予以具体规定。分则性条文对罚金(瑞尔)额度档次的设定主要是:① 重罪。自然人不适用罚金。对法人罚金有三个档次,最低额度 1000 万,最高额度 2 亿。② 轻罪。法人没有轻微罪。对自然人罚金有 15 个档次,最低额度 1 万,最高额度 2000 万;对法人罚金有 5 个档次,最低额度 100 万,最高额度 1 亿。③ 轻微罪。对自然人罚金有 5 个档次,最低额度 1000,最高额度 1000 万。

《柬埔寨王国刑法典》第 45 条规定,"监禁刑和罚金刑的下限和上限,可以根据本法的规定予以增减。"根据第 97 条,对于两种主刑,既可以仅适用监禁刑,也可以仅适用罚金刑,还可以同时适用监禁刑与罚金刑。

与很少的主刑种类形成鲜明对照的是,《柬埔寨王国刑法典》规定的附加刑种类达 19 种之多,涉及对权利、资格、自由、财产和名誉的剥夺或者限制。例如,剥夺选举权和被选举权以及担任公务员的权利,禁止从事与犯罪有关的职业,禁止离境,没收机动车,在印刷媒体上公布量刑结果,等等。此外,根据第 53 条第 2 款,还可以通过特别条款规定其他附加刑。多种附加刑的好处在于,可以根据犯罪及犯罪人的具体情况,着眼于惩治和预防,有针对性地选择适当的剥夺和限制措施。不过,将"没收犯罪所得的收益或者财产"作为附加刑,与我国关于刑罚与财产的观念不相吻合——刑罚应当针对合法财产,没收非法所得不具有刑罚性质。当然,"没收用于或者意图用于实施犯罪的任何工具、材料或者物品"、"没收涉及犯罪的物品或者资金"、"没收犯罪发生场所的器具、材料和家具"等附加刑规定,对于我国刑事司法如何合理处置这些财产,还是很有启发意义的。

(2)刑罚替代。这是《柬埔寨王国刑法典》规定的一种尽量使刑罚适用轻缓的制度,即在一定情况下,对被告人的处刑,可以用非刑罚措施替代刑罚或者用较轻的刑种替代较重的刑种——前者即为"刑罚替代措施",后者则为"附加刑替代主刑"。

刑罚替代措施包括"社区服务"和"斥责"。其一,社区服务。根据第72条,社区服务是为国家、地方当局或者公共机构、协会或者非政府团体提供30至200小时无偿服务的一项义务。如果被告人可被判处的监禁刑期最高为三年或者以上,法院可以对罪犯下达社区服务令。其二,斥责。类同于我国刑法中的训诫。根据第76条,如果满足三个条件,法庭可以对最高监禁期为三年或者以上的被告人予以斥责。三个条件是:① 犯罪引起的社会混乱已经平息;② 损害已经得到修复;③ 被告人为其重归社会提供了保证。关于刑罚替代措施的性质,第98条很明确:"社区服务可作为主刑的替代措施。一经法庭发出社区服务令,不得再适用监禁刑或者罚金刑。斥责可作为主刑的替代措施。一经法庭发出斥责令,不得再适用监禁刑或者罚金刑。"可见,刑罚替代措施就是替代较重主刑的非刑罚措施。

附加刑替代主刑,不同于适用主刑基础上适用附加刑。关于后者,根据第54条,被起诉的重罪、轻罪或者轻微罪明确规定了附加刑的场合,可以宣告附加刑的适用。根据第71条,适用于监禁刑的附加刑,或者在监禁刑期满后执行,或者与监禁刑同时执行。然而,第100条第2款规定:"如果法庭决定用一项或者多项附加刑替代主刑,则不得适用监禁刑或者罚金刑。"也就是说,附加刑替代主刑,则不再执行主刑。该条还规定了替代条件:"下列情况,法庭可以决定用一项或者多项附加刑替代主刑:(一)如果被告人应当被判处的主刑只能是罚金刑;(二)如果被告人应当被判处的主刑为最高刑期三年或者三年以下监禁刑。"可见,附加刑只能替代较轻的主刑。

(3)量刑情节。《柬埔寨王国刑法典》总则性条文规定了刑罚加重和减轻的一般情节。其中,对若干加重情节给予具体定义,包括有组织的犯罪集团、预谋、强行进入、非法进入、武器和被视为武器的物品、埋伏、累犯。相比之下,第93条规定的"减轻情节的定义"并不具体,只是要求"根据犯罪的性质和被告人的特性,法庭可以确认有利于被告人的减轻情节。"这里反映出现代刑法有利于被告人原则,即对加重被告人刑罚给予具体限制,加重的场合与范围由刑法典直接规定,相反,对减轻被告人刑罚相对开放,减轻的场合与范围不由刑法典规定,交给法庭自行确认,灵活掌握,刑法典仅提供确认的原则。为此,第96条规定:"在判处刑罚时,法庭应当考虑罪行的严重程度和情节,被告人的特性、心理状态、财产、开支和动机,以及犯罪后的表现,特别是针对被害人的表现。"这一取向也体现在分则性条文中。尽管不是所有罪名都有量刑情节的专门规定,但专门规定了量刑情节的罪名,均为"加重情节"。不同的是,对一些犯罪,刑法典用一个分则性条文规定加重情节,对另一些犯罪,刑法典用多个分则性条文规定加重情节。

不过,第 124 条"可以延迟量刑的情形"可以被视为具体减轻情节。该条规定,轻罪案件同时满足下列条件,法庭可以在认定被告人有罪后延迟量刑:① 犯罪导致的社会混乱已经停止;② 被告人为其回归社会提供了保证;③ 被告人请求给予其修复损害的时间。显然,这几项条件表明犯罪造成的危害得到平复且被告人的人身危险性很小,对此,法庭在延迟后的量刑中不可能不加以考虑,意味着这几项条件起到了减轻刑罚的作用。

此外,"未成年人"的身份也是一项具体减轻情节。第 160 条规定:凡未成年人犯罪,"应当对被指控罪行所适用的主刑作如下减轻:(一)所适用的监禁最高刑应当减少二分之一;(二)如果所适用的最高刑是终身监禁,应被减少为二十年监禁;(三)如果所适用的最低刑是超过一天的监禁,应当被减少二分之一;(四)罚金下限和上限减少二分之一;(五)在指控重罪的情况下,如果因本条规定所适用的监禁最高刑减至五年以下,被指控的罪行仍应当是重罪。"

(4)刑罚执行。《柬埔寨王国刑法典》规定的刑罚执行方式包括缓刑、附考验期缓刑、日间释放、分期服刑。

缓刑是指对主刑的暂缓或者延迟执行。对于重罪和轻罪,可以适用缓刑的主刑是 5 年以下监禁刑和罚金刑。如果被告人犯罪之前 5 年内不存在其他有罪判决,可以适用缓刑。针对所判刑罚,既可以全部适用缓刑,也可以部分适用缓刑。适用缓刑后5年内,如果被告人没有因重罪或者轻罪获得新的有效判决,原判刑罚可以不再执行。在这一前提下,如果只是部分所判刑罚适用缓刑,则未适用缓刑的那一部分刑罚也应当被视为没有执行,并且也不再执行。对于轻微罪,可以适用缓刑的是任何监禁刑和罚金刑。如果被告人犯罪之前1年内未发生过判处被告人监禁刑的有罪判决,可适用缓刑。适用缓刑后1年内,如果被告人没有因重罪、轻罪或者轻微罪获得新的有效判决,可以不再执行原判刑罚。

附考验期缓刑是要求犯罪人在缓刑期限内服从缓刑措施以及一项或者多项特定义务。如果本应当判处的监禁刑期是6个月以上5年以下,法庭可以适用缓刑并附1年至3年的考验期。犯罪人在考验期内应当服从的缓刑措施包括:及时接受检察官的传唤和到访,向其提供重归社会的证明或者报告地址、工作的变动以及提交出国申请。可以加予罪犯的特定义务则有10余项,包括不得离职、接受指导或者培训、在特定地点居住、接受体检或者治疗、为家庭开支做贡献、修复犯罪带来的危害、支付因被定罪而欠国家的款项、不得从事有助于实施犯罪的职业或者社会活动、不得出现在被禁止的场合、不得前往经常赌博或者喝酒的场所、不得与犯罪分子或者被害人交往、不得拥有或者携带任何武器、爆炸品或者弹药。对于适用缓刑的罪犯,可以加予这些义务中的一项或者多项。

日间释放即白天不予关押而在夜晚收监的服刑方式。第127条规定:"法庭处以六个月及以下监禁刑,可以决定采取日间释放的方式服刑,以使罪犯能够经营或者从业、参加辅导课程或者职业培训、接受治疗,或者满足其家庭的需要。"第128条规定:"被决定日间释放的罪犯,应当获准在规定时段离开监狱。法庭应当在日间释放决定中设定罪犯被允许离开监狱的天数和时段。"第129条规定:"应当将日间释放所耗时间从正在执行的刑期中扣除。"

分期服刑是不将刑期一次执行完毕,而是分段间隔执行。第132条规定:"法庭处以一年及以下监禁刑,可以出于家庭、医疗、职业或者社会原因,决定分期服刑。"第133条规定:"分期服刑的时段不得少于一个月。包括间隔时间在内,服刑用时总计不得超过二年。法庭的决定应当载明分期服刑的方式。"

此外,《柬埔寨王国刑法典》还规定了赦免和特赦制度,但没有规定减刑和假释。对比《法国刑法典》,柬埔寨刑法中的刑罚执行措施如出一辙,明显受其影响。

五

中国和柬埔寨王国有着悠久的传统友谊。1958年7月两国正式建交。两国在经贸、文化、教育等方面一直保持密切的交往与合作。2010年12月,两国建立全面战略合作伙伴关系。2019年4月,两国签署《构建中柬命运共同体行动计划》。2022年1月1日,两国双边自贸协定正式生效。中柬关系进入新的发展阶段。然而,两国在法律文化上的交流相对薄弱。目前,我国刑法学者已经翻译出版了包括泰国、越南、菲律宾、新加坡等东南亚国家在内的几十个国家的刑法典,柬埔寨刑法的中文译本至今未在国内出版,也鲜见国内学者撰著的相关专著和学术论文。为了填补这方面的空白,我们基于英文版本翻译了《柬埔寨王国刑法典》。

目 录

第一编　一般规定　/1
第一部分　刑法　/3
- 第一章　一般原则　/3
- 第二章　刑法适用的时间效力　/4
- 第三章　柬埔寨刑法适用的空间效力　/5

第二部分　刑事责任　/8
- 第一章　一般规定　/8
- 第二章　刑事责任的免除或者减轻　/10
- 第三章　未成年人的刑事责任　/12
- 第四章　法人的刑事责任　/13

第三部分　刑罚　/14
- 第一章　刑罚的种类　/14
- 第二章　加重和减轻情节　/22
- 第三章　量刑原则　/27
- 第四章　适用于并发犯罪的规则　/35
- 第五章　影响刑罚执行的若干因素　/37
- 第六章　适用于未成年人的刑罚　/40
- 第七章　适用于法人的刑罚　/43

第二编　侵犯人身的犯罪 /49

第一部分　灭绝种族罪，危害人类罪，战争罪 /51

第一章　灭绝种族罪 /51

第二章　危害人类罪 /53

第三章　战争罪 /56

第二部分　侵犯个人的犯罪 /60

第一章　杀人罪 /60

第二章　侵犯人身完整性的犯罪 /64

第三章　性侵罪 /74

第四章　非法剥夺自由的犯罪 /78

第五章　亵渎人格尊严的犯罪 /81

第六章　侵犯个人自由的犯罪 /95

第三部分　侵害未成年人和亲属的犯罪 /102

第一章　遗弃未成年人的犯罪 /102

第二章　遗弃亲属的犯罪 /103

第三章　干扰对未成年人监护的犯罪 /103

第四章　侵犯亲属关系的犯罪 /104

第五章　伤害未成年人的犯罪 /106

第六章　其他侵害亲属的犯罪 /109

第三编　侵犯财产的犯罪 /111

第一部分　诈取财产的犯罪 /113

第一章　窃取及相关犯罪 /113

第二章　诈骗及相关犯罪 /119

第三章　违反诚信及相关犯罪 /124

第四章　衍生的犯罪 /126

第二部分　毁损财产的犯罪　/132
第一章　破坏、污损和损坏财产的犯罪　/132
第二章　与信息技术有关的犯罪　/138

第四编　危害国家的犯罪　/141
第一部分　侵犯重要国家机构的犯罪　/143
第一章　侵害国王的犯罪　/143
第二章　危害国家安全的犯罪　/144
第三章　危害公共安全的犯罪　/156
第四章　危害国家权力的犯罪　/162
第五章　侵犯国教的犯罪　/163

第二部分　侵犯司法的犯罪　/166
第一章　危害司法制度的犯罪　/166
第二章　侵犯司法程序的犯罪　/169
第三章　有关羁押的犯罪　/178
第四章　不服从某些司法判决的犯罪　/183

第三部分　侵害行政管理的犯罪　/185
第一章　公共代表侵害行政管理的犯罪　/185
第二章　个人侵犯行政管理的犯罪　/190

第四部分　损害公众信心的犯罪　/197
第一章　伪造罪　/197
第二章　伪造政府机关文件的犯罪　/204

第五编　衔接性规定　/209
独一章　衔接性规定　/211

第六编　生效规定　/213
独一章　生效规定　/215

BOOK 1　General Provisions　/217

Title 1　The Criminal Law　/219

- Chapter 1　General Principles　/219
- Chapter 2　Temporal Application of Criminal Law　/221
- Chapter 3　Territorial Application of Cambodian Criminal Law　/222

Title 2　Criminal Responsibility　/226

- Chapter 1　General Provisions　/226
- Chapter 2　Exclusion of or Diminished Criminal Responsibility　/229
- Chapter 3　Criminal Responsibility of Minors　/231
- Chapter 4　Criminal Responsibility of Legal Entities　/233

Title 3　Penalties　/234

- Chapter 1　Categories of Penalties　/234
- Chapter 2　Aggravating and Mitigating Circumstances　/245
- Chapter 3　Sentencing Principles　/252
- Chapter 4　Rules Applicable in Case of Concurrent Offences　/263
- Chapter 5　General Factors Relevant to The Enforcement of Penalties　/265
- Chapter 6　Penalties Applicable to Minors　/270
- Chapter 7　Penalties Applicable to Legal Entities　/274

BOOK 2　Crimes Against Persons　/281

Title 1　Genocide, Crimes Against Humanity, War Crimes　/283

- Chapter 1　Genocide　/283
- Chapter 2　Crimes Against Humanity　/286
- Chapter 3　War Crimes　/289

Title 2　Offences Against the Person　/294

- Chapter 1　Homicide　/294

Chapter 2	Violations of Personal Integrity	/299
Chapter 3	Sexual Assaults	/313
Chapter 4	Unlawful Deprivation of Liberty	/318
Chapter 5	Violation of Personal Dignity	/323
Chapter 6	Violations of Personal Liberty	/341

Title 3　Offences Against Minors and The Family　/350

Chapter 1	Abandonment of Minors	/350
Chapter 2	Abandonment of Family	/351
Chapter 3	Interference with The Custody of Minors	/352
Chapter 4	Offences Against Familial Relationships	/353
Chapter 5	Endangerment of Minors	/356
Chapter 6	Other Offences Against the Family	/360

BOOK 3　Offences Against Properties　/361

Title 1　Fraudulent Appropriation　/363

Chapter 1	Theft and Related Offences	/363
Chapter 2	Fraud and Related Offences	/371
Chapter 3	Breach of Trust and Related Offences	/378
Chapter 4	Additional Offences	/381

Title 2　Infringements on Property　/388

Chapter 1	Destruction, Defacement and Damage	/388
Chapter 2	Offences Related to Information Technology	/396

BOOK 4　Offences Against the Nation　/399

Title 1　Infringements Against Major Institutions of State　/401

Chapter 1	Offences Against the King	/401
Chapter 2	Breach of State Security	/403
Chapter 3	Violation of Public Security	/419

Chapter 4	Offences Against State Authorities	/427
Chapter 5	Offences Against State Religion	/429

Title 2　Infringement of Justice /432
    Chapter 1　Offences Against Judicial Institution　/432
    Chapter 2　Offences Against Judicial Processes　/436
    Chapter 3　Offences Related to Detention　/449
    Chapter 4　Breach of Certain Judicial Decisions　/455

Title 3　Infringement of The Functioning of Public Administration /458
    Chapter 1　Infringement of Public Administration by Representative of Public Authorities　/458
    Chapter 2　Offences Against Public Administration by Individuals　/464

Title 4　Infringement of Public Confidence /473
    Chapter 1　Forgery　/473
    Chapter 2　Forging Documents of Public Authorities　/482

BOOK 5　Transitional Provisions　/487
    Single Chapter　Transitional Provisions　/489

BOOK 6　Final Provision　/491
    Single Chapter　Final Provision　/493

刑法典修正案　/495

第一编

一 般 规 定

第一部分　刑法

第一章　一般原则

第一条　刑法适用范围

刑法规定犯罪，明确何人可以被认定实施了犯罪，设定刑罚并明确其执行方式。

必要时，行政部门发布的规范性文件可以规定仅能处以罚金的轻微犯罪。

第二条　犯罪的定义和分类

本法规定，犯罪是由自然人或者法人实施的引起社会混乱的特定行为。

根据严重程度，犯罪可以分为重罪、轻罪和轻微罪。

第三条　法定主义原则

只有在发生之时构成犯罪的行为才能被定罪。

只有在犯罪之时合法适当的刑罚才能被适用。

第四条　蓄意

没有犯罪意图的，不构成犯罪。

但是，在法律有规定的场合，可因轻率、大意、疏忽或者未履行特定义务而构成犯罪。

第五条　刑法的解释

在刑事领域，应当严格解释法律。法官既不能扩大其适用范围，也不能类推解释。

第六条　刑罚的宣告

未经法庭宣告，不得执行刑罚。

第七条　柬埔寨刑法典的适用

在刑事领域，柬埔寨法律的空间适用范围应当依照本法典的条款确定，并与国际条约一致。

第八条　对违反国际人道主义法的严重犯罪不得豁免

根据特别立法，对于那些触犯柬埔寨王国承认的国际人道主义法、国际习惯或者国际公约的严重罪行，本法典具有为被害人诉诸司法的效力。

第二章　刑法适用的时间效力

第九条　轻法的适用

废除一项犯罪的新规定应当立即适用。新规定生效前实施的行为，不应当被追诉，且任何正在进行的追诉应当终止。

已经作出的终审判决所产生的刑罚应当不再执行或者停止执行。

第十条　较轻或者较重的刑罚

较轻刑罚的新条款应当立即适用。但是，无论相关刑罚的轻重，生效判决都必须执行。

规定了较重刑罚的新条款仅适用于新条款生效后实施的行为。

第十一条　程序的有效性

新条款的立即适用不影响根据原规定采取的程序的有效性。

第三章　柬埔寨刑法适用的空间效力

第一节　在或者被视为在柬埔寨王国领土内实施犯罪

第十二条　柬埔寨王国领土的含义

在刑事领域，柬埔寨法律适用于所有在柬埔寨王国领土内实施的犯罪。

柬埔寨王国领土包括相应的空域和海域。

第十三条　实施犯罪的地点

如果犯罪中的一项事实发生在柬埔寨王国领土内，则该犯罪应当被视为在柬埔寨王国领土内实施。

第十四条　在柬埔寨船舶上实施犯罪

在刑事领域，柬埔寨法律适用于在悬挂柬埔寨国旗的船舶上实施的犯罪，无论这些船舶位于何处。

第十五条　在悬挂外国旗帜船舶上实施犯罪

在刑事领域，柬埔寨法律适用于经国际协议授权柬埔寨官方检查或者登临的外国船舶。

第十六条　在柬埔寨注册的航空器内实施犯罪

在刑事领域，柬埔寨法律适用于在柬埔寨注册的航空器内实施的犯罪，无论这些航空器位于何处。

第十七条　柬埔寨刑法适用于在柬埔寨启动的行为

在刑事领域，任何人在柬埔寨王国领土内教唆或者帮助在柬埔寨王国领土外实施的重罪或者轻罪，如果满足以下两个条件，可以适用柬埔寨法律：

根据柬埔寨法律和外国法律，该犯罪均应当被处罚；并且

实施犯罪的事实得到了外国法院生效判决的确定。

第十八条　法人实施犯罪的属性

法人实施的犯罪属于重罪、轻罪还是轻微罪，应当根据自然人可以判处的刑罚确定。

第二节　在柬埔寨王国领土外实施的犯罪

第十九条　柬埔寨公民实施重罪或者轻罪

在刑事领域，柬埔寨法律适用于任何在柬埔寨王国领土外实施任何重罪的柬埔寨公民。

柬埔寨法律适用于柬埔寨公民在外国实施的轻罪，如果其行为根据所在国法律同样会受到处罚。

即使被告人是在实施了被指控的犯罪行为之后才取得柬埔寨国籍，上述规定亦适用。

第二十条　被害人是柬埔寨公民的情形

在刑事领域，如果犯罪时被害人是柬埔寨公民，则柬埔

寨法律适用于任何柬埔寨公民或者外国人在柬埔寨王国领土外实施的任何重罪。

第二十一条　提起诉讼

第十九条（柬埔寨公民实施重罪或者轻罪）和第二十条（被害人是柬埔寨公民的情形）规定的情形，只能由公诉机关提起诉讼。起诉需满足以下前提：

被害人或者其指定的人举报；或者

犯罪发生国当局的正式照会。

第二十二条　特定重罪的特别司法管辖

在刑事领域，柬埔寨法律适用于在柬埔寨王国领土外实施的符合以下特征的任何重罪：

（一）危害柬埔寨王国安全的犯罪；

（二）伪造柬埔寨王国的印章；

（三）伪造柬埔寨王国的国家货币和合法存在于柬埔寨王国的法定货币；

（四）侵害柬埔寨王国外交或者领事人员的犯罪；

（五）侵犯柬埔寨王国外交或者领事机构的犯罪。

第二十三条　禁止重复指控和定罪

行为人已在国外获得终审判决，并且在定罪之后已经服刑完毕或者依照追诉时效其刑罚归于消灭，则不得因同一行为再被追诉。

第二部分　刑事责任

第一章　一般规定

第二十四条　个人刑事责任原则

任何人只对自己的行为承担刑事责任。

第二十五条　实行犯的定义

任何人实施刑事法律所禁止的行为，即为某种犯罪的实行犯。

实行犯的定义包括任何实施重罪而未遂的人或者在法律规定的情况下实施轻罪而未遂的人。

第二十六条　共同实行犯的定义

任何多人共同谋划并实施某种重罪或者在法律规定的情形下实施某种轻罪而未遂，即为该犯罪的共同实行犯。

第二十七条　未遂的定义

实施某种重罪或者在法律规定的情形下实施某种轻罪而未遂，在满足下述条件时应当受刑事处罚：

实行犯已经开始实施犯罪，即其本人已经实施了直接导致该犯罪得以完成的行为；

实行犯并未自愿停止自己的行为，犯罪行为仅仅因其不能控制的情况而中断。

不能直接导致实施犯罪的准备行为不是实行行为的开始。

实施轻微罪的未遂不应当受刑事处罚。

第二十八条 教唆犯的定义

凡实施下列行为的人即为重罪或者轻罪的教唆犯：

（一）唆使或者命令他人实施重罪或者轻罪；

（二）以送礼、许诺、威胁、鼓动、劝说、滥用职权或者权力等手段引发重罪或者轻罪。

只有实施了重罪或者轻罪或者重罪、轻罪未遂的教唆犯才可以受到处罚。

重罪或者轻罪的教唆犯应当承担与实行犯同样的刑罚。

第二十九条 帮助犯的定义

任何人在明知的情况下帮助或者支持、促成实施某种重罪或者轻罪的意愿或者实行该犯罪的，即为帮助犯。

只有实施了重罪或者轻罪或者重罪、轻罪未遂的帮助犯才可以受到处罚。

重罪或者轻罪的帮助犯应当承担与实行犯同样的刑罚。

第三十条 "公务员"和民选公职人员的定义

"公务员"是指：

（一）任何由法律文件任命的，在立法机关、行政机关或者司法机关临时或者长期工作的人员，不论其是否获得薪酬，也不论其身份或者年龄；

（二）任何在柬埔寨王国法律范围内的公共机构或者企业以及其他公共团体担任公职的其他人员。

民选公职人员包括参议员、国民议会议员、首都市政议员、省议员、市议员、区或者坎①的议员、公社或者桑吉②的议员以及任何被选出的以其他身份担任公职的人员。

第二章　刑事责任的免除或者减轻

第三十一条　因精神错乱不负刑事责任

实施犯罪时发生精神错乱而丧失认知能力的人，不负刑事责任。

实施犯罪时发生精神错乱而减弱认知能力的人，仍应当承担刑事责任。但是，法庭在判处刑罚时，应当对这种情况予以考虑。

实施犯罪时因饮酒、吸毒或者使用违禁物品而导致精神错乱的人，仍应当承担刑事责任。

第三十二条　法律或者合法机构的授权

基于法律规定或者授权实施行为的，不负刑事责任。

执行合法机构的命令实施行为的，不负刑事责任，除非该行为明显不合法。

种族灭绝罪、反人类罪或者战争罪的实行犯、共同实行犯、教唆犯或者帮助犯，在任何情况下都不得基于以下理由

---

①　坎（Khan），柬埔寨王国行政区划名称，指直辖市管辖的下一级行政区划。——译者注

②　公社或者桑吉（Sangkat），柬埔寨王国行政区划名称，指坎管辖的下一级行政区划。——译者注

被免除刑事责任：

（一）其实施的是现行法律规定的、授权的或者并不禁止的行为。

（二）其行为的依据是合法机构的命令。

第三十三条　防卫

出于防卫而实施犯罪的人，不负刑事责任。

防卫必须符合以下条件：

为了保护自身或者他人，或者为了保护财产，抵抗不当侵袭而被迫犯罪；

犯罪与侵袭必须同时发生；并且

用于防卫的手段要与侵袭的严重程度相适应。

第三十四条　防卫的推定

如有以下行为，应当推定行为人是在正当防卫：

（一）对夜晚强行进入住宅、施以暴力或者欺骗的行为进行抵抗；

（二）为保护自身，对窃取或者暴力掠夺财产的行为进行反抗。

防卫的推定不具有绝对性，可以被相反的证据推翻。

第三十五条　避险防卫

因避险而实施犯罪的人不应当承担刑事责任。

构成避险必须满足下列条件：

为保护自身、保护他人或者财产免遭正在发生或者迫在眉睫的危险，不得已实施犯罪；并且

所使用的保护手段要与危险的严重程度相适应。

第三十六条　强制或者强迫的效果

在无法抗拒的强制或者强迫的压力下实施犯罪的，不应当承担刑事责任。

强制或者强迫只能发生在超出人的控制能力的情形下。必须是无法预见和不可避免的。

第三十七条　不承担刑事责任

不承担刑事责任的人不应当受到刑事处罚。

第三章　未成年人的刑事责任

第三十八条　刑事责任年龄

刑事责任年龄为十八岁及以上。

第三十九条　适用于未成年人的措施

实施了犯罪的未成年人应当接受监督、教育、保护和援助。

但是，根据犯罪的情节或者未成年人的特点，法院可以对已满十四岁的未成年人处以刑罚。

第四十条　措施的种类

监督、教育、保护和援助措施应当包括：

（一）将未成年人送返其父母、法定监护人、委托监护人或者其他值得信赖的人；

（二）将未成年人送交照管未成年人的社会服务机构；

（三）将未成年人送交具有接收未成年人资质的民间组织；

（四）将未成年人送交专门医院或者机构；

（五）对未成年人采取司法保护措施。

第四十一条　采取司法保护

对未成年人采取司法保护，法院应当指定一人进行监督。监督人员应当定期向检察官报告未成年人的表现。监督人应当将所有可能导致措施变更的事件通知检察官。

第四章　法人的刑事责任

第四十二条　法人的刑事责任

依照法律和法规性文件的明文规定，法人的机构或者代表人以法人的名义实施犯罪的，法人可以承担刑事责任，但国家除外。

法人的刑事责任不排除自然人对同一行为的刑事责任。

第三部分　刑罚

第一章　刑罚的种类

第一节　主刑

第四十三条　主刑

主刑包括监禁刑和罚金刑。

罚金刑以瑞尔①计算。

第四十四条　最轻和最重的主刑

如果犯罪的刑罚是监禁，法律应当设定可以判处的最短和最长刑期。

如果犯罪的刑罚是罚金，法律应当设定可以判处的最小和最大数额。

第四十五条　刑罚的加重和减轻

监禁刑和罚金刑的下限和上限，可以根据本法的规定予以增减。

---

①　瑞尔（Riel），柬埔寨王国法定货币。1 瑞尔约合 0.0017 人民币，或者 1 人民币约合 600 瑞尔。——译者注

第四十六条 重罪的定义

重罪是可以判处以下最高监禁刑期的犯罪：

（一）终身监禁；

（二）五年以上三十年以下监禁。

罚金刑可以与监禁刑并处。

第四十七条 轻罪的定义

轻罪是可以判处六天以上五年以下监禁刑期的犯罪。

罚金刑可以与监禁刑并处。

第四十八条 轻微罪的定义

轻微罪是下列犯罪：

（一）可以判处六天以下监禁刑期的犯罪。罚金刑可以与监禁刑并处；

（二）只能处以罚金的犯罪。

第四十九条 刑期的计算

一天监禁期为二十四小时。

一个月监禁期为三十天。

超过一个月的监禁期，应当以相关月份的实际天数进行计算。

一年监禁期为十二个月。

第五十条 监禁刑期结束日期的计算

监禁刑本将于周六、周日或者法律和法规性文件规定范围内的公共假日到期的，则应当提前一天释放犯罪人。

第五十一条 审前羁押时间的扣除

全部审前羁押时间须从应当执行的刑期中扣除。

第五十二条　罚金收益

应当将罚金收益上缴国库。

第二节　附加刑

第五十三条　附加刑

附加刑包括：

（一）剥夺特定权利；

（二）禁止从事在从业期间实施了犯罪或者与犯罪有密切关联的职业；

（三）禁止驾驶任何机动车辆；

（四）吊销驾驶执照；

（五）本地驱逐；

（六）禁止离开柬埔寨王国领土；

（七）禁止被定罪的外国人进入或者停留于柬埔寨王国领土；

（八）没收用于或者打算用于实施犯罪的任何工具、材料或者物品；

（九）没收涉及犯罪的物品或者资金；

（十）没收犯罪所得的收益或者财产；

（十一）没收犯罪发生场所的器具、材料和家具；

（十二）没收罪犯拥有的一辆或者多辆机动车；

（十三）禁止拥有或者携带任何武器、爆炸物或者弹药；

（十四）取消公开招投标资格；

（十五）关闭用于谋划或者实施犯罪的设施；

（十六）禁止经营向公众开放或者供公众使用的设施；

（十七）公布量刑结果；

（十八）在印刷媒体上公布量刑结果；

（十九）通过视听传媒播报量刑结果。

可以通过特别条款规定其他附加刑。

第五十四条　可以宣告附加刑的情形

只有被起诉的重罪、轻罪或者轻微罪明确规定了附加刑，才能予以宣告。

可以宣告附加刑，也可以不宣告附加刑。但是，法律有明确规定时必须宣告。

第五十五条　剥夺权利

根据第五十三条（附加刑）第一项，可以剥夺以下权利：

（一）选举权；

（二）被选举权；

（三）担任公务员的权利；

（四）被任命为专家、仲裁人员或者委任司法官员的权利；

（五）获得官方勋章和荣誉的权利；

（六）在法庭上宣誓作证的权利。

剥夺特定权利的刑罚可以是永久性的，也可以是暂时性的。暂时剥夺权利的期限不应当超过五年。

第五十六条　禁止从事某种职业

禁止从事某种职业，不适用于民选职位或者工会岗位，亦不适用于新闻犯罪。

禁止可以是永久性的，也可以是暂时性的。暂时禁止的期限不应当超过五年。

法院应当明确禁止从事何种职业。

第五十七条　禁止驾驶

禁止驾驶机动车辆的期限不应当超过五年。

第五十八条　吊销驾驶执照

吊销驾驶执照的处罚不应当超过五年。罪犯须将其驾驶执照上交法庭登记人员。应当按照司法部长签署的规章保管驾驶执照。

第五十九条　驱逐出柬埔寨王国领土内的特定地方

本地驱逐，即禁止被定罪的人出现在柬埔寨王国领土内的特定地方。该种刑罚的期限，重罪在十年以内，轻罪在五年以内。

法庭应当列明适用驱逐刑的地域和期限。

本地驱逐刑应当有监督配合。罪犯应当：

（一）在法庭指定的司法或者行政机构传唤时现身；

（二）定期向法庭指定的王国警察或者王国宪兵办公室报告。

法庭应当确定监督的方式。

检察官应当将法庭的决定通知内务部和国防部。

第六十条　禁止离开柬埔寨王国领土

禁止离开柬埔寨领土的期限不应当超过五年。

罪犯须将其护照上交法庭登记人员。应当按照司法部长签署的规章保管护照。

罪犯在刑罚执行期间不能获得护照。

第六十一条　禁止被定罪的外国人进入或者停留于柬埔寨王国领土

禁止被定罪的外国人进入或者停留于柬埔寨王国领土,可以是永久性的,也可以是暂时性的。暂时禁止的期限不应当超过五年。此种禁止系指被定罪的外国人监禁服刑期满后将被驱逐出境。

第六十二条　没收

可以下令没收下列物品:

(一) 任何用于或者打算用于犯罪的工具、材料或者物品;

(二) 用于犯罪的物品或者资金;

(三) 犯罪所得收益或者财产;

(四) 犯罪发生场所的器具、材料和家具。

但是,如果涉及第三方权利,不得下达没收令。

第六十三条　没收物品的处理

没收一经完成,没收的物品即应当成为国家财产,除非另有特别规定。

国家可以依照售卖国家财产的规定出售或者销毁没收的物品。

第六十四条　禁止拥有或者携带任何武器、爆炸物或者任何种类的弹药

禁止拥有或者携带任何武器、爆炸物或者任何种类的弹药,可以是永久性的,也可以是暂时性的。暂时禁止的期限

不应当超过五年。此种禁止适用于柬埔寨王国内的任何种类的武器、爆炸物或者弹药。

第六十五条 取消公开招投标资格

取消公开招投标资格的刑罚包括禁止直接或者间接地参加由下列主体举办的招投标活动：

（一）国家；

（二）地方当局；

（三）公共机构；以及

（四）国家或者地方当局特许的或者控制的企业。

取消公开招投标资格可以是永久性的，也可以是暂时性的。暂时取消的期限不得超过五年。

第六十六条 关闭机构

关闭机构的刑罚系指禁止在该机构内从事与实施犯罪有关的活动。

关闭机构可以是永久性的，也可以是暂时性的。暂时关闭的期限不得超过五年。

第六十七条 禁止运营机构

禁止运营向公众开放或者供公众使用的机构，可以是永久性的，也可以是暂时性的。暂时禁止运营的期限不得超过五年。

第六十八条 公布量刑裁决

应当在法庭确定的场所和时间内公布量刑裁决。公布期限不应当超过两个月。可以公布量刑裁决的全部或者部分，亦可仅对其有所提及。公布的费用应当由犯罪人承担。

如果裁决公告被移除、隐藏或者撕毁，则移除、隐藏或者撕毁公告的人承担制作新公告的费用。

第六十九条　印刷媒体上公布量刑裁决

应当依照法庭确定的方式和时段，在印刷媒体上公布量刑裁决。

印刷媒体公布裁决的费用由犯罪人承担。可以将不支付费用的犯罪人收监。

法庭命令公布裁决，报社不得拒绝。

第七十条　视听传媒播报量刑裁决

应当依照法庭确定的方式，通过视听传媒播报量刑裁决。执行播发不应当超过八天。可以播发裁决的全部内容，也可以播发裁决的部分内容，或者可以仅有所提及。播发的费用应当由犯罪人承担。

第七十一条　执行附加刑的日期

第五十三条（附加刑）第（一）、（二）、（三）、（四）、（五）、（六）和（七）项规定的附加刑，应当在监禁期满后执行，法院另行决定的除外。

第三节　刑罚替代措施

第一分节　社区服务

第七十二条　社区服务的含义

如果被告人可被判处的监禁刑期最高为三年或者以上，法庭可以对罪犯下达社区服务令。

社区服务是为国家、地方当局或者公共机构、协会或者非政府团体提供三十至二百小时无偿服务的一项义务。

第七十三条 社区服务不得使自然人受益

任何情况下都不得为自然人的利益执行社区服务。

第七十四条 社区服务的相关规定

社区服务受《劳动法典》(尤其该法中涉及夜间工作、职业健康、安全和女工的条款)规制。

社区服务可以与职业活动一并进行。

第七十五条 赔偿第三方损失

罪犯在进行社区服务过程中造成第三方损害的,国家应予赔偿。依照现行法律,国家应当代为行使被害人的权利。

第二分节 斥责

第七十六条 斥责的相关规定

如果满足以下三个条件,法庭可以对最高监禁期为三年或者以上的被告人予以斥责:

——犯罪引起的社会混乱已经平息;

——损害已经得到修复;

——被告人为其重归社会提供了保证。

第二章 加重和减轻情节

第一节 加重情节

第一分节 若干加重情节的定义

第七十七条 有组织犯罪集团

有组织犯罪集团是为策划或者实施一项或者多项犯罪而

成立的任何团体或者阴谋集团。

第七十八条　预谋

预谋是指先于行为的实施犯罪的蓄意。

第七十九条　强行进入

强行进入包括强力破坏或者损毁任何类型的锁闭装置或者围栏。

强行进入亦包括以下情形：

（一）使用配制的钥匙；

（二）使用非法获取的钥匙；

（三）使用任何可用于操控而非破坏、损伤或者毁坏锁闭装置的工具。

第八十条　非法进入

非法进入是通过攀越围栏或者穿过任何本不是入口的洞孔而进入任何场所的行为。

第八十一条　武器和被视为武器的物品

武器是指任何被设计用于杀伤的物品。

下列情况，武器包括可能给人身带来危险的任何其他物品：

（一）用于杀人、伤害或者威胁的物品；

（二）意图用于杀人、伤害或者威胁的物品。

武器亦包括用于杀人、伤害或者威胁的动物。

第八十二条　埋伏

埋伏是以实施犯罪为目的，而在任何场所潜伏守候被害人的行为。

第二分节 累犯

第八十三条 累犯：刑罚

依照本分节，实施新的犯罪，无论重罪还是轻罪，都应当提升监禁刑期的上限。

第八十四条 累犯的适用

以下情形构成累犯：

（一）终审认定重罪的人在十年内实施新的重罪；

（二）终审认定重罪的人在五年内实施轻罪；

（三）终审认定轻罪并判处三年或者以上监禁的人，在五年内实施重罪；

（四）终审认定轻罪的人在五年内实施同样的轻罪。

十年和五年的期限应当从上一次犯罪被定罪时起算。

第八十五条 重罪累犯

终审认定重罪的人在十年以内实施新的重罪，新罪可被处以的监禁刑最高刑期应当作如下提升：

（一）如果新罪可被处以的监禁刑刑期本来不超过二十年，则最高刑期应当加倍；

（二）如果新罪可被处以的监禁刑刑期本来不超过三十年，则最高刑期应当为终身监禁。

第八十六条 犯重罪被判刑后又犯轻罪

终审认定重罪的人五年内又犯轻罪的，轻罪可被处以的监禁刑最高刑期应当加倍。

如果因累犯导致监禁刑最高刑期超过五年，即使刑罚提升，该犯罪在法律上仍然属于轻罪。

第八十七条　犯轻罪被判刑后又犯重罪

因轻罪被判三年或者以上监禁刑的人五年内又犯重罪的，重罪可以被处以的刑罚应当作如下提升：

（一）如果重罪可被处以的监禁刑刑期本来不超过二十年，则最高刑期应当加倍；

（二）如果重罪可被处以的监禁刑刑期本来不超过三十年，则最高刑期应当为终身监禁。

第八十八条　因轻罪被判刑后又犯轻罪

终审认定轻罪的人五年内又犯相同轻罪的，新罪可被处以的监禁刑最高刑期应当加倍。

如果因累犯导致监禁刑最高刑期超过五年，即使刑罚提升，该犯罪在法律上仍然属于轻罪。

第八十九条　视同

基于累犯的相关规定，窃取罪、违反诚信罪与诈骗罪应当被视为相同的犯罪。

收受赃物罪与获取赃物罪应当被视为相同的犯罪。

洗钱罪与洗钱得以发生的相关犯罪应当被视为相同的犯罪。

第九十条　前罪与起诉

只有起诉书明确指出前罪，法庭才能予以考虑并用作加重监禁刑期的根据。

第九十一条　前罪与终审判决

终审判决不可上诉。

从累犯规则的目的出发，只能考虑刑事诉讼中的终审判决。

第九十二条　特别规定

即使时效规定适用于相应量刑结果，亦可考虑先前的定罪。

如果根据《柬埔寨王国宪法》第九十条新规定的第（二）项和第（四）项对前罪进行了赦免，则不得考虑前罪。

第二节　减轻情节

第九十三条　减轻情节的定义

根据犯罪的性质和被告人的特性，法庭可以确认有利于被告人的减轻情节。

即使被告人先前被判决有罪，也可以适用减轻情节。

第九十四条　减轻情节的效果

如果法庭核准了被告人的减轻情节，则应当对重罪或者轻罪可以被判处的最轻主刑作出如下降低：

（一）可被处以的监禁刑最低刑期为十年以上的，减为二年；

（二）可被处以的监禁刑最低刑期为五年以上不满十年的，减为一年；

（三）可被处以的监禁刑最低刑期为二年以上不满五年的，减为六个月；

（四）可被处以的监禁刑最低刑期为六天以上不满二年的，减为一天；

（五）可被处以的罚金最低额度减半。

第九十五条　终身监禁与减轻情节

如果一项犯罪可被处以的刑罚是终身监禁，法官可以根据其确认的减轻情节判处十五年至三十年监禁。

第三章　量刑原则

第一节　一般原则

第九十六条　刑罚个别化原则

在判处刑罚时，法庭应当考虑罪行的严重程度和情节、被告人的特性、心理状态、财产、开支和动机，以及犯罪后的表现，特别是针对被害人的表现。

第九十七条　主刑的宣告

在既可以处以监禁刑也可以处以罚金刑的案件中，法庭可以判处：

——同时适用监禁刑和罚金刑；或者

——仅适用监禁刑；或者

——仅适用罚金刑。

第九十八条　刑罚替代措施的宣告

社区服务可作为主刑的替代措施。一经法庭发出社区服务令，不再适用监禁刑或者罚金刑。

斥责可作为主刑的替代措施。一经法庭发出斥责令，不再适用监禁刑或者罚金刑。

第九十九条　主刑之外附加刑的宣告

如果可以适用一项或者多项附加刑，应当按本法典第一百条（附加刑替代主刑的宣告）的规定，在主刑之外予以判处。

第一百条　附加刑替代主刑的宣告

下列情况，法庭可以决定用一项或者多项附加刑替代主刑：

（一）被告人应当被判处的主刑只能是罚金刑；

（二）被告人应当被判处的主刑为最高刑期三年或者三年以下监禁刑。

如果法庭决定用一项或者多项附加刑替代主刑，则不再适用监禁刑或者罚金刑。

第一百零一条　适用于社区服务令宣告的特别规则

社区服务仅在被告人出庭并接受服务工作时才可以适用。作出裁判之前，法庭应当告知被告人有权拒绝实施社区服务。应当将被告人的回答记录在案。

第一百零二条　社区服务的期限

法庭发出社区服务令，应当确定期限和起止时间。期限不超过一年。

第一百零三条　社区服务的实施

社区服务的实施方式应当由检察官决定。

检察官应当指定法人作为社区服务的受益方。

社区服务应当在检察官的监督下实施。

第二节 缓刑

第一分节 一般规定

第一百零四条 缓刑的宣告

法庭可以暂缓本节所涉主刑的执行。

第一百零五条 关于缓刑的规则

适用缓刑条款,仅与刑事诉讼的终审判决有关。

第二分节 重罪或者轻罪案件

第一百零六条 先前的定罪

被告人被指控犯重罪或者轻罪而被处以刑罚,如果犯罪之前五年内未发生过针对该被告人的终审有罪判决,则可适用缓刑。

第一百零七条 可以适用缓刑的刑罚

下列刑罚可以适用缓刑:

(一)五年或者不满五年的监禁刑;

(二)罚金刑。

第一百零八条 部分缓刑

法庭可以依其确定的时间暂缓执行部分监禁刑,或者依其确定的数额暂缓执行部分罚金刑。

第一百零九条 缓刑撤销

对重罪或者轻罪的终审判决适用缓刑,如果缓刑宣告后五年内出现针对重罪或者轻罪的新的终审判决,缓刑应当自动撤销。

原先判处的前一个刑罚应予执行,但不得与新判处的后一个刑罚同时执行。

第一百一十条　缓刑不予撤销

尽管有第一百零九条（缓刑撤销）的规定，法院仍然可以作出特别理由的裁判，决定新判处的刑罚并不意味着撤销正在适用的缓刑。

第一百一十一条　适用缓刑的刑罚被视为从未执行

对重罪或者轻罪的有效判决适用缓刑后五年内，如果没有针对重罪或者轻罪的新的终审判决，则可以不再执行原判刑罚。

如果只是部分所判刑罚适用缓刑，则全部所判刑罚都应当被认为从未执行。可以不再执行原判刑罚。

第三分节　轻微罪案件

第一百一十二条　先前的定罪

被告人被指控犯轻微罪而被处以刑罚，如果犯罪之前一年内未受到处以监禁刑的终审有罪判决，可以适用缓刑。

第一百一十三条　可以适用缓刑的刑罚

下列轻微罪的刑罚可以适用缓刑：

（一）监禁刑；

（二）罚金刑。

第一百一十四条　缓刑撤销

对轻微罪的终审判决适用缓刑，如果缓刑宣告后一年内出现针对重罪、轻罪或者轻微罪的新的终审判决，缓刑应当自动撤销。原先判处的前一个刑罚应当予以执行，但不得与新判处的后一个刑罚同时执行。

第一百一十五条　缓刑不予撤销

尽管有第一百一十四条（缓刑撤销）的规定，法院仍然可以作出特别理由的裁判，决定新判处的刑罚并不意味着撤销正在适用的缓刑。

第一百一十六条　适用缓刑的刑罚被视为从未执行

缓刑宣告一年内，如果没有针对重罪、轻罪或者轻微罪的新的定罪，则针对终审判决适用缓刑的刑罚应当被视为从未执行。该刑罚可以不再执行。

第三节　附考验期缓刑

第一百一十七条　附考验期缓刑的含义

如果本应当判处的监禁刑是六个月以上五年以下，则法庭可以适用缓刑并附考验期。

附考验期缓刑要求犯罪人在确定期限内服从缓刑措施以及一项或者多项特定义务。

第一百一十八条　缓刑考验期的时限

法庭确定缓刑考验期的时限应当不少于一年，不超过三年。

第一百一十九条　缓刑措施

犯罪人应当服从下列缓刑措施：

（一）在检察官或者其指定的代表传唤时到位；

（二）接受检察官指定的任何人的到访；

（三）向检察官或者其指定的代表提供其重新融入社会的证明文件；

（四）向检察官及时报告地址的变动；

（五）向检察官及时报告工作的变动；以及

（六）出国旅行须事先获得检察官的批准。

第一百二十条 可以加予罪犯的特定义务

可以加予罪犯下列特定义务：

（一）不得离职；

（二）接受指导课程或者职业培训；

（三）在特定地点居住；

（四）接受体检或者治疗；

（五）证明自己为家庭开支做出了贡献；

（六）以自己的方式修复其犯罪带来的危害；

（七）证明其正在以自己的方式支付因被定罪而欠国家的款项；

（八）不得从事法院明确禁止的、有助于或者方便于实施犯罪的职业或者社会活动；

（九）不得出现在法院明确禁止的场合；

（十）不得前往常去赌博的地方；

（十一）不得前往常去喝酒的场所；

（十二）不得与法庭指定的人员交往，特别是实行犯、共同实行犯、教唆犯、帮助犯或者犯罪的被害人；

（十三）不得拥有或者携带任何武器、爆炸物或者弹药。

法庭的判决应当包括将这些特定义务中的一项或者多项加予罪犯。

第一百二十一条 法院对特定义务的变更

法院可以随时对罪犯加予特定义务。

依照《刑事诉讼法典》的规定适用。

第一百二十二条 附考验期缓刑的撤销

下列情形，法院可以撤销附考验期缓刑：

（一）罪犯在考验期内没有遵守缓刑措施或者特定义务；

（二）罪犯在考验期内再次实施重罪或者轻罪。

法院可以撤销全部或者部分附考验期缓刑。此种情况下，原判刑罚的全部或者部分应当予以执行。

依照《刑事诉讼法典》的规定适用。

第一百二十三条 附缓刑考验期的刑罚被视为从未执行

直到考验期满，缓刑未被请求撤销且未作出撤销决定的，适用缓刑的刑罚被认为从未执行。

第四节 延迟量刑

第一百二十四条 可以延迟量刑的情形

指控轻罪的案件，如果同时满足下列条件，法庭可以在认定被告人有罪后延迟量刑：

——犯罪导致的社会混乱已经停止；

——被告人为其回归社会提供了保证；并且

——被告人请求给予其修复损害的时间。

第一百二十五条 推迟判决

只有在被告人出庭的情况下，才可以准予推迟。

法庭应当在决定推迟判决时设定处刑日期。

须在作出推迟决定后一年内宣判刑罚。

第一百二十六条　押后聆讯

法庭应当在押后聆讯时宣判刑罚。

第五节　日间释放

第一百二十七条　日间释放的适用

法庭处以六个月及以下监禁刑,可以决定采取日间释放的方式服刑,以使罪犯能够经营或者从业、参加辅导课程或者职业培训、接受治疗,或者满足其家庭的需要。

第一百二十八条　日间释放的安排

被决定日间释放的罪犯,应当获准在规定时段离开监狱。

法庭应当在日间释放决定中设定允许罪犯离开监狱的天数和时段。

第一百二十九条　从刑罚中扣除日间释放时间

应当将日间释放所耗时间从正在执行的刑期中扣除。

第一百三十条　条件和撤销

经检察官请求,法院可以随时设定条件或者撤销日间释放的安排。

依照《刑事诉讼法典》的规定适用。

第一百三十一条　逮捕和羁押

检察官可以下令逮捕并羁押日间释放逾期未回监狱的罪犯。

第六节　分期服刑

第一百三十二条　可以分期服刑的情形

法庭判处一年及以下监禁刑,可以出于家庭、医疗、职业或者社会原因，决定分期服刑。

第一百三十三条　服刑

分期服刑的时间不得少于一个月。

包括间隔时间在内，服刑时间总计不得超过二年。

法庭的判决应当明确分期服刑的方式。

第一百三十四条　条件和撤销

经检察官请求，法院可以随时安排或者撤销分期服刑。

依照《刑事诉讼法典》的规定适用。

第一百三十五条　逮捕和监禁

检察官可以下令对分期服刑间隔结束后未回到监狱的罪犯进行逮捕和监禁。

第四章　适用于并发犯罪的规则

第一节　一般规则

第一百三十六条　并发犯罪

行为人在其犯罪受到终审判决之前又实施了另一个犯罪，称为并发犯罪。

第一百三十七条　分别追究

分别追究是指，如果认定被告人有并发的若干犯罪，可以分别判处应受的若干刑罚。但是，如果判处多个同类性质的应受刑罚，则对其中任何一个刑罚的判处都不得超出法律允许的上限。

在法律允许判处的每个罪行的刑罚上限内判处的每个刑罚都应当被视为同时适用于并发犯罪。

第一百三十八条　并合追究

并合追究是指，如果认定被告人有并发的若干犯罪，则判处的多个刑罚累计不得超过法律允许的刑罚上限。但是，处理这类案件的终审法院可以命令一并执行全部或者部分同类性质的刑罚。

基于本条，如果被告人的罪责符合终身监禁刑却未被判处终身监禁刑，则法律允许的最高监禁刑期为三十年。

针对并发犯罪判处的每一个刑罚全部或者部分适用缓刑，不应当妨碍未适用缓刑的同类性质刑罚的执行。

第二节　特别规则

第一百三十九条　刑罚赦免和减轻的效果

根据《柬埔寨王国宪法》第二十七条的有关规定，在有权赦免刑罚的情况下，应当基于并发犯罪案件的适用规则，考虑应予判处的刑罚。

如果存在并处的刑罚，应当从中扣除减免的部分。

第一百四十条　罚金的累计性质

虽有前述规定，对轻微罪的罚金刑也应当累计，包括与并发的重罪和轻罪所判处的罚金刑累加。

第一百四十一条　不得同时执行越狱罪的刑罚

对越狱罪判处的刑罚应当与对导致罪犯入狱的犯罪判处的刑罚相加，二者不能同时执行。

第五章　影响刑罚执行的若干因素

第一节　刑罚时效

第一百四十二条　时效的影响

如果刑罚时效到期，可以不再执行该刑罚。

第一百四十三条　某些犯罪不受时效限制

对种族灭绝罪、危害人类罪和战争罪判处的刑罚不受任何时效的限制。

除上述罪行外，特别法可以规定对其他犯罪判处的刑罚不适用时效规定。

第一百四十四条　时效的适用

重罪的时效为二十年。

轻罪的时效为五年。

轻微罪的时效为一年。

第一百四十五条　时效的起算

第一百四十四条规定的二十年、五年和一年的时效期间均应当从终审有罪判决之日起算。

第一百四十六条　刑事判决所生民事义务的时效适用

有效刑事判决产生的民事义务适用《民事法典》设定的时效规则。

第二节 赦免

第一百四十七条 赦免的效果

《柬埔寨王国宪法》第二十七条规定的赦免使得罪犯免于服刑。

第一百四十八条 赦免对被害人索赔权利的影响

除非王国法令另有规定,赦免不应当妨碍被害人就其所受损失获得赔偿的权利。

第三节 特赦

第一百四十九条 特赦的效果

《柬埔寨王国宪法》第九十条新规定的第(二)项和第(四)项使得相关定罪归于消灭。

刑罚不再执行。

如果刑罚正在执行,应当停止。

但是,国家不应当返还任何已经缴纳的罚金和诉讼费用。

第一百五十条 特赦和缓刑的撤销

如果缓刑因新的定罪而被撤销,则对新的定罪的赦免恢复缓刑待遇。

第一百五十一条 特赦对被害人索赔权利的影响

除非法律另有规定,特赦不应当妨碍被害人就其受到的损失获取赔偿的权利。

第四节　若干附加刑的调整和免除

第一百五十二条　可适用的情形

依照第五十三条（附加刑）第（一）、（二）、（三）、（四）、（五）、（六）、（七）、（十四）、（十五）或者（十六）项判处附加刑，如果满足下列条件，法院可以调整或者免除一项或者多项刑罚：

——犯罪引起的社会混乱已经停止；

——损害已经得到修复；

——调整或者免除刑罚的决定能够促进犯罪人重返社会。

调整或者免除刑罚的申请由检察机关自行提出或者由犯罪人提出。法院应当在听取检察机关的代表、犯罪人及其律师的意见后视情公开作出决定。

第一百五十三条　全部或者部分权利的恢复

如果本法典第五十五条（剥夺权利）涉及的权利被剥夺，法院可以全部或者部分予以恢复。

第一百五十四条　禁止令的调整或者解除

法院可以调整或者解除：

（一）对从业或者社会活动的禁止令；

（二）对驾驶机动车的禁止令。

第一百五十五条　驾驶执照的恢复

如果驾驶执照被吊销，法院可以下令恢复。

第一百五十六条　本地驱逐措施的变更

采取本地驱逐，法院可以变更监管措施。

如果情况紧急，检察官可以准许在被禁止的地方临时居住最多八天。检察官应当将其决定通知法院。

法院和检察官应当将决定告知内政部和国防部。

第一百五十七条　不得离开柬埔寨王国领土禁止令的变更

法院可以解除不得离开柬埔寨王国领土的禁止令。法庭在必要时可以附加某些条件。

第一百五十八条　不得进入柬埔寨王国领土禁止令的变更

法院可以解除被认定有罪的外国人不得进入和停留于柬埔寨王国领土的禁止令。但是，检察官必须在征求外交部和国际合作部的意见后告知法庭。

法院不受该意见的约束。

第一百五十九条　吊销公开招投标资质、关闭经营机构以及禁止营业的变更

法院可以变更或者终止下列刑罚：

（一）吊销公开招投标资质；

（二）关闭经营机构；

（三）禁止经营向公众开放或者供公众使用的场所。

第六章　适用于未成年人的刑罚

第一节　一般规定

第一百六十条　适用于十四岁以上未成年人的主刑

法庭决定对年龄超过十四岁的未成年人判处刑罚，应当

对指控罪行所适用的主刑作如下减轻：

（一）所适用的监禁最高刑应当减少二分之一；

（二）如果所适用的最高刑是终身监禁，应当被减少为二十年监禁；

（三）如果所适用的最低刑是超过一天的监禁，应当被减少二分之一；

（四）罚金最低数额和最高数额减少二分之一。

在指控重罪的情况下，如果因本条规定所适用的监禁最高刑减至五年以下，被指控的罪行仍应当是重罪。

第一百六十一条　附加刑

对未成年人，应当只适用下列附加刑：

（一）没收用于或者打算用于实施犯罪的任何工具、材料或者物品；

（二）没收作为犯罪对象的物品或者资金；

（三）没收因犯罪而产生的收益或者财产；

（四）没收犯罪发生场所的器具、材料和家具；

（五）禁止持有或者携带任何种类的任何武器、爆炸物或者弹药。

第一百六十二条　社区服务

社区服务应当适用于十六岁以上的未成年人。但是，社区服务的持续时间不得超过一百小时。

社区服务必须适合未成年人；必须具有教育作用并能够促进其回归社会。

第一百六十三条 未成年人不适用有关前科的规定

有关前科的规定不应当适用于未成年人。

第一百六十四条 未成年人有权获得减轻

有关减轻情节的规定应当适用于未成年人。

如果法庭准许未成年人适用减轻情节,未成年人因犯重罪或者轻罪所适用的主刑下限应当作如下减轻:

(一) 如果所适用的监禁最低刑为十年以上,应当被减至一年;

(二) 如果所适用的监禁最低刑为五年以上十年以下,应当被减至六个月;

(三) 如果所适用的监禁最低刑为二年以上五年以下,应当被减至三个月;

(四) 如果所适用的监禁最低刑为六天以上二年以下,应当被减至一天;

(五) 所适用的最低数额的罚金应当减少二分之一。

第一百六十五条 未成年人附考验期缓刑的具体义务

未成年人执行附考验期缓刑只承担以下义务:

(一) 参加指导课程或者职业培训;

(二) 在指定地方居住;

(三) 接受医学检查或者治疗;

(四) 力所能及地修复犯罪导致的损失;

(五) 证明自己正在力所能及地支付因定罪而欠国家的款项;

（六）不得出现在指定地点；

（七）不得前往常去喝酒的场所；

（八）不得与法庭指定的某些人交往，特别是共同实行犯、教唆犯、帮助犯或者犯罪的被害人；

（九）不得拥有或者携带任何种类的任何武器、爆炸物或者弹药。

第二节 特别规定

第一百六十六条 为未成年人单独设立的监狱设施

应当为被监禁的未成年人安排与成年罪犯相区隔的特殊监室。未成年人受制于一种非常强调教育和职业训练的特殊且个性化的制度。

关押制度应当由司法部长和相关部长签署的规章决定。

第七章 适用于法人的刑罚

第一节 一般规定

第一百六十七条 可以对法人判处的刑罚

可以对法人判处的具体刑罚是：

（一）作为主刑的罚金；

（二）第一百六十八条（适用于法人的附加刑）规定的附加刑。

第二节 附加刑

第一百六十八条 适用于法人的附加刑

适用于法人的附加刑包括:

(一) 解散;

(二) 置于司法监视;

(三) 禁止开展一项或者多项活动;

(四) 取消公开招投标的资格;

(五) 禁止公开上市;

(六) 禁止发行未经银行出证的支票;

(七) 禁止使用支付卡;

(八) 关闭用于策划或者实施犯罪的场所;

(九) 禁止运营向公众开放或者由公众使用的场所;

(十) 没收用于或者计划用于实施犯罪的任何工具、材料或者物品;

(十一) 没收犯罪涉及的物品或者资金;

(十二) 没收犯罪所得收益或者财产;

(十三) 没收实施犯罪场所的器具、材料和家具;

(十四) 公布量刑结果,在印刷媒体上公布量刑结果或者通过视听传媒公布量刑结果。

特别条款可以规定其他附加刑。

第一百六十九条 可以适用的场合

只有针对所指控的犯罪规定了具体附加刑的场合,法庭才可以宣告附加刑。

第一百七十条　法人的解散和清算

命令解散法人的判决应当包含将法人移送到负责司法清算的法庭。

第一百七十一条　置于司法监视

司法监视的期限不得超过五年。将法人置于司法监视的判决包括指定一名经司法任命的官员，其职责范围由法庭决定。经司法任命的官员应当至少每六个月向检察官报告其履行职责的情况。

检察官审查履职报告后，可以将案件移交给命令司法监视的法庭。法庭可以判处新的刑罚。

法庭应当在听取来自检察部门、经司法任命的官员和法人的律师的意见后，当庭作出判决。

第一百七十二条　禁止活动的开展

对开展活动的禁止可以是永久性的，也可以是临时性的。后一种情况，禁止期限不得超过五年。

法庭应当具体指明所禁止的活动。

第一百七十三条　取消公开招投标的资格

取消公开招投标的资格包括禁止直接或者间接参与由以下主体发起的任何招投标：

（一）国家；

（二）地方当局；

（三）公共团体；

（四）国家或者地方当局特许的或者控制的企业。

取消公开招投标的资格可以是永久性的，也可以是临时性的。后一种情况，取消资格，期限不得超过五年。

第一百七十四条　禁止公开上市

禁止公开上市可以是永久性的，也可以是暂时性的。后一种情况，禁止的期限不得超过五年。

禁止公开上市应当包括禁止法人使用任何信用机构、金融机构或者经纪人出售其证券。

禁止公开上市亦应当包括禁止发布广告。

第一百七十五条　禁止签发支票

禁止签发支票可以是永久性的，也可以是暂时性的。后一种情况，禁止的期限不得超过五年。

上述规定同样适用于禁止使用支付卡。

第一百七十六条　关闭场所

关闭场所的刑罚应当包括禁止在场所中进行与实施犯罪有关的活动。

关闭场所可以是永久性的，也可以是暂时性的。后一种情况，关闭的期限不得超过五年。

第一百七十七条　禁止场所的运营

禁止运营向公众开放或者由公众使用的场所，可以是永久性的，也可以是暂时性的。后一种情况，禁止的期限不得超过五年。

第一百七十八条　没收物品的所有权、出售和销毁

没收确定后，没收的物品应当属于国家财产，但另有特别规定的除外。

国家可以依照出售国家财产的程序出售或者销毁没收的物品。法律亦可规定某些物品的销毁。

如果应当没收的物品尚未被查获并且不能被制造，犯罪人应当支付由法庭估价的金额。出于弥补损失的目的，应当适用有关不履行债务相关犯罪的监禁刑规定。

第一百七十九条　没收与第三方权利

可以就下列物品发出没收令：

（一）用于或者打算用于实施犯罪的任何工具、材料或者物品；

（二）涉及犯罪的物品或者资金；

（三）犯罪产生的收益或者财产；

（四）实施犯罪的处所内的器具、材料和家具。

但是，如果影响到第三方的权利，不得下令没收。

第一百八十条　公布判决

公布判决的刑罚，应当在法庭确定的地点和时间进行。延迟公布不得超过两个月。可以公布判决的全部内容，也可以公布判决的部分内容，或者仅仅公布其附件。公布的费用应当由被定罪的法人承担。

如果公告被移除、隐藏或者撕毁，则移除、隐藏或者撕毁公告的人承担制作新公告的费用。

第一百八十一条　通过视听传媒播放判决

通过视听传媒播放判决刑应当依照法庭决定的方式执行。播放的执行不得超过八天。可以播放判决的全部内容，也可以播放判决的部分内容，或者仅仅播放其附件。播放的费用应当由被定罪的法人承担。

公布判决的刑罚应当依照法庭确定的方式和期限以书面媒体的形式执行。公布的费用应当由被定罪的法人承担。报纸不得拒绝在法庭命令的版面位置公布判决。

第一百八十二条　有关自然人的条款适用于法人

本法典第一编第一、第二和第三部分有关自然人的条款，只要与本章规定不相冲突，应当适用于法人。

第二编

侵犯人身的犯罪

第一部分 灭绝种族罪，危害人类罪，战争罪

第一章 灭绝种族罪

第一百八十三条 灭绝种族罪的定义

"灭绝种族罪"系指意图全部或者部分消灭一个国家、民族、种族或者宗教团体的下列行为之一：

（一）杀害团体成员；

（二）导致团体成员严重的身体或者精神伤害；

（三）有意迫使团体成员处于旨在导致其受到不同程度摧残的环境；

（四）采取强制措施或者志愿者形式，蓄意阻止团体内的生育；

（五）强制转移一个团体的孩子至另一个团体。

第一百八十四条 刑罚

犯灭绝种族罪，应当处以终身监禁。

第一百八十五条 计划灭绝种族罪

有组织地参与或者以共谋方式计划灭绝种族的，应当处

以二十年至三十年监禁。

计划必须表现为一项或者多项实际行为。

第一百八十六条 附加刑（种类及期限）

对于本章规定的重罪，可以判处下列附加刑：

（一）剥夺特定权利，或者永久剥夺，或者剥夺期限在五年以内；

（二）禁止从事在从业期间实施了犯罪或者与犯罪有密切关联的职业，或者永久禁止，或者禁止期限在五年以内；

（三）期限在十年以内的本地驱逐；

（四）禁止离开柬埔寨王国领土，期限为五年以内；

（五）禁止被定罪的外国人进入和停留于柬埔寨王国领土，或者永久禁止，或者禁止期限在五年以内；

（六）没收用于或者打算用于实施犯罪的任何工具、材料或者物品；

（七）禁止拥有或者携带任何种类的任何武器、爆炸物或者弹药，或者永久禁止，或者禁止期限在五年以内；

（八）公布量刑结果，期限为二个月以内；

（九）以印刷媒体公布量刑结果；

（十）通过任何视听传媒公布量刑结果，期限为八天以内。

第一百八十七条 法人的刑事责任

根据本法典第四十二条（法人的刑事责任），可以确定法人对本法典第一百八十三条（灭绝种族罪）和第一百八十五条（计划灭绝种族罪）规定的犯罪承担刑事责任。

应当对法人处以五千万瑞尔至五亿瑞尔的罚金,并处下列附加刑中的一项或者多项:

(一)依照本法典第一百七十条(法人的解散和清算)予以解散;

(二)依照本法典第一百七十一条(置于司法监视)予以司法监视;

(三)依照本法典第一百七十二条(禁止活动的开展),禁止进行一项或者多项活动;

(四)依照本法典第一百七十三条(取消公开招投标的资格),取消公开招投标资格;

(五)依照本法典第一百七十四条(禁止公开上市),禁止公开上市;

(六)依照本法典第一百八十条(公布判决),公布量刑结果;

(七)依照本法典第一百八十一条(通过视听传媒播放判决),以印刷媒体公布量刑结果,或者以任何视听传媒播放量刑结果。

第二章 危害人类罪

第一百八十八条 危害人类罪的定义

"危害人类罪"系指作为直接针对任何平民的广泛或者系统侵害的一部分而实施的下列任何行为:

(一)谋杀;

（二）灭绝；

（三）奴役；

（四）驱逐或者强行迁徙人口；

（五）违反国际法基本准则的监禁或者其他严重剥夺人身自由的行为；

（六）酷刑；

（七）强奸、性奴役、强迫卖淫、强迫怀孕、强迫绝育或者具有同样严重性的其他形式的性暴力；

（八）以政治、种族、民族、文化、宗教或者性别为由迫害任何可识别的团体或者集体；

（九）强迫失踪；

（十）种族隔离；

（十一）其他蓄意导致身体巨大痛苦或者严重伤害的不人道行为。

第一百八十九条　刑罚

犯危害人类罪，应当处以终身监禁。

第一百九十条　计划危害人类罪

有组织地参与或者以共谋方式计划危害人类的，应当处以二十年至三十年监禁。

计划必须表现为一项或者多项实际行为。

第一百九十一条　附加刑（种类及期限）

对于本章规定的重罪，可以判处下列附加刑：

（一）剥夺特定权利，或者永久剥夺，或者剥夺期限在五年以内；

（二）禁止从事在从业期间实施了犯罪或者与犯罪有密切关联的职业，或者永久禁止，或者禁止期限在五年以内；

（三）期限在十年以内的本地驱逐；

（四）禁止离开柬埔寨王国领土，期限为五年以内；

（五）禁止被定罪外国人进入和停留于柬埔寨王国领土，或者永久禁止，或者禁止期限在五年以内；

（六）没收用于或者打算用于实施罪行的任何工具、材料或者物品；

（七）禁止拥有或者携带任何种类的任何武器、爆炸物或者弹药，或者永久禁止，或者禁止期限在五年以内；

（八）公布量刑结果的期限为二个月以内；

（九）以印刷媒体公布量刑结果；

（十）通过任何视听传媒公布量刑结果的期限为八天以内。

第一百九十二条　法人的刑事责任

根据本法典第四十二条（法人的刑事责任），可以确定法人对本法典第一百八十八条（危害人类罪）和第一百九十条（计划危害人类罪）规定的犯罪承担刑事责任。

应当对法人处以五千万瑞尔至五亿瑞尔的罚金，并处下列附加刑中的一项或者多项：

（一）依照本法典第一百七十条（法人的解散和清算）予以解散；

（二）依照本法典第一百七十一条（置于司法监视）予以司法监视；

（三）依照本法典第一百七十二条（禁止活动的开展），禁止进行一项或者多项活动；

（四）依照本法典第一百七十三条（取消公开招投标的资格），取消公开招投标资格；

（五）依照本法典第一百七十四条（禁止公开上市），禁止公开上市；

（六）依照本法典第一百八十条（公布判决），公布量刑结果；

（七）依照本法典第一百八十一条（通过视听传媒播放判决），以印刷媒体公布量刑结果，或者以任何视听传媒播放量刑结果。

第三章　战争罪

第一百九十三条　战争罪的定义

"战争罪"系指直接针对受 1949 年 8 月 12 日《日内瓦公约》保护的人员或者财产所实施的任何下列行为：

（一）谋杀；

（二）酷刑或者包括生物实验在内的其他不人道对待；

（三）有意对身体或者健康造成巨大痛苦或者严重伤害；

（四）并非出于军事必要，非法和恣意地对财产进行大规模破坏和侵占；

（五）强迫战俘或者平民在敌国部队中服役；

（六）剥夺战俘或者平民受到公正和规范审判的权利；

（七）非法驱逐、迁徙或者拘禁平民；

（八）劫持平民作为人质。

第一百九十四条　其他战争罪

在国际或者非国际武装冲突中实施下列任何行为，也构成战争罪：

（一）使用有毒武器或者旨在造成不必要痛苦的其他武器；

（二）蓄意以任何方式攻击、轰炸非军事目标的不设防城镇、村庄、民居或者建筑物；

（三）蓄意攻击依照《联合国宪章》参与人道主义任务的人员或者物资；

（四）蓄意剥夺平民生存必需的物品，使其陷于饥饿；

（五）利用平民使某些建筑物、领土区域或者部队免于军事行动的影响；

（六）蓄意摧毁或者破坏作为宗教、慈善事业、教育、艺术、科学、历史古迹、艺术作品或者科学作品的建筑物；

（七）对自然环境造成广泛、长期和严重破坏，明显超出实际的和直接的预期军事利益；

（八）掠夺公共或者私人财产。

第一百九十五条　刑罚

犯战争罪，应当处以终身监禁。

第一百九十六条　策划战争罪

有组织地参与或者以共谋方式策划战争的，应当处以二十年至三十年监禁。

计划必须表现为一项或者多项实际行为。

第一百九十七条　附加刑（种类及期限）

对于本章规定的重罪，可以判处下列附加刑：

（一）剥夺特定权利，或者永久剥夺，或者剥夺期限在五年以内；

（二）禁止从事在从业期间实施了犯罪或者与犯罪有密切关联的职业，或者永久禁止，或者禁止期限在五年以内；

（三）期限在十年以内的本地驱逐；

（四）禁止离开柬埔寨王国领土，期限为五年以内；

（五）禁止被定罪的外国人进入和停留于柬埔寨王国领土，或者永久禁止，或者禁止期限在五年以内；

（六）没收用于或者打算用于实施犯罪的任何工具、材料或者物品；

（七）禁止拥有或者携带任何种类的任何武器、爆炸物或者弹药，或者永久禁止，或者禁止期限在五年以内；

（八）公布量刑结果，期限为二个月以内；

（九）以印刷媒体公布量刑结果；

（十）通过任何视听传媒公布量刑结果，期限为八天以内。

第一百九十八条　法人的刑事责任

根据本法典第四十二条（法人的刑事责任），可以确定法人对本法典第一百九十三条（战争罪），第一百九十四条（其他战争罪）和第一百九十六条（策划战争罪）规定的犯罪承担刑事责任。

应当对法人处以五千万瑞尔至五亿瑞尔的罚金，并处下列附加刑中的一项或者多项：

（一）依照本法典第一百七十条（法人的解散和清算）予以解散；

（二）依照本法典第一百七十一条（置于司法监视）予以司法监视；

（三）依照本法典第一百七十二条（禁止活动的开展），禁止进行一项或者多项活动；

（四）依照本法典第一百七十三条（取消公开招投标的资格），取消公开招投标资格；

（五）依照本法典第一百七十四条（禁止公开上市），禁止公开上市；

（六）依照本法典第一百八十条（公布判决），公布量刑结果；

（七）依照本法典第一百八十一条（通过视听传媒播放判决），以印刷媒体公布量刑结果，或者以任何视听传媒播放量刑结果。

第二部分 侵犯个人的犯罪

第一章 杀人罪

第一节 蓄意杀人罪

第一百九十九条 谋杀罪的定义

"谋杀罪"系指有意使用武器或者不使用武器地杀害他人,不包括本法典第二百条(有准备谋杀的定义)至第二百零五条(伴有酷刑、虐待或者强奸的谋杀罪)范围内有加重情节的情形。

犯谋杀罪,应当处以十年至十五年监禁。

第二百条 有准备谋杀的定义

"有准备谋杀"系指预先策划或者通过埋伏实施的谋杀罪。

预先策划包括针对被害人人身设想的侵害预案。

埋伏是指为了实施暴力而守候被害人的行为。

有准备谋杀的,应当处以终身监禁。

第二百零一条 投毒谋杀的定义

"投毒谋杀"的,应当处以十五年至三十年监禁。

第二百零二条　加重情节（被害人身份）

下列情形的谋杀罪,应当处以十五年至三十年监禁：

（一）侵害因年龄而特别脆弱的人；

（二）侵害明显是怀孕或者犯罪人明知是怀孕的妇女；

（三）侵害明显是或者犯罪人明知是因患病或者残疾而特别脆弱的人；

（四）侵害正在履行职责或者从事相关活动的公务人员。

第二百零三条　加重情节（动机）

下列情形的谋杀罪,应当处以十五年至三十年监禁：

（一）为避免举报或者索赔而对被害人或者当事人进行侵害；

（二）为避免调查、司法调查、审理或者其他诉讼程序中的举证而对被害人或者当事人进行侵害；

（三）对正在举报犯罪或者追索损害赔偿的被害人或者当事人进行侵害；

（四）对正在调查、司法调查、审理或者其他诉讼程序中举证的证人进行侵害。

第二百零四条　公务员实施的谋杀罪

正在履行职责或者进行相关活动的公务员实施谋杀罪,应当处以十五年至三十年监禁。

第二百零五条　伴有酷刑、虐待或者强奸的谋杀罪

实施谋杀之前或者之后存在酷刑、虐待或者强奸的,应当处以终身监禁。

第二百零六条 附加刑（种类及期限）

对于本节规定的重罪，可以判处下列附加刑：

（一）剥夺特定权利，或者永久剥夺，或者剥夺期限在五年以内；

（二）禁止从事在从业期间实施了犯罪或者与犯罪有密切关联的职业，或者永久禁止，或者禁止期限在五年以内；

（三）期限在十年以内的本地驱逐；

（四）禁止被定罪的外国人进入和停留于柬埔寨王国领土，或者永久禁止，或者禁止期限在五年以内；

（五）没收用于或者打算用于实施犯罪的任何工具、材料或者物品；

（六）禁止拥有或者携带任何种类的任何武器、爆炸物或者弹药，或者永久禁止，或者禁止期限在五年以内；

（七）公布量刑结果，期限为二个月以内；

（八）以印刷媒体公布量刑结果；

（九）通过任何视听传媒公布量刑结果，期限为八天以内。

第二节 非蓄意的杀人罪

第二百零七条 普通杀人罪的定义

"普通杀人罪"系指因下列情形导致他人死亡的行为：

（一）疏忽、轻率或者大意；

（二）违反法律强调的安全要求或者检查职责。

犯普通杀人罪，应当处以一年至三年监禁，并处二百万瑞尔至六百万瑞尔的罚金。

第二百零八条　附加刑（种类及期限）

普通杀人罪可以判处下列附加刑：

（一）禁止从事在从业期间实施了犯罪或者与犯罪有密切关联的职业，或者永久禁止，或者禁止期限在五年以内；

（二）禁止驾驶任何机动车辆，期限为五年以内；

（三）吊销驾驶执照，期限为五年以内；

（四）禁止拥有或者携带任何种类的任何武器、爆炸物或者弹药，或者永久禁止，或者禁止期限在五年以内；

（五）公布量刑结果，期限为二个月以内；

（六）以印刷媒体公布量刑结果；

（七）通过任何视听传媒公布量刑结果，期限为八天以内。

第二百零九条　法人的刑事责任

根据本法典第四十二条（法人的刑事责任），可以确定法人对本法典第二百零七条（普通杀人罪的定义）规定的犯罪承担刑事责任。

应当对法人处以一千万瑞尔至五千万瑞尔的罚金，并处下列附加刑中的一项或者多项：

（一）依照本法典第一百七十条（法人的解散和清算）予以解散；

（二）依照本法典第一百七十一条（置于司法监视）予以司法监视；

（三）依照本法典第一百七十二条（禁止活动的开展），禁止进行一项或者多项活动；

（四）依照本法典第一百七十六条（关闭场所）关闭场所；

（五）依照本法典第一百七十七条（禁止场所的运营）禁止场所向公众开放；

（六）依照本法典第一百八十条（公布判决），公布量刑结果；

（七）依照本法典第一百八十一条（通过视听传媒播放判决），以印刷媒体公布量刑结果，或者以任何视听传媒播放量刑结果。

第二章 侵犯人身完整性的犯罪

第一节 酷刑和虐待罪

第二百一十条 酷刑和虐待罪

对他人实施酷刑和虐待行为的，应当处以七年至十五年监禁。

第二百一十一条 加重情节（被害人身份）

第二百一十条（酷刑和虐待罪）规定的犯罪，如有下列情形应当处以十年至二十年监禁：

（一）侵害因年龄而特别脆弱的人；

（二）侵害明显是怀孕或者犯罪人明知是怀孕的妇女；

（三）侵害明显是或者犯罪人明知是因患病或者残疾而特别脆弱的人；

第二百一十二条　加重情节（动机）

第二百一十条（酷刑和虐待罪）规定的犯罪，如有下列情形，应当处以十年至二十年监禁：

（一）为避免举报或者索赔而对被害人或者当事人进行侵害；

（二）为避免调查、司法调查、审理或者其他诉讼程序中的举证而对被害人或者当事人进行侵害；

（三）对正在举报犯罪或者追索损害赔偿的被害人或者当事人进行侵害；

（四）对正在调查、司法调查、审理或者其他诉讼程序中举证的证人进行侵害。

第二百一十三条　加重情节（犯罪人身份）

正在履行公务或者从事相关活动的公务人员实施第二百一十条（酷刑和虐待罪）规定的犯罪的，应当处以十年至二十年监禁。

第二百一十四条　加重情节（肢残或者伤残）

第二百一十条（酷刑和虐待罪）规定的犯罪造成被害人肢残或者伤残的，应当处以十年至二十年监禁。

第二百一十五条　加重情节（被害人死亡）

第二百一十条（酷刑和虐待罪）规定的犯罪，如果不具有杀害他人的蓄意，造成被害人死亡或者导致被害人自杀的，应当处以十五年至三十年监禁。

第二百一十六条　附加刑（种类及期限）

对于本节规定的重罪，可以判处下列附加刑：

（一）剥夺特定权利，或者永久剥夺，或者剥夺期限在五年以内；

（二）禁止从事在从业期间实施了犯罪或者与犯罪有密切关联的职业，或者永久禁止，或者禁止期限在五年以内；

（三）期限在十年以内的本地驱逐；

（四）禁止被定罪外国人进入和停留于柬埔寨王国领土，或者永久禁止，或者禁止期限在五年以内；

（五）没收用于或者打算用于实施犯罪的任何工具、材料或者物品；

（六）禁止拥有或者携带任何种类的任何武器、爆炸物或者弹药，或者永久禁止，或者禁止期限在五年以内；

（七）公布量刑结果，期限为二个月以内；

（八）以印刷媒体公布量刑结果；

（九）通过任何视听传媒公布量刑结果，期限为八天以内。

第二节 暴行罪

第二百一十七条 蓄意施暴罪

蓄意对他人实施暴行的，应当处以一年至三年监禁，并处二百万瑞尔至六百万瑞尔的罚金。

第二百一十八条 加重情节

下列情形的蓄意施暴罪，应当处以二年至五年监禁，并处四百万瑞尔至一千万瑞尔的罚金：

（一）预先策划的；

（二）使用或者威胁使用武器的；

（三）分别作为实行犯、共司实行犯、教唆犯或者帮助犯的多人犯罪。

第二百一十九条　加重情节（被害人身份）

下列情形的蓄意施暴罪，应当处以二年至五年监禁，并处四百万瑞尔至一千万瑞尔的罚金：

（一）侵害因年龄而特别脆弱的人；

（二）侵害明显是怀孕或者犯罪人明知是怀孕的妇女；

（三）侵害明显是或者犯罪人明知是因患病或者残疾而特别脆弱的人；

第二百二十条　加重情节（动机）

下列情形的蓄意施暴罪，应当处以二年至五年监禁，并处四百万瑞尔至一千万瑞尔的罚金：

（一）为避免举报或者索赔而对被害人或者当事人进行侵害；

（二）为避免调查、司法调查、审理或者其他诉讼程序中的举证而对被害人或者当事人进行侵害；

（三）对正在举报犯罪或者追索损害赔偿的被害人或者当事人进行侵害；

（四）对正在调查、司法调查、审理或者其他诉讼程序中举证的证人进行侵害。

第二百二十一条　加重情节（犯罪人身份）

公务员执行其公务或者从事相关活动时实施暴行的，应当处以二年至五年监禁，并处四百万瑞尔至一千万瑞尔的罚金。

第二百二十二条　配偶或者伴侣实施的蓄意施暴罪

被害人的配偶或者伴侣蓄意施暴的，应当处以二年至五年监禁，并处四百万瑞尔至一千万瑞尔的罚金。

第二百二十三条　加重情节（肢残或者伤残）

蓄意施暴罪造成被害人肢残或者伤残的，应当处以五年至十年监禁。

第二百二十四条　加重情节（被害人死亡）

蓄意施暴而不具有杀害他人的蓄意，造成被害人死亡的，应当处以七年至十五年监禁。

第二百二十五条　视为蓄意施暴罪的有毒物质

对他人投放有毒物质的，应当视为蓄意施暴罪。

第二百二十六条　视为蓄意施暴罪的有毒食品

明知食品或者饮料会毒害身体而进行售卖、发放或者给予的，应当视为蓄意施暴罪。

第二百二十七条　视为蓄意施暴罪的对饮用水投毒

将有害身体的任何物质投入公共饮用水的，应当视为蓄意施暴罪。

第二百二十八条　轻微暴行罪的定义

未对他人造成任何伤害的轻微暴行罪，应当处以五千瑞尔至十万瑞尔的罚金。

第二百二十九条　附加刑（种类及期限）

对于本章规定的重罪，可以判处下列附加刑：

（一）剥夺特定权利，或者永久剥夺，或者剥夺期限在五年以内；

（二）禁止从事在从业期间实施了犯罪或者与犯罪有密切关联的职业，或者永久禁止，或者禁止期限在五年以内；

（三）如是重罪，期限在十年以内的本地驱逐，如是轻罪，期限为五年以内的本地驱逐；

（四）禁止被定罪外国人进入和停留于柬埔寨王国领土，或者永久禁止，或者禁止期限在五年以内；

（五）没收用于或者打算用于实施罪行的任何工具、材料或者物品；

（六）禁止拥有或者携带任何种类的任何武器、爆炸物或者弹药，或者永久禁止，或者禁止期限在五年以内；

（七）公布量刑结果，期限为二个月以内；

（八）以印刷媒体公布量刑结果；

（九）通过任何视听传媒公布量刑结果，期限为八天以内。

第二百三十条　法人的刑事责任

根据本法典第四十二条（法人的刑事责任），可以确定法人对本法典第二百二十六条（视为蓄意施暴罪的有毒食品）和第二百二十七条（视为蓄意施暴罪的对饮用水投毒）规定的犯罪承担刑事责任。

应当对法人处以一千万瑞尔至五千万瑞尔的罚金，并处下列附加刑中的一项或者多项：

（一）依照本法典第一百七十条（法人的解散和清算）予以解散；

（二）依照本法典第一百七十一条（置于司法监视）予以司法监视；

（三）依照本法典第一百七十二条（禁止活动的开展），禁止进行一项或者多项活动；

（四）依照本法典第一百七十三条（取消公开招投标的资格），取消公开招投标资格；

（五）依照本法典第一百七十四条（禁止公开上市），禁止公开上市；

（六）依照本法典第一百七十六条（关闭场所）关闭场所；

（七）依照本法典第一百七十七条（禁止场所的运营）禁止场所向公众开放；

（八）依照本法典第一百七十八条（没收物品的所有权、出售和销毁）和第一百七十九条（没收与第三方权利）没收用于或者打算用于实施罪行的任何工具、材料或者物品；

（九）依照本法典第一百七十八条（没收物品的所有权、出售和销毁）和第一百七十九条（没收与第三方权利）没收涉及犯罪的物品或者资金；

（十）依照本法典第一百七十八条（没收物品的所有权、出售和销毁）和第一百七十九条（没收与第三方权利）没收犯罪产生的收益或者财产；

（十一）依照本法典第一百八十条（公布判决），公布量刑结果；

（十二）依照本法典第一百八十一条（通过视听传媒播放判决），以印刷媒体公布量刑结果，或者以任何视听传媒播放量刑结果。

第三节　威胁罪

第二百三十一条　威胁罪

多次或者以书面文件、影像或者任何种类的物品威胁要对他人实施重罪或者轻罪的,应当处以一个月至六个月监禁,并处十万瑞尔至一百万瑞尔的罚金。

第二百三十二条　勒索威胁罪

以任何方式威胁对他人实施重罪或者轻罪,并有勒索行为的,应当处以六个月至二年监禁,并处一百万瑞尔至四百万瑞尔的罚金。

第二百三十三条　死亡威胁罪

多次或者以书面文件、影像或者任何种类的物品进行死亡威胁的,应当处以六个月至二年监禁,并处一百万瑞尔至四百万瑞尔的罚金。

第二百三十四条　伴有勒索的死亡威胁罪

以任何方式进行死亡威胁　并有勒索行为的,应当处以一年至三年监禁,并处二百万瑞尔至六百万瑞尔的罚金。

第二百三十五条　附加刑(种类及期限)

对于本节规定的犯罪,可以判处下列附加刑:

(一)剥夺特定权利,或者永久剥夺,或者剥夺期限在五年以内;

(二)禁止从事在从业期间实施了犯罪或者与犯罪有密切关联的职业,或者永久禁止,或者禁止期限在五年以内;

(三)如是重罪,期限为一年以内的本地驱逐,如是轻罪，期限为五年以内的本地驱逐；

（四）禁止被定罪外国人进入和停留于柬埔寨王国领土，或者永久禁止，或者禁止期限在五年以内；

（五）没收用于或者打算用于实施罪行的任何工具、材料或者物品；

（六）禁止拥有或者携带任何种类的任何武器、爆炸物或者弹药，或者永久禁止，或者禁止期限在五年以内；

（七）公布量刑结果，期限为二个月以内；

（八）以印刷媒体公布量刑结果；

（九）通过任何视听传媒公布量刑结果，期限为八天以内。

第四节　不慎致人伤害罪

第二百三十六条　不慎致人伤害罪

因下列情形致人伤害的，构成不慎致人伤害罪：

（一）因疏忽、轻率或者大意而造成被害人身体损伤达八天或者以上的；

（二）违反法律规定的安全要求或者检查职责的。

不慎致人身体伤害的，应当处以六个月至二年监禁，并处一百万瑞尔至四百万瑞尔的罚金。

第二百三十七条　附加刑（种类及期限）

犯不慎致人伤害罪，可以判处下列附加刑：

（一）禁止从事在从业期间实施了犯罪或者与犯罪有密切关联的职业，禁止期限在五年以内；

（二）禁止驾驶任何机动车辆，期限为五年以内；

（三）吊销驾驶执照，期限为五年以内；

（四）禁止拥有或者携带任何种类的任何武器、爆炸物或者弹药，禁止期限在五年以内；

（五）公布量刑结果，期限为二个月以内；

（六）以印刷媒体公布量刑结果；

（七）通过任何视听传媒公布量刑结果，期限为八天以内。

第二百三十八条　法人的刑事责任

根据本法典第四十二条（法人的刑事责任），可以确定法人对本法典第二百三十六条（不慎致人伤害罪）规定的犯罪承担刑事责任。

应当对法人处以五百万瑞尔至二千万瑞尔的罚金，并处下列附加刑中的一项或者多项：

（一）依照本法典第一百七十条（法人的解散和清算）予以解散；

（二）依照本法典第一百七十一条（置于司法监视）予以司法监视；

（三）依照本法典第一百七十二条（禁止活动的开展），禁止进行一项或者多项活动；

（四）依照本法典第一百七十六条（关闭场所）关闭场所；

（五）依照本法典第一百七十七条（禁止场所的运营）禁止场所向公众开放；

（六）依照本法典第一百八十条（公布判决），公布量刑结果；

（七）依照本法典第一百八十一条（通过视听传媒播放判决），以印刷媒体公布量刑结果，或者以任何视听传媒播放量刑结果。

第三章　性侵罪

第一节　强奸罪

第二百三十九条　强奸罪的定义

"强奸罪"系指以暴力、胁迫、威胁或者乘机的方式，以性器官或者物体对任何性别的他人实施的任何性插入行为。

犯强奸罪，应当处以五年至十年监禁。

性成熟的年龄应当为十五岁。

第二百四十条　加重情节（使用的手段或者犯罪人身份）

下列情形的强奸罪，应当处以七年至十五年监禁：

（一）使用或者威胁使用武器；

（二）使用麻醉品或者任何能够压制或者削弱被害人抵抗的手段；

（三）行为人是对被害人拥有权威的人；

（四）行为人滥用因其职责而对被害人拥有的权威；

（五）多个实行犯、共同实行犯、教唆犯或者帮助犯。

第二百四十一条 加重情节（被害人身份）

下列情形的强奸罪，应当处以七年至十五年监禁：

（一）侵害因年龄而特别脆弱的人；

（二）侵害明显是怀孕或者犯罪人明知是怀孕的妇女；

（三）侵害明显是或者犯罪人明知是因患病或者残疾而特别脆弱的人。

第二百四十二条 加重情节（肢残或者伤残）

强奸造成被害人肢残或者伤残的，应当处以十年至二十年监禁。

第二百四十三条 加重情节（酷刑或虐待行为）

实施强奸之前、之中或者之后有酷刑或者虐待行为的，应当处以十至三十年监禁。

第二百四十四条 加重情节（被害人死亡）

强奸罪，如果不具有杀害他人的蓄意，造成被害人死亡或者导致被害人自杀的，应当处以十五年至三十年监禁。

第二百四十五条 附加刑（种类及期限）

对于本节规定的重罪，可以判处下列附加刑：

（一）剥夺特定权利，或者永久剥夺，或者剥夺期限在五年以内；

（二）禁止从事在从业期间实施了犯罪或者与犯罪有密切关联的职业，或者永久禁止，或者禁止期限在五年以内；

（三）期限在十年以内的本地驱逐；

（四）禁止被定罪外国人进入和停留于柬埔寨王国领土，或者永久禁止，或者禁止期限在五年以内；

（五）没收用于或者打算用于实施罪行的任何工具、材料或者物品；

（六）公布量刑结果，期限为二个月以内；

（七）以印刷媒体公布量刑结果；

（八）通过任何视听传媒公布量刑结果，期限为八天以内。

第二节 其他性侵罪

第二百四十六条 强制猥亵罪的定义

未经他人同意，以获得刺激或者性快感为目的，触碰、爱抚或者抚摸其性器官或者其他部位的，或者强迫他人对侵害人自身或者第三人实施上述行为的，构成强制猥亵罪。

犯强制猥亵罪，应当处以一年至三年监禁，二百万瑞尔至六百万瑞尔的罚金。

第二百四十七条 加重情节（使用的手段或者犯罪人身份）

本法典第二百四十六条（强制猥亵罪的定义）规定的犯罪，有下列情形的，应当处以二年至五年监禁，并处四百万瑞尔至一千万瑞尔的罚金：

（一）使用或者威胁使用武器；

（二）使用麻醉品或者任何能够压制或者削弱被害人抵抗的手段；

（三）行为人是对被害人拥有权威的人；

（四）行为人滥用因其职责而对被害人拥有的权威；

（五）多个实行犯、共同实行犯、教唆犯或者帮助犯。

第二百四十八条　加重情节（被害人身份）

本法典第二百四十六条（强制猥亵罪的定义）规定的犯罪，有下列情形的，应当处以二年至五年监禁，并处四百万瑞尔至一千万瑞尔的罚金：

（一）侵害因年龄而特别脆弱的人；

（二）侵害明显是怀孕或者犯罪人明知是怀孕的妇女；

（三）侵害明显是或者犯罪人明知是因患病或者残疾而特别脆弱的人。

第二百四十九条　有伤风化的暴露罪

在公共场所对他人实施有伤风化的暴露行为的，应当处以六天至三个月的监禁，并处十万瑞尔至五十万瑞尔的罚金。

第二百五十条　性骚扰罪的定义

"性骚扰罪"系指行为人为满足性趣味而滥用职权对他人经常性地施加压力。

犯性骚扰罪，应当处以六天至三个月监禁，并处十万瑞尔至五十万瑞尔的罚金。

第二百五十一条　未遂

实施本节规定的轻罪而未遂的，应当处以同样的刑罚。

第二百五十二条　附加刑（种类及期限）

对于本节规定的犯罪，可以判处下列附加刑：

（一）剥夺特定权利，或者永久剥夺，或者剥夺期限在五年以内；

（二）禁止从事在从业期间实施了犯罪或者与犯罪有密切

关联的职业，或者永久禁止，或者禁止期限在五年以内；

（三）期限在五年以内的本地驱逐；

（四）禁止被定罪外国人进入和停留于柬埔寨王国领土，或者永久禁止，或者禁止期限在五年以内；

（五）禁止拥有或者携带任何种类的任何武器、爆炸物或者弹药，或者永久禁止，或者禁止期限在五年以内；

（六）公布量刑结果，期限为二个月以内；

（七）以印刷媒体公布量刑结果；

（八）通过任何视听传媒公布量刑结果，期限为八天以内。

第四章 非法剥夺自由的犯罪

第一节 擅自逮捕、拘留和非法拘禁罪

第二百五十三条 擅自逮捕、拘留和非法拘禁罪

未经司法程序，擅自逮捕、拘留或者非法拘禁他人的，应当处以以下期限的监禁刑：

（一）擅自逮捕、拘留或者非法拘禁未超过四十八小时的，刑期一年至三年；

（二）擅自逮捕、拘留或者非法拘禁超过四十八小时不到一个月的，刑期三年至五年；

（三）擅自逮捕、拘留或者非法拘禁超过一个月的，刑期五年至十年。

第二百五十四条　加重情节

未经司法程序，擅自逮捕、拘留和非法拘禁，如有下列情形的，应当处以十五年至三十年监禁：

（一）擅自逮捕、拘留和非法拘禁，伴有酷刑或者虐待行为；

（二）擅自逮捕、拘留和非法拘禁，非蓄意地造成他人死亡；

（三）擅自逮捕、拘留和非法拘禁，旨在确保赎金的支付或者条件的满足。

第二百五十五条　附加刑（种类及期限）

对于本节规定的犯罪，可以判处下列附加刑：

（一）剥夺特定权利，或者永久剥夺，或者剥夺期限在五年以内；

（二）禁止从事在从业期间实施了犯罪或者与犯罪有密切关联的职业，或者永久禁止，或者禁止期限在五年以内；

（三）如是重罪，期限在十年以内的本地驱逐，如是轻罪，期限在五年以内的本地驱逐；

（四）禁止被定罪外国人进入和停留于柬埔寨王国领土，或者永久禁止，或者禁止期限在五年以内；

（五）没收用于或者打算用于实施罪行的任何工具、材料或者物品；

（六）没收犯罪所得的收益或者财产；

（七）没收罪犯拥有的一辆或者多辆机动车；

（八）禁止拥有或者携带任何种类的任何武器、爆炸物或

者弹药,或者永久禁止,或者禁止期限在五年以内;

(九)公布量刑结果,期限为二个月以内;

(十)以印刷媒体公布量刑结果;

(十一)通过任何视听传媒公布量刑结果,期限为八天以内。

第二节 其他剥夺自由的犯罪

第二百五十六条 劫持交通工具罪

以暴力或者以暴力相威胁,夺取对任何种类的载人交通工具的控制的,应当处以五年至十年监禁。

第二百五十七条 加重情节(肢残或者伤残)

本法典第二百五十六条(劫持交通工具罪)规定的犯罪造成被害人肢残或者伤残的,应当处以十年至二十年监禁。

第二百五十八条 加重情节(酷刑或者虐待行为)

本法典第二百五十六条(劫持交通工具罪)规定的犯罪,如在实施之前、之中或者之后有酷刑或者虐待行为的,应当处以十五年至三十年监禁。

第二百五十九条 加重情节(被害人死亡)

本法典第二百五十六条(劫持交通工具罪)规定的犯罪,如果造成一人或者多人死亡的,应当处以十五年至三十年监禁。

第二百六十条 附加刑罚(种类和期限)

对于本节规定的犯罪,可以判处下列附加刑:

(一)剥夺特定权利,或者永久剥夺,或者剥夺期限在五年以内；

（二）禁止从事在从业期间实施了犯罪或者与犯罪有密切关联的职业，或者永久禁止，或者禁止期限在五年以内；

（三）期限在十年以内的本地驱逐；

（四）禁止被定罪外国人进入和停留于柬埔寨王国领土，或者永久禁止，或者禁止期限在五年以内；

（五）没收用于或者打算用于实施罪行的任何工具、材料或者物品；

（六）没收犯罪所得的收益或者财产；

（七）没收罪犯拥有的一辆或者多辆机动车；

（八）禁止拥有或者携带任何种类的任何武器、爆炸物或者弹药，或者永久禁止，或者禁止期限在五年以内；

（九）公布量刑结果，期限为二个月以内；

（十）以印刷媒体公布量刑结果；

（十一）通过任何视听传媒公布量刑结果，期限为八天以内。

第五章　亵渎人格尊严的犯罪

第一节　对死者不敬的犯罪

第二百六十一条　损害尸体完整性罪

损害尸体物理完整性的，应当处以一个月至一年监禁，并处十万瑞尔至二百万瑞尔的罚金。

第二百六十二条 亵渎墓地罪

以任何方式亵渎坟墓、墓园、为纪念死者而建的佛塔或者纪念碑的,应当处以一个月至一年监禁,并处十万瑞尔至二百万瑞尔的罚金。

第二百六十三条 未遂

实施本节规定的轻罪而未遂的,应当处以同样的刑罚。

第二百六十四条 附加刑(种类及期限)

对于本节规定的犯罪,可以判处下列附加刑:

(一)剥夺特定权利,或者永久剥夺,或者剥夺期限在五年以内;

(二)禁止从事在从业期间实施了犯罪或者与犯罪有密切关联的职业,或者永久禁止,或者禁止期限在五年以内;

(三)公布量刑结果,期限为二个月以内;

(四)以印刷媒体公布量刑结果;

(五)通过任何视听传媒公布量刑结果,期限为八天以内。

第二节 歧视罪

第二百六十五条 拒不提供商品或者服务罪

以下列任何理由拒不向他人提供商品或者服务的,应当处以一个月至一年监禁,并处一万瑞尔至二百万瑞尔的罚金:

(一)是或者不是特定族群、国籍或者人种的成员;

(二)是或者不是特定宗教的成员;

(三)政治立场;

（四）工会活动；

（五）家庭状况；

（六）性别；

（七）健康状态；

（八）残疾。

第二百六十六条　有差别地提供商品或者服务罪

因任何下列情形而有差别地提供商品或者服务的，应当处以一个月至一年监禁，并处一万瑞尔至二百万瑞尔的罚金：

（一）是或者不是特定族群、国籍或者人种的成员；

（二）是或者不是特定宗教的成员；

（三）政治立场；

（四）工会活动；

（五）家庭状况；

（六）性别；

（七）健康状态；

（八）残疾。

第二百六十七条　拒不雇用罪

出于本法典第二百六十五条（拒不提供商品或者服务罪）第一项至第八项的理由，拒不雇用他人的，应当处以一个月至一年监禁，并处一万瑞尔至二百万瑞尔的罚金。

第二百六十八条　有差别地雇用罪

出于本法典第二百六十六条（有差别地提供商品或者服务罪）第一项至第八项的理由，有差别地雇用他人的，应当处以一个月至一年监禁，并处一万瑞尔至二百万瑞尔的罚金。

第二百六十九条　因歧视停职或者开除罪

出于本法典第二百六十五条（拒不提供商品或者服务罪）第一项至第八项的理由，终止雇用或者开除他人的，应当处以一个月至一年监禁，并处一万瑞尔至二百万瑞尔的罚金。

第二百七十条　公务员因歧视拒不行使职权罪

出于本法典第二百六十五条（拒不提供商品或者服务罪）第一项至第八项的理由，拒不行使职权或者从事与他人权利有关的公务的，应当处以六个月至二年监禁，并处一百万瑞尔至四百万瑞尔的罚金。

第二百七十一条　法律允许的区别对待

法律允许的区别对待不应当构成本节规定的犯罪。

下列区别对待不适用本节的规定：

（一）出于健康的考虑，为了防止人身安全的风险、工作能力的丧失或者导致残疾；

（二）由于健康状况或者残疾，并且根据医学证明的丧失能力而拒不雇用或者终止雇用；

（三）雇用取决于性别，是男性还是女性成为聘用或者就业的决定性因素。

第二百七十二条　附加刑（种类及期限）

对于本节规定的犯罪，可以判处下列附加刑：

（一）剥夺特定权利，或者永久剥夺，或者剥夺期限在五年以内；

（二）禁止从事在从业期间实施了犯罪或者与犯罪有密切关联的职业，或者永久禁止，或者禁止期限在五年以内；

（三）公布量刑结果，期限为二个月以内；

（四）以印刷媒体公布量刑结果；

（五）通过任何视听传媒公布量刑结果，期限为八天以内。

第二百七十三条　法人的刑事责任

根据本法典第四十二条（法人的刑事责任），可以确定法人对本法典第二百六十五条（拒不提供商品或者服务罪）和第二百六十九条（因歧视停职或者开除罪）规定的犯罪承担刑事责任。

应当对法人处以一百万瑞尔至一千万瑞尔的罚金，并处下列附加刑中的一项或者多项：

（一）依照本法典第一百七十一条（置于司法监视）予以司法监视；

（二）依照本法典第一百七十二条（禁止活动的开展），禁止进行一项或者多项活动；

（三）依照本法典第一百八十条（公布判决），公布量刑结果；

（四）依照本法典第一百八十一条（通过视听传媒播放判决），以印刷媒体公布量刑结果，或者以任何视听传媒播放量刑结果。

第三节　强加有辱人类尊严的工作条件罪

第二百七十四条　强加有辱人类尊严的工作条件罪

利用他人弱势或者依赖地位，迫使其在有辱人类尊严的条件下工作的,应当处以一个月至一年监禁,并处十万瑞尔至二百万瑞尔的罚金。

第二百七十五条 未遂

实施本法典第二百七十四条(强加有辱人类尊严的工作条件罪)规定的轻罪而未遂的,应当处以同样的刑罚。

第二百七十六条 附加刑(种类及期限)

对于本节规定的犯罪,可以判处下列附加刑:

(一)剥夺特定权利,或者永久剥夺,或者剥夺期限在五年以内;

(二)禁止从事在从业期间实施了犯罪或者与犯罪有密切关联的职业,或者永久禁止,或者禁止期限在五年以内;

(三)公布量刑结果,期限为二个月以内;

(四)以印刷媒体公布量刑结果;

(五)通过任何视听传媒公布量刑结果,期限为八天以内。

第二百七十七条 法人的刑事责任

根据本法典第四十二条(法人的刑事责任),可以确定法人对本法典第二百七十四条(强加有辱人类尊严的工作条件罪)规定的犯罪承担刑事责任。

应当对法人处以一百万瑞尔至一千万瑞尔的罚金,并处下列附加刑中的一项或者多项:

(一)依照本法典第一百七十条(法人的解散和清算)予以解散;

(二)依照本法典第一百七十一条(置于司法监视)予以司法监视;

（三）依照本法典第一百七十二条（禁止活动的开展），禁止进行一项或者多项活动；

（四）依照本法典第一百七十三条（取消公开招投标的资格），取消公开招投标资格；

（五）依照本法典第一百七十四条（禁止公开上市），禁止公开上市；

（六）依照本法典第一百七十六条（关闭场所）关闭场所；

（七）依照本法典第一百七十七条（禁止场所的运营）禁止场所向公众开放；

（八）依照本法典第一百七十八条（没收物品的所有权、出售和销毁）和第一百七十九条（没收与第三方权利）没收用于或者打算用于实施罪行的任何工具、材料或者物品；

（九）依照本法典第一百七十八条（没收物品的所有权、出售和销毁）和第一百七十九条（没收与第三方权利）没收涉及犯罪的物品或者资金；

（十）依照本法典第一百七十八条（没收物品的所有权、出售和销毁）和第一百七十九条（没收与第三方权利）没收犯罪产生的收益或者财产；

（十一）依照本法典第一百八十条（公布判决），公布量刑结果；

（十二）依照本法典第一百八十一条（通过视听传媒播放判决），以印刷媒体公布量刑结果，或者以任何视听传媒播放量刑结果。

第四节 雇员和管理者腐败的犯罪

第二百七十八条 雇员索取或者收受贿赂罪

雇员在雇主不知情时或者未经雇主准许而索要或者接受任何捐赠、礼品、许诺或者报酬，作为其履行或者不履行职责的条件的，应当处以六个月至二年监禁，并处一百万瑞尔至四百万瑞尔的罚金。

第二百七十九条 对雇员行贿罪

任何人在雇主不知情时或者未经雇主准许而向雇员提供任何捐赠、礼品、许诺或者报酬，以此作为雇员履行或者不履行职责的条件的，应当处以六个月至二年监禁，并处一百万瑞尔至四百万瑞尔的罚金。

第二百八十条 管理者贿赂罪

（一）本法典第三百九十三条（管理者或者其他人员违反特别信用罪）第一款和第二款提及的任何人或者督察人员接受非法请托，收取或者索要物质利益，或者答应因非法请托收取利益的，应当处以五年至十年监禁。

（二）任何人配送、提供或者承诺上述第一款利益的，同样适用该项刑罚。

（三）上述第一款规定的任何物质利益都应当没收。如果无法没收全部利益或者部分利益，应当由收受利益者补偿。

第二百八十一条 未遂

实施本法典第二百七十八条（雇员索取或者收受贿赂罪）和第二百七十九条（对雇员行贿罪）规定的轻罪而未遂的，

应当处以同样的刑罚。

第二百八十二条 附加刑（种类及期限）

对于本节规定的犯罪，可以判处下列附加刑：

（一）剥夺特定权利，或者永久剥夺，或者剥夺期限在五年以内；

（二）禁止从事在从业期间实施了犯罪或者与犯罪有密切关联的职业，或者永久禁止，或者禁止期限在五年以内；

（三）公布量刑结果，期限为二个月以内；

（四）以印刷媒体公布量刑结果；

（五）通过任何视听传媒公布量刑结果，期限为八天以内。

第二百八十三条 法人的刑事责任

根据本法典第四十二条（法人的刑事责任），可以确定法人对本法典第二百七十九条（对雇员行贿罪）规定的犯罪承担刑事责任。

应当对法人处以五百万瑞尔至二千万瑞尔的罚金，并处下列附加刑中的一项或者多项：

（一）依照本法典第一百七十条（法人的解散和清算）予以解散；

（二）依照本法典第一百七十一条（置于司法监视）予以司法监视；

（三）依照本法典第一百七十二条（禁止活动的开展），禁止进行一项或者多项活动；

（四）依照本法典第一百七十三条（取消公开招投标的资

格），取消公开招投标资格；

（五）依照本法典第一百七十四条（禁止公开上市），禁止公开上市；

（六）依照本法典第一百七十八条（没收物品的所有权、出售和销毁）和第一百七十九条（没收与第三方权利）没收用于或者打算用于实施罪行的任何工具、材料或者物品；

（七）依照本法典第一百八十条（公布判决），公布量刑结果；

（八）依照本法典第一百八十一条（通过视听传媒播放判决），以印刷媒体公布量刑结果，或者以任何视听传媒播放量刑结果。

第五节　淫媒罪

第二百八十四条　淫媒罪

"淫媒罪"系指：

（一）通过他人卖淫牟利；

（二）协助或者保护他人卖淫，或者以任何方式组织卖淫；

（三）招募、诱拐或者引诱他人卖淫；

（四）逼迫任何人成为娼妓。

犯淫媒罪应当处以二年至五年监禁，并处四百万瑞尔至一千万瑞尔的罚金。

第二百八十五条　居间介绍娼妓罪

在卖淫者与淫媒者之间从事居间介绍活动的，应当处以二年至五年监禁,并处四百万瑞尔至一千万瑞尔的罚金。

第二百八十六条 粉饰淫媒收益罪

帮助粉饰或者掩盖淫媒收益的,应当处以二年至五年监禁,并处四百万瑞尔至一千万瑞尔的罚金。

与经常从事卖淫活动的人一起居住或者与一名或者多名从事卖淫的人保持经常往来的任何人,如果不能说明其收益与其生活方式相匹配,则应当被处以同样的刑罚。

第二百八十七条 妨碍施行预防卖淫措施罪

任何妨碍公共服务机构或者有资质的私人机构向从事卖淫或者有卖淫危险的人提供预防性援助或者再教育的行为,均可处以二年至五年监禁,并处四百万瑞尔至一千万瑞尔的罚金。

第二百八十八条 加重情节(犯罪人身份)

下列情况的淫媒罪,应当处以五年至十年监禁:

(一)淫媒者是卖淫者的后代或者长辈;

(二)淫媒者滥用其对卖淫者所具有的职权;

(三)淫媒者对卖淫者进行强制或者施用暴力;

(四)有组织犯罪集团实施;

(五)多人卖淫。

第二百八十九条 加重情节(被害人身份)

卖淫者是未成年人的,淫媒者应当处以七年至十五年监禁。

第二百九十条 加重情节(酷刑或者虐待行为)

淫媒者对卖淫者施加酷刑或者虐待行为的,应当处以十年至二十年监禁。

第二百九十一条　经营卖淫场所罪

直接或者通过中间人管理、运作、指挥、经营或者资助卖淫场所的，应当处以二年至五年监禁，并处四百万瑞尔至一千万瑞尔的罚金。

第二百九十二条　容留卖淫活动罪

任何管理、运作、支配或者经营向公众开放场所的人，直接或者通过中介，接纳或者容留任何人从事下列活动的，应当处以二年至五年监禁，并处四百万瑞尔至一千万瑞尔的罚金：

（一）在处所或者附属建筑内卖淫；

（二）在处所内定期招徕嫖客，以期在该处所或者其附属建筑内卖淫。

第二百九十三条　提供卖淫场所罪

向任何人出售或者提供任何不向公众开放的处所或者场地，且明知他人将在此处从事卖淫的，应当处以二年至五年监禁，并处四百万瑞尔至一千万瑞尔的罚金。

第二百九十四条　未遂

实施本节规定的轻罪而未遂的，应当处以同样的刑罚。

第二百九十五条　附加刑（种类及期限）

对于本节规定的犯罪，可以判处下列附加刑：

（一）剥夺特定权利，或者永久剥夺，或者剥夺期限在五年以内；

（二）禁止从事在从业期间实施了犯罪或者与犯罪有密切

关联的职业，或者永久禁止，或者禁止期限在五年以内；

（三）如是重罪，期限在十年以内的本地驱逐，如是轻罪，期限在五年以内的本地驱逐；

（四）禁止被定罪外国人进入和停留于柬埔寨王国领土，或者永久禁止，或者禁止期限在五年以内；

（五）没收用于或者打算用于实施罪行的任何工具、材料或者物品；

（六）没收涉及犯罪的物品或者资金；

（七）没收犯罪所得的收益或者财产；

（八）没收犯罪发生场所的器具、材料和家具；

（九）没收罪犯拥有的一辆或者多辆机动车；

（十）禁止拥有或者携带任何种类的任何武器、爆炸物或者弹药，或者永久禁止，或者禁止期限在五年以内；

（十一）关闭用于谋划或者实施犯罪的设施，或者永久禁止，或者禁止期限在五年以内；

（十二）禁止经营向公众开放或者供公众使用的设施，或者永久禁止，或者禁止期限在五年以内；

（十三）公布量刑结果，期限为二个月以内；

（十四）以印刷媒体公布量刑结果；

（十五）通过任何视听传媒公布量刑结果，期限为八天以内。

第二百九十六条　法人的刑事责任

根据本法典第四十二条（法人的刑事责任），可以确定法人对本节规定的犯罪承担刑事责任。

应当对法人处以一千万瑞尔至五千万瑞尔的罚金，并处下列附加刑中的一项或者多项：

（一）依照本法典第一百七十条（法人的解散和清算）予以解散；

（二）依照本法典第一百七十一条（置于司法监视）予以司法监视；

（三）依照本法典第一百七十二条（禁止活动的开展），禁止进行一项或者多项活动；

（四）依照本法典第一百七十六条（关闭场所）关闭场所；

（五）依照本法典第一百七十七条（禁止场所的运营）禁止场所向公众开放；

（六）依照本法典第一百七十八条（没收物品的所有权、出售和销毁）和第一百七十九条（没收与第三方权利）没收用于或者打算用于实施罪行的任何工具、材料或者物品；

（七）依照本法典第一百七十八条（没收物品的所有权、出售和销毁）和第一百七十九条（没收与第三方权利）没收涉及犯罪的物品或者资金；

（八）依照本法典第一百七十八条（没收物品的所有权、出售和销毁）和第一百七十九条（没收与第三方权利）没收犯罪产生的收益或者财产；

（九）依照本法典第一百八十条（公布判决），公布量刑结果；

（十）依照本法典第一百八十一条（通过视听传媒播放判决），以印刷媒体公布量刑结果，或者以任何视听传媒播放量刑结果。

第六节　其他有辱尊严的犯罪

第二百九十七条　醉酒罪

任何人在公共道路上明显醉酒的，应当处以五千瑞尔至一万瑞尔的罚金。

第二百九十八条　在公共场所招嫖罪

以诱使他人从事性交易为目的，在公共场所招引他人的，应当处以五千瑞尔至五万瑞尔的罚金。

第六章　侵犯个人自由的犯罪

第一节　侵犯隐私罪

第二百九十九条　破门入户罪

未经法律授权，采取暴力或者强制、威胁、欺骗的方法进入他人住所的，应当处以一个月至一年的监禁，并处一万瑞尔至二百万瑞尔的罚金。

第三百条　加重情节（犯罪人身份）

未经法律授权，公务员执行其公务或者从事相关活动时违反他人意志进入他人住所的，应当处以一年至二年监禁，二百万瑞尔至四百万瑞尔的罚金。

第三百零一条　窃听或者偷录私人谈话罪

除非在法律有规定的场合，否则未经他人同意，窃听或者偷录其在私密场合所述话语的，应当处以一个月至一年监禁，并处十万瑞尔至二百万瑞尔的罚金。

如果当事者已经得知自己的谈话受到窃听或者被偷录，却未表示反对，应当推定为同意。

第三百零二条　侵犯隐私罪（偷录他人影像）

除非在法律有规定的场合，否则未经他人同意，偷录其在私密场所的影像的，应当处以一个月至一年监禁，并处十万瑞尔至二百万瑞尔的罚金。

如果当事者已经得知自己的影像被偷录，却未表示反对，应当推定为同意。

第三百零三条　未遂

实施本节规定的轻罪而未遂的，应当处以同样的刑罚。

第三百零四条　附加刑（种类及期限）

对于本节规定的犯罪，可以判处下列附加刑：

（一）剥夺特定权利，或者永久剥夺，或者剥夺期限在五年以内；

（二）禁止从事在从业期间实施了犯罪或者与犯罪有密切关联的职业，或者永久禁止，或者禁止期限在五年以内；

（三）公布量刑结果，期限为二个月以内；

（四）以印刷媒体公布量刑结果；

（五）通过任何视听传媒公布量刑结果，期限为八天以内。

第二节　诽谤罪和公然侮辱罪

第三百零五条　诽谤罪的定义

"诽谤罪"系指恶意作出的任何有损个人或者机构的品格或者声望的指责。

以下列任何方式实施诽谤的，应当处以十万瑞尔至一千万瑞尔的罚金：

（一）在公共场所或者公共集会上发表任何言论；

（二）向公众发布或者展示任何形式的书面文件或者图像；

（三）面向公众的任何视听交流。

第三百零六条　利用媒体诽谤罪

利用媒体实施诽谤的，应当适用《新闻法》的规定。

第三百零七条　公然侮辱罪的定义

"侮辱罪"系指粗暴的表达、轻蔑的用语或者脱离任何事实归咎的谩骂。

以下列任何方式实施侮辱罪的，应当处以十万瑞尔至一千万瑞尔的罚金：

（一）在公共场所或者公共集会上发表任何言论；

（二）向公众发布或者展示任何形式的书面文件或者图像；

（三）面向公众的任何视听交流。

第三百零八条　利用媒体侮辱罪

利用媒体实施侮辱的，应当适用《新闻法》的规定。

第三百零九条　诽谤罪和公然侮辱罪的审理程序

对王国政府、公务人员或者执行公共任务或者命令的任何公民进行诽谤或者公然侮辱的，应当在涉事对象提出控告的基础上起诉，或者由涉事个人或者涉事机构的负责人在提出控告后自行起诉。

诽谤或者侮辱个人的，应当由遭受诽谤或者侮辱的人提起诉讼。

第三百零九条上述两款规定的个人或者机构负责人提出控告作为检察机关提起刑事诉讼的必备条件的，则撤回控告即终结刑事诉讼。

但是，针对个人或者群体的出身、民族、种族、国籍或者宗教进行诽谤或者公然侮辱的，可以由检察官自主提起诉讼。将这类案件移送审判的程序应当符合《刑事诉讼法典》的规定。

第三百一十条　附加刑（种类及期限）

对于本节规定的犯罪，可以判处下列附加刑：

（一）公布量刑结果；

（二）以印刷媒体公布量刑结果；

（三）通过任何视听传媒公布量刑结果，期限为八天以内。

第三节　诬告罪

第三百一十一条　诬告罪的定义

"诬告罪"指明知是虚假的情况而向下列人员举报以期引

起刑事处罚或者纪律制裁的行为：

——有追诉权的法官、司法警官或者雇主；

——任何有权将举报提交给追诉人员的人。

第三百一十二条　适用的刑罚和起诉条件

犯诬告罪，应当处以一个月至一年监禁，并处十万瑞尔至二百万瑞尔的罚金。

此种案件的诉讼时效为一年。

此种犯罪的时效期间自诬告被人所知或者提交主管机关之日起计算。

诬告内容导致刑事诉讼的，结案前应当中止该刑事诉讼。

第三百一十三条　附加刑（种类及期限）

对于本节规定的轻罪，可以判处下列附加刑：

（一）公布量刑结果，期限为二个月以内；

（二）以印刷媒体公布量刑结果；

（三）通过任何视听传媒公布量刑结果，期限为八天以内。

第四节　泄露职业秘密罪

第三百一十四条　泄露职业秘密罪

任何因其职位或者职业、职责或者职能而掌握秘密信息的人向无权获取该信息的人泄露该信息的，应当处以一个月至一年监禁，并处十万瑞尔至二百万瑞尔的罚金。

法律授权或者强制披露秘密的，不构成犯罪。

第三百一十五条　不适用第三百一十四条的情形

向任何司法部门、医疗机构或者行政当局揭露其从事职业过程中获知的虐待十五岁以下未成年人的情况的，不应当被视为本法典第三百一十四条（泄露职业秘密罪）规定的犯罪。

第三百一十六条　附加刑（种类及期限）

对于本节规定的轻罪，可以判处下列附加刑：

（一）禁止从事在从业期间实施了犯罪或者与犯罪有密切关联的职业，或者永久禁止，或者禁止期限在五年以内；

（二）公布量刑结果，期限为二个月以内；

（三）以印刷媒体公布量刑结果；

（四）通过任何视听传媒公布量刑结果，期限为八天以内。

第五节　侵犯私密通信和通信罪

第三百一十七条　侵犯通信罪

恶意将寄给第三方的信件拆封、损毁、延迟或者转移的，应当处以一个月至一年监禁，并处十万瑞尔至二百万瑞尔的罚金。

恶意截取寄给第三方信件的，应当处以同样的刑罚。

第三百一十八条　侵犯私密电讯通话罪

偷听或者干扰电讯通话的，应当处以一个月至一年监禁，并处十万瑞尔至二百万瑞尔的罚金。

窃听或者干扰，偷看或者偷听以电讯方式传送的信息的，应当处以同样的刑罚。

第三百一十九条 未遂

实施本节规定的轻罪而未遂的,应当处以同样的刑罚。

第三百二十条 附加刑(种类及期限)

对于本节规定的犯罪,可以判处下列附加刑:

(一)禁止从事在从业期间实施了犯罪或者与犯罪有密切关联的职业,或者永久禁止,或者禁止期限在五年以内;

(二)没收用于或者打算用于实施犯罪的任何工具、材料或者物品;

(三)公布量刑结果,期限为二个月以内;

(四)以印刷媒体公布量刑结果;

(五)通过任何视听传媒公布量刑结果,期限为八天以内。

第三部分　侵害未成年人和亲属的犯罪

第一章　遗弃未成年人的犯罪

第三百二十一条　遗弃未成年人罪的刑罚

法定监护人遗弃十五岁以下未成年人，危及未成年人健康或者安全的，应当处以一年至五年监禁，并处二百万瑞尔至一千万瑞尔的罚金。

第三百二十二条　未遂

实施本章规定的轻罪而未遂的，应当处以同样的刑罚。

第三百二十三条　附加刑（种类及期限）

对于本章规定的轻罪，可以判处下列附加刑：

（一）剥夺特定权利，期限在五年以内；

（二）公布量刑结果，期限为二个月以内；

（三）以印刷媒体公布量刑结果；

（四）通过任何视听传媒公布量刑结果，期限为八天以内。

第二章　遗弃亲属的犯罪

第三百二十四条　遗弃亲属罪

违反生效判决，不向配偶或者原配偶、未成年人、后代、长辈或者其他亲属支付抚养费超过二个月的，应当处以一个月至一年监禁，并处十万瑞尔至二百万瑞尔的罚金。

第三百二十五条　附加刑（种类及期限）

对于本章规定的轻罪，可以判处下列附加刑：

（一）剥夺特定权利，期限在五年以内；

（二）公布量刑结果，期限为二个月以内；

（三）以印刷媒体公布量刑结果；

（四）通过任何视听传媒公布量刑结果，期限为八天以内。

第三章　干扰对未成年人监护的犯罪

第三百二十六条　不移交未成年人罪

恶意地不向有监护权的人移交未成年人的，应当处以一个月至一年监禁，并处十万瑞尔至二百万瑞尔的罚金。

第三百二十七条　擅自带走未成年人罪

擅自将未成年人从法定监护人处带走的，应当处以一个月至一年监禁，并处十万瑞尔至二百万瑞尔的罚金。

将未成年人带至柬埔寨王国领土外的，应当处以一年至三年监禁，并处二百万瑞尔至六百万瑞尔的罚金。

第三百二十八条　未遂

实施本章规定的轻罪而未遂的，应当处以同样的刑罚。

第三百二十九条　附加刑（种类及期限）

对于本章规定的轻罪，可以判处下列附加刑：

（一）剥夺特定权利，期限在五年以内；

（二）公布量刑结果，期限为二个月以内；

（三）以印刷媒体公布量刑结果；

（四）通过任何视听传媒公布量刑结果，期限为八天以内。

第四章　侵犯亲属关系的犯罪

第三百三十条　诱使他人遗弃子女罪

直接以金钱利益为诱饵，唆使父母遗弃已经出生或者将要出生的子女的，应当处以一个月至六个月监禁，并处十万瑞尔至一百万瑞尔的罚金。

第三百三十一条　介绍领养或者遗弃罪

为了金钱利益，在打算收养孩子的个人或者夫妻与打算遗弃已经出生或者尚未出生孩子的夫妻之间充当中介的，应当处以一个月至六个月监禁，并处十万瑞尔至一百万瑞尔的罚金。

第三百三十二条　在领养人与孕妇之间充当掮客罪

为了金钱利益，在打算收养孩子的个人或者夫妻与打算孩子出生后将其出让的孕妇之间充当掮客的，应当处以一个月至六个月监禁，并处十万瑞尔至一百万瑞尔的罚金。

第三百三十三条　替换、虚构或者隐瞒新生儿罪

替换、虚构或者隐瞒新生儿，侵犯其公民身份的，应当处以一个月至一年监禁，并处一万瑞尔至二百万瑞尔的罚金。

第三百三十四条　未遂

实施本章规定的轻罪而未遂的，应当处以同样的刑罚。

第三百三十五条　附加刑（种类及期限）

对于本章规定的犯罪，可以判处下列附加刑：

（一）剥夺特定权利，期限在五年以内；

（二）公布量刑结果，期限为二个月以内；

（三）以印刷媒体公布量刑结果；

（四）通过任何视听传媒公布量刑结果，期限为八天以内。

第三百三十六条　法人的刑事责任

根据本法典第四十二条（法人的刑事责任），可以确定法人对本法典第三百三十条（诱使他人遗弃子女罪）、第三百三十一条（介绍领养或者遗弃罪）和第三百三十二条（在领养人与孕妇之间充当掮客罪）规定的犯罪承担刑事责任。

应当对法人处以一百万瑞尔至五百万瑞尔的罚金，并处下列附加刑中的一项或者多项：

（一）依照本法典第一百七十一条（置于司法监视）予以司法监视；

（二）依照本法典第一百七十二条（禁止活动的开展），禁止进行一项或者多项活动；

(三)依照本法典第一百七十六条(关闭场所)关闭场所;

(四)依照本法典第一百七十八条(没收物品的所有权、出售和销毁)和第一百七十九条(没收与第三方权利)没收涉及犯罪的物品或者资金;

(五)依照本法典第一百八十条(公布判决),公布量刑结果;

(六)依照本法典第一百八十一条(通过视听传媒播放判决),以印刷媒体公布量刑结果,或者以任何视听传媒播放量刑结果。

第五章 伤害未成年人的犯罪

第一节 损害身心健康的犯罪

第三百三十七条 使十五岁以下未成年人失去食物或者照料罪

对十五岁以下未成年人拥有管理权力的任何人,使未成年人失去食物或者照料,足以危害其健康的,应当处以二年至五年监禁,并处四百万瑞尔至一千万瑞尔的罚金。

第三百三十八条 加重情节(被害人死亡)

实施本法典第三百三十七条(使十五岁以下未成年人失去食物或者照料罪)规定的犯罪,造成被害人死亡的,应当处以七年至十五年监禁。

第三百三十九条　将未成年人置于有害健康的工作环境罪

将未成年人置于有害健康或者身体发育的工作环境的，应当处以二年至五年监禁，并处四百万瑞尔至一千万瑞尔的罚金。

第三百四十条　造成未成年人死亡的加重情节

实施本法典第三百三十九条（将未成年人置于有害健康的工作环境罪）规定的犯罪，如果造成被害人死亡的，应当处以七年至十五年监禁。

第三百四十一条　猥亵十五岁以下未成年人罪

猥亵是以自身获得性刺激或者性快感为目的，触摸或者暴露性器官或者他人身体其他部位，或者让他人触摸行为人性器官或者身体其他部位的行为。

犯猥亵十五岁以下未成年人罪，应当处以一年至三年监禁，并处二百万瑞尔至六百万瑞尔的罚金。

第三百四十二条　加重情节

本法典第三百四十一条（猥亵十五岁以下未成年人罪）规定的犯罪，如有下列情形，应当处以二年至五年监禁，并处四百万瑞尔至一千万瑞尔的罚金：

（一）侵害人是被害人的长辈；

（二）侵害人是对被害人拥有权威的人；

（三）分别作为实行犯、共同实行犯、教唆犯或者帮助犯的多人犯罪。

（四）涉及金钱支付。

第二节　唆使未成年人实施违法或者危险行为的犯罪

第三百四十三条　唆使未成年人吸食毒品罪

直接唆使未成年人非法地和经常地吸食大量毒品的，应当处以六个月至二年监禁，并处一百万瑞尔至四百万瑞尔的罚金。

第三百四十四条　唆使未成年人赌博罪

直接唆使未成年人赌博的，应当处以一个月至一年监禁，并处十万瑞尔至二百万瑞尔的罚金。

第三百四十五条　诱使未成年人实施重罪或者轻罪

直接诱使未成年人实施重罪或者轻罪的，应当处以二年至五年监禁，并处四百万瑞尔至一千万瑞尔的罚金。

第三百四十六条　成年人安排涉及未成年人的不雅暴露或者性交罪

成年人安排涉及不雅暴露或者性交的聚会，有未成年人在场或者参与的，应当处以一年至五年监禁，并处二百万瑞尔至一千万瑞尔的罚金。

第三节　滥用亲权的犯罪

第三百四十七条　滥用亲权罪

滥用基于法律、自然或者收养关系形成的对未成年人的支配地位，足以使未成年人丧失人身自由，因此导致未成年人的健康、安全或者精神状况面临危险的，应当处以一个月至一年监禁，并处十万瑞尔至二百万瑞尔的罚金。

第四节 未遂和刑罚

第三百四十八条 未遂

实施本章规定的轻罪而未遂的,应当处以同样的刑罚。

第三百四十九条 附加刑(种类及期限)

对于本章规定的犯罪,可以判处下列附加刑:

(一)剥夺特定权利,或者永久剥夺,或者剥夺期限在五年以内;

(二)禁止从事在从业期间实施了犯罪或者与犯罪有密切关联的职业,或者永久禁止,或者禁止期限在五年以内;

(三)如是重罪,期限在十年以内的本地驱逐,如是轻罪,期限在五年以内的本地驱逐;

(四)公布量刑结果,期限为二个月以内;

(五)以印刷媒体公布量刑结果;

(六)通过任何视听传媒公布量刑结果,期限为八天以内。

第六章 其他侵害亲属的犯罪

第三百五十条 重婚罪

前一个婚姻尚未解除又结婚的,应当处以一个月至一年监禁,并处十万瑞尔至二百万瑞尔的罚金。

民事身份登记官员知道当事人的前一个婚姻尚未解除仍准予登记结婚的,应当适用同样的刑罚。

第三百五十一条　长辈性侵未成年人罪

十八岁以下未成年人的长辈，与该未成年人性交的，应当处以五年至十年监禁。

第三百五十二条　血亲或者姻亲性侵罪

三代以内血亲或者姻亲之间发生性交的，应当处以一个月至一年监禁，并处十万瑞尔至二百万瑞尔的罚金。

第三编

侵犯财产的犯罪

第一部分　诈取财产的犯罪

第一章　窃取及相关犯罪

第一节　窃取罪

第三百五十三条　窃取罪的定义

窃取罪是指以占有为目的，以任何方式偷取他人财产的行为。

第三百五十四条　窃取能源罪

偷用能源，造成他人损失的，应当被视为窃取罪。

第三百五十五条　亲属豁免

行为人实施的窃取行为属于下列情形的，不应当提起刑事追诉：

（一）受到损害的是行为人的长辈或者晚辈；

（二）受到损害的是行为人的配偶。

第三百五十六条　适用的刑罚

犯窃取罪，应当处以六个月至三年监禁，并处一百万瑞尔至六百万瑞尔的罚金。

第三百五十七条 加重情节（暴力）

下列情形的窃取罪，应当处以三年至十年监禁：

（一）窃取之前、之中或者之后有暴力行为的；

（二）破门入户实施窃取的。

第三百五十八条 加重情节（肢残或者伤残）

窃取之前、之中或者之后有暴力行为，造成他人肢残或者伤残的，应当处以十年至二十年监禁。

第三百五十九条 加重情节（酷刑或者虐待行为）

如果窃取之前、之中或者之后有酷刑或者虐待行为的，应当处以十五年至三十年监禁。

第三百六十条 加重情节（被害人死亡）

如果窃取之前、之中或者之后有暴力行为，意外造成被害人死亡的，应当处以十五年至三十年监禁。

第三百六十一条 未遂

实施本节规定的轻罪而未遂的，应当处以同样的刑罚。

第三百六十二条 附加刑（种类及期限）

对于本节规定的犯罪，可以判处下列附加刑：

（一）剥夺特定权利，或者永久剥夺，或者剥夺期限在五年以内；

（二）禁止从事在从业期间实施了犯罪或者与犯罪有密切关联的职业，或者永久禁止，或者禁止期限在五年以内；

（三）禁止驾驶任何机动车辆，或者永久禁止，或者禁止期限在五年以内；

（四）如是重罪，期限在十年以内的本地驱逐，如是轻罪，期限在五年以内的本地驱逐；

（五）禁止被定罪外国人进入和停留于柬埔寨王国领土，或者永久禁止，或者禁止期限在五年以内；

（六）没收用于或者打算用于实施罪行的任何工具、材料或者物品；

（七）没收涉及犯罪的物品或者资金；

（八）没收犯罪所得的收益或者财产；

（九）没收犯罪发生场所的器具、材料和家具；

（十）没收罪犯拥有的一辆或者多辆机动车；

（十一）禁止拥有或者携带任何种类的任何武器、爆炸物或者弹药；

（十二）关闭用于谋划或者实施犯罪的设施，或者永久禁止，或者禁止期限在五年以内；

（十三）禁止经营向公众开放或者供公众使用的设施，或者永久禁止，或者禁止期限在五年以内；

（十四）公布量刑结果，期限为二个月以内；

（十五）以印刷媒体公布量刑结果；

（十六）通过任何视听传媒公布量刑结果，期限为八天以内。

第二节　勒索罪

第三百六十三条　勒索罪的定义

勒索罪是以暴力、暴力威胁或者胁迫的方式达成下列目标的行为：

(一）签名或者指印；

(二）承诺或者放弃；

(三）披露秘密；

(四）交付资金、贵重物品或者任何财产。

第三百六十四条　适用的刑罚

犯勒索罪，应当处以二年至五年监禁，并处四百万瑞尔至一千万瑞尔的罚金。

第三百六十五条　加重情节（被害人身份）

下列情形的勒索罪，应当处以五年至十年监禁：

(一）侵害因年龄而特别脆弱的人；

(二）侵害明显是怀孕或者犯罪人明知是怀孕的妇女；

(三）侵害明显是或者犯罪人明知是因患病或者残疾而特别脆弱的人；

第三百六十六条　加重情节（使用武器）

实施勒索罪，使用或者威胁使用武器的，应当处以七年至十五年监禁。

第三百六十七条　加重情节（肢残或者伤残）

勒索之前、之中或者之后有暴力行为，造成他人肢残或者伤残的，应当处以十年至二十年监禁。

第三百六十八条　加重情节（酷刑或者虐待行为）

如果勒索之前、之中或者之后有酷刑或者虐待行为的，应当处以十五年至三十年监禁。

第三百六十九条　加重情节（被害人死亡）

勒索之前、之中或者之后有暴力行为，意外造成被害人死亡的，应当处以十五年至三十年监禁。

第三百七十条 未遂

实施本节规定的轻罪而未遂的，应当处以同样的刑罚。

第三百七十一条 附加刑（种类及期限）

对于本节规定的犯罪，可以判处下列附加刑：

（一）剥夺特定权利，或者永久剥夺，或者剥夺期限在五年以内；

（二）禁止从事在从业期间实施了犯罪或者与犯罪有密切关联的职业，或者永久禁止，或者禁止期限在五年以内；

（三）如是重罪，期限在十年以内的本地驱逐，如是轻罪，期限在五年以内的本地驱逐；

（四）禁止被定罪外国人进入和停留于柬埔寨王国领土，或者永久禁止，或者禁止期限在五年以内；

（五）没收用于或者打算用于实施罪行的任何工具、材料或者物品；

（六）没收涉及犯罪的物品或者资金；

（七）没收犯罪所得的收益或者财产；

（八）没收犯罪发生场所的器具、材料和家具；

（九）没收罪犯拥有的一辆或者多辆机动车；

（十）禁止拥有或者携带任何种类的任何武器、爆炸物或者弹药，或者永久禁止，或者禁止期限在五年以内；

（十一）公布量刑结果，期限为二个月以内；

（十二）以印刷媒体公布量刑结果；

（十三）通过任何视听传媒公布量刑结果，期限为八天以内。

第三节　敲诈罪

第三百七十二条　敲诈罪的定义

敲诈是以披露或者嫁祸有损于他人品格或者名誉的事实相威胁而实现下列事项的行为：

(一) 签名或者指印；

(二) 承诺或者放弃；

(三) 披露秘密；

(四) 交付资金、贵重物品或者任何财产。

第三百七十三条　适用的刑罚

犯敲诈罪，应当处以二年至五年监禁，并处四百万瑞尔至一千万瑞尔的罚金。

第三百七十四条　将威胁付诸实行的加重情节

威胁要披露或者嫁祸有损于他人品格或者名誉的事实并付诸实行的，犯罪人应当处以五年至十年监禁。

第三百七十五条　未遂

实施本节规定的轻罪而未遂的，应当处以同样的刑罚。

第三百七十六条　附加刑（种类及期限）

对于本节规定的犯罪，可以判处下列附加刑：

(一) 剥夺特定权利，或者永久剥夺，或者剥夺期限在五年以内；

(二) 禁止从事在从业期间实施了犯罪或者与犯罪有密切关联的职业，或者永久禁止，或者禁止期限在五年以内；

(三) 如是重罪，期限在十年以内的本地驱逐，如是轻罪，期限在五年以内的本地驱逐；

（四）禁止被定罪外国人进入和停留于柬埔寨王国领土，或者永久禁止，或者禁止期限在五年以内；

（五）没收用于或者打算用于实施罪行的任何工具、材料或者物品；

（六）没收涉及犯罪的物品或者资金；

（七）没收犯罪所得的收益或者财产；

（八）没收犯罪发生场所的器具、材料和家具；

（九）没收罪犯拥有的一辆或者多辆机动车；

（十）禁止拥有或者携带任何种类的任何武器、爆炸物或者弹药，或者永久禁止，或者禁止期限在五年以内；

（十一）公布量刑结果，期限为二个月以内；

（十二）以印刷媒体公布量刑结果；

（十三）通过任何视听传媒公布量刑结果，期限为八天以内。

第二章　诈骗及相关犯罪

第一节　诈骗罪

第三百七十七条　诈骗罪的定义

"诈骗罪"是使用虚假名义或者虚构身份，滥用真实身份或者非法操控手段欺骗自然人或者法人，从而实现以下目的，造成对方或者第三人损失的行为：

（一）转移资金、贵重物品或者任何财产；

（二）提供服务；或者

（三）制作承担或者履行义务的文书。

第三百七十八条 适用的刑罚

犯诈骗罪，应当处以六个月至三年监禁，并处一百万瑞尔至六百万瑞尔的罚金。

第三百七十九条 加重情节（被害人身份）

下列情形的诈骗罪，应当处以二年至五年监禁：

（一）侵害因年龄而特别脆弱的人；

（二）侵害明显是怀孕或者犯罪人明知是怀孕的妇女；

（三）侵害明显是或者犯罪人明知是因患病或者残疾而特别脆弱的人。

第三百八十条 其他加重情节

下列人员实施的诈骗罪，应当处以二年至五年监禁：

（一）正在履行民事或者军事职责或者从事相关活动的公职人员；

（二）非法冒充公职人员的人；

（三）公开发行证券的发起人；

（四）公开募集人道主义或者社会援助资金的发起人；

（五）有组织犯罪集团。

第三百八十一条 未遂

实施本节规定的犯罪而未遂的，应当处以同样的刑罚。

第三百八十二条 附加刑（种类及期限）

对于本节规定的犯罪，可以判处下列附加刑：

（一）剥夺特定权利，或者永久剥夺，或者剥夺期限在五年以内；

（二）禁止从事在从业期间实施了犯罪或者与犯罪有密切关联的职业，或者永久禁止，或者禁止期限在五年以内；

（三）如是轻罪，期限在五年以内的本地驱逐；

（四）禁止被定罪外国人进入和停留于柬埔寨王国领土，或者永久禁止，或者禁止期限在五年以内；

（五）没收用于或者打算用于实施罪行的任何工具、材料或者物品；

（六）没收涉及犯罪的物品或者资金；

（七）没收犯罪所得的收益或者财产；

（八）没收犯罪发生场所的器具、材料和家具；

（九）没收罪犯拥有的一辆或者多辆机动车；

（十）禁止拥有或者携带任何种类的任何武器、爆炸物或者弹药，或者永久禁止，或者禁止期限在五年以内；

（十一）公布量刑结果，期限为二个月以内；

（十二）以印刷媒体公布量刑结果；

（十三）通过任何视听传媒公布量刑结果，期限为八天以内。

第二节　类似诈骗的犯罪

第一分节　利用弱点的犯罪

第三百八十三条　利用无知或者弱点罪

明知他人因年龄、怀孕或者残疾而特别脆弱，利用其无知或者弱点，迫使其实施或者不实施可能造成其严重损害的行为的，应当处以一个月至一年监禁，并处十万瑞尔至二百万瑞尔的罚金。

第二分节　失信罪

第三百八十四条　失信罪的定义

"失信罪"是明知自己完全不具有支付能力或者决定不支付而实施的下列行为：

（一）在酒吧、餐馆或者其他向公众开放的场所点餐食品或者饮料；

（二）在旅馆或者其他向公众开放的场所预定或者占据房间；

（三）搭乘三轮车、出租车或者其他类型的交通工具。

犯失信罪，应当处以六天至三个月监禁，并处十万瑞尔至五十万瑞尔的罚金。

第三百八十五条　未遂

实施本分节规定的轻罪而未遂的，应当处以同样的刑罚。

第三百八十六条　附加刑（种类及期限）

对于本分节规定的犯罪，可以判处下列附加刑：

（一）剥夺特定权利，或者永久剥夺，或者剥夺期限在五年以内；

（二）禁止从事在从业期间实施了犯罪或者与犯罪有密切关联的职业，或者永久禁止，或者禁止期限在五年以内；

（三）没收犯罪所得的收益或者财产；

（四）没收罪犯拥有的一辆或者多辆机动车；

（五）公布量刑结果，期限为二个月以内；

（六）以印刷媒体公布量刑结果；

（七）通过任何视听传媒公布量刑结果，期限为八天以内。

第三分节 干扰竞拍的犯罪

第三百八十七条 不当投标罪

在公开拍卖中，以礼物、承诺、谅解或者任何其他欺诈手段拒绝投标或者篡改投标的，应当处以六个月至二年监禁，并处一百万瑞尔至四百万瑞尔的罚金。

第三百八十八条 妨碍投标自由罪

竞标拍卖期间，以暴力或者威胁妨碍投标自由的，应当处以一年至三年监禁，并处二百万瑞尔至六百万瑞尔的罚金。

第三百八十九条 未遂

实施本节规定的轻罪而未遂的，应当处以同样的刑罚。

第三百九十条 附加刑（种类及期限）

对于本节规定的犯罪，可以判处下列附加刑：

（一）剥夺特定权利，或者永久剥夺，或者剥夺期限在五年以内；

（二）禁止从事在从业期间实施了犯罪或者与犯罪有密切关联的职业，或者永久禁止，或者禁止期限在五年以内；

（三）没收犯罪所得的收益或者财产；

（四）没收罪犯拥有的一辆或者多辆机动车；

（五）公布量刑结果，期限为二个月以内；

（六）以印刷媒体公布量刑结果；

（七）通过任何视听传媒公布量刑结果，期限为八天以内。

第三章　违反诚信及相关犯罪

第一节　违反诚信罪

第三百九十一条　违反诚信罪的定义

违反诚信罪是行为人对其经手的、被要求返还或者交还的、以特定方式展示或者使用的资金、贵重物品或者任何财产进行挪用，给他人造成损失的行为。

第三百九十二条　适用的刑罚

犯违反诚信罪，应当处以六个月至三年监禁，一百万瑞尔至六百万瑞尔的罚金。

第三百九十三条　行政人员或者其他人员违反特定诚信罪

有限责任公司或者股份有限公司的董事或者经理、依法任命的官员或者法人授权的人员违反诚信，意图牟取个人私利或者第三人利益，或者意图造成法人的损失并且已经造成了财产损失，应当处以二年至五年监禁，并处四百万瑞尔至一千万瑞尔的罚金。

有限责任公司或者股份有限公司的清算人，或者依法指定的清算人的代表，实施第一款行为并且导致法人财产损失的，应当适用第一款的规定。

实施第三百九十三条第一款和第二款规定的犯罪而未遂的，应当处以同样的刑罚。

第三百九十四条　加重情节（犯罪人身份）

下列情形的违反诚信罪，应当处以二年至五年监禁，并处四百万瑞尔至一千万瑞尔的罚金：

（一）以本人或者工商企业的名义募集资金或者资产的过程中实施行为；

（二）依法任命的官员或者法院工作人员在履行职责或者从事与职责有关工作中实施行为；

（三）政府文职人员或者军职人员在履行职责或者从事与职责有关工作中实施行为。

第三百九十五条　未遂

实施本节规定的轻罪而未遂的，应当处以同样的刑罚。

第三百九十六条　附加刑（种类及期限）

对于本节规定的犯罪，可以判处下列附加刑：

（一）剥夺特定权利，或者永久剥夺，或者剥夺期限在五年以内；

（二）禁止从事在从业期间实施了犯罪或者与犯罪有密切关联的职业，或者永久禁止，或者禁止期限在五年以内；

（三）没收用于或者打算用于实施罪行的任何工具、材料或者物品；

（四）没收涉及犯罪的物品或者资金；

（五）没收犯罪所得的收益或者财产；

（六）没收犯罪发生场所的器具、材料和家具；

（七）没收罪犯拥有的一辆或者多辆机动车；

（八）公布量刑结果，期限为二个月以内；

（九）以印刷媒体公布量刑结果；

（十）通过任何视听传媒公布量刑结果，期限为八天以内。

第二节 挪用查封或者担保物品的犯罪

第三百九十七条 挪用查封或者担保物品罪

债务人损毁或者动用主管部门查封或者作为诉讼担保的物品的，应当处以一个月至一年监禁，并处十万瑞尔至二百万瑞尔的罚金。

第三百九十八条 未遂

实施轻罪而未遂的，应当处以同样的刑罚。

第四章 衍生的犯罪

第一节 收赃罪

第三百九十九条 收赃罪

"收赃罪"是明知物品是重罪或者轻罪所得而接收、隐藏、保存或者转移的行为。

"收赃罪"亦指：

（一）为了转移明知是重罪或者轻罪所得的物品而充当中间人；

(二) 明知是重罪或者轻罪所得而从中获益。

第四百条 适用的刑罚

犯收赃罪,应当处以二年至五年监禁,并处四百万瑞尔至一千万瑞尔的罚金。

第四百零一条 加重情节

下列情形的收赃罪,应当处以五年至十年监禁:

(一) 惯犯;

(二) 利用职务之便实施的;

(三) 有组织犯罪集团实施的;

第四百零二条 罚金刑上限

可以判处的罚金刑上限可与所涉赃物的价值相当。

第四百零三条 附加刑(种类及期限)

对于本节规定的犯罪,可以判处下列附加刑:

(一) 剥夺特定权利,或者永久剥夺,或者剥夺期限在五年以内;

(二) 禁止从事在从业期间实施了犯罪或者与犯罪有密切关联的职业,或者永久禁止,或者禁止期限在五年以内;

(三) 禁止驾驶任何机动车辆,或者永久禁止,或者禁止期限在五年以内;

(四) 如是重罪,期限在十年以内的本地驱逐,如是轻罪,期限在五年以内的本地驱逐;

(五) 禁止被定罪外国人进入和停留于柬埔寨王国领土,或者永久禁止,或者禁止期限在五年以内;

（六）没收用于或者打算用于实施罪行的任何工具、材料或者物品；

（七）没收涉及犯罪的物品或者资金；

（八）没收犯罪所得的收益或者财产；

（九）没收犯罪发生场所的器具、材料和家具；

（十）没收罪犯拥有的一辆或者多辆机动车；

（十一）禁止拥有或者携带任何种类的任何武器、爆炸物或者弹药；

（十二）关闭用于谋划或者实施犯罪的设施，或者永久禁止，或者禁止期限在五年以内；

（十三）禁止经营向公众开放或者供公众使用的设施，或者永久禁止，或者禁止期限在五年以内；

（十四）公布量刑结果，期限为二个月以内；

（十五）以印刷媒体公布量刑结果；

（十六）通过任何视听传媒公布量刑结果，期限为八天以内。

第二节 洗钱罪

第四百零四条 洗钱罪的定义

"洗钱罪"是以任何方式对来源于重罪或者轻罪的直接或者间接收益予以虚假正当化的行为。

"洗钱罪"亦应当包括协助将重罪或者轻罪的直接或者间接收益用于投资、加以掩饰或者进行兑换的行为。

第四百零五条　适用的刑罚

犯洗钱罪，应当处以二年至五年监禁，并处四百万瑞尔的罚金。罚金上限可以与洗钱所涉资金或者财产的价值相当。

在产生作为洗钱对象的财产或者资金的犯罪可以处以高于上文第一款所判处的监禁的情况下，洗钱罪应当处以作为实行犯的前罪的刑罚，如果前罪存在加重情节，相应的刑罚亦适用于洗钱犯罪人。

第四百零六条　加重情节

下列情形的洗钱罪应当处以五年至十年监禁：

（一）惯犯；

（二）利用职务之便实施的；

（三）有组织犯罪集团实施的；

第四百零七条　未遂

实施本节规定的轻罪而未遂的，应当处以同样的刑罚。

第四百零八条　附加刑（种类及期限）

对于本节规定的犯罪，可以判处下列附加刑：

（一）剥夺特定权利，或者永久剥夺，或者剥夺期限在五年以内；

（二）禁止从事在从业期间实施了犯罪或者与犯罪有密切关联的职业，或者永久禁止，或者禁止期限在五年以内；

（三）没收用于或者打算用于实施罪行的任何工具、材料或者物品；

（四）没收涉及犯罪的物品或者资金；

（五）没收犯罪所得的收益或者财产；

（六）没收犯罪发生场所的器具、材料和家具；

（七）没收罪犯拥有的一辆或者多辆机动车；

（八）公布量刑结果，期限为二个月以内；

（九）以印刷媒体公布量刑结果；

（十）通过任何视听传媒公布量刑结果，期限为八天以内。

第四百零九条　法人的刑事责任

根据本法典第四十二条（法人的刑事责任），可以确定法人对本法典第四百零四条（洗钱罪的定义）规定的犯罪承担刑事责任。

应当对法人处以一百万瑞尔至五百万瑞尔的罚金，并处下列附加刑中的一项或者多项：

（一）依照本法典第一百七十条（法人的解散和清算）予以解散；

（二）依照本法典第一百七十一条（置于司法监视）予以司法监视；

（三）依照本法典第一百七十二条（禁止活动的开展），禁止进行一项或者多项活动；

（四）依照本法典第一百七十三条（取消公开招投标的资格），取消公开招投标资格；

（五）依照本法典第一百七十四条（禁止公开上市），禁止公开上市；

（六）依照本法典第一百七十八条（没收物品的所有权、出售和销毁）和第一百七十九条（没收与第三方权利）没收用于或者打算用于实施罪行的任何工具、材料或者物品；

（七）依照本法典第一百七十八条（没收物品的所有权、出售和销毁）和第一百七十九条（没收与第三方权利）没收犯罪产生的收益或者财产；

（八）依照本法典第一百八十条（公布判决），公布量刑结果；

（九）依照本法典第一百八十一条（通过视听传媒播放判决），以印刷媒体公布量刑结果，或者以任何视听传媒播放量刑结果。

第二部分 毁损财产的犯罪

第一章 破坏、污损和损坏财产的犯罪

第一节 破坏、污损和损坏财产的犯罪

第四百一十条 蓄意损坏财产罪

蓄意破坏、污损或者损坏他人财产的,应当处以六个月至二年监禁,并处一百万瑞尔至四百万瑞尔的罚金,仅造成轻微损害的除外。

第四百一十一条 加重情节

如有下列情形,第四百一十条(蓄意损坏财产罪)规定的犯罪应当处以二年至五年监禁,并处四百万瑞尔至一千万瑞尔的罚金:

(一)犯罪是由多个实行犯、共同实行犯、教唆犯或者帮助犯实施的;

(二)在住所内实施犯罪的;

(三)在用于保存资金、有价证券、货物或者设备的场所实施犯罪的;

(四)犯罪导致公共建筑或者道路损坏的;

（五）犯罪造成农作物或者庄稼损坏的；

（六）犯罪导致柬埔寨王国国境标志损坏的。

第四百一十二条　加重情节（被害人身份）

第四百一十条（蓄意损坏财产罪）规定的犯罪，如有下列有害表现，应当处以二年至五年监禁，并处四百万瑞尔至一千万瑞尔的罚金：

（一）蓄意影响法官、公职人员或者律师的履职活动；

（二）阻止被害人或者当事人举报犯罪或者追索损害赔偿；

（三）阻止证人在司法调查、询问、案件审理或者其他法律程序中提供证言，或者影响其作证；

（四）对提起诉讼或者追索损害赔偿的被害人或者当事人发生影响；

（五）对证人在司法调查、询问、案件审理或者其他法律程序中提供的证言发生影响。

第四百一十三条　加重情节（使用危及人身的方法）

蓄意使用爆炸、纵火或者其他可能危及人身的方法破坏、污损或者损坏他人财产的，应当处以二年至五年监禁，并处四百万瑞尔至一千万瑞尔的罚金。

第四百一十四条　加重情节（造成他人受伤）

本法典第四百一十三条加重情节（使用危及人身的方法）规定的犯罪，如造成他人受伤的，应当处以五年至十年监禁。

第四百一十五条　加重情节（肢残或者伤残）

本法典第四百一十三条加重情节（使用危及人身的方法）

规定的犯罪，如造成他人肢残或者伤残的，应当处以七年至十五年监禁。

第四百一十六条 加重情节（有组织犯罪集团实施的犯罪）

本法典第四百一十三条加重情节（使用危及人身的方法）规定的犯罪，如由有组织犯罪集团实施，应当处以七年至十五年监禁。

第四百一十七条 加重情节（致人死亡）

本法典第四百一十三条 加重情节（使用危及人身的方法）规定的犯罪，如意外致人死亡的，应当处以十年至二十年监禁。

第四百一十八条 轻微损坏罪

蓄意破坏、污损或者损坏他人财产，仅造成轻微损坏的，应当处以一天至六天监禁，并处一千瑞尔至十万瑞尔的罚金。

本条规定不适用于属于柬埔寨王国国家财产组成部分的公有或者私有的文化遗产。

第四百一十九条 轻率或者违规导致其他损坏罪

使用爆炸或者纵火方法破坏、污损或者损坏他人财产的，如果出于下列原因，应当处以一个月至一年监禁，并处十万瑞尔至二百万瑞尔的罚金：

（一）疏忽、轻率或者大意；

（二）不遵守安全要求或者不履行法律规定的安全检查职责。

第四百二十条 损坏官方海报或者告示罪

意外破坏、污损或者损坏行政部门张贴的官方海报或者告示的，应当处以一天至六天监禁，一千瑞尔至十万瑞尔的罚金。

第四百二十一条 未遂

除本法典第四百一十九条（轻率或者违规导致的其他损坏罪）规定的犯罪外，实施本节规定的轻罪而未遂的，应当处以同样的刑罚。

第四百二十二条 附加刑（种类及期限）

对于本节规定的犯罪，可以判处下列附加刑：

（一）剥夺特定权利，或者永久剥夺，或者剥夺期限在五年以内；

（二）禁止从事在从业期间实施了犯罪或者与犯罪有密切关联的职业，或者永久禁止，或者禁止期限在五年以内；

（三）禁止驾驶任何机动车辆，或者永久禁止，或者禁止期限在五年以内；

（四）如是重罪，期限在十年以内的本地驱逐，如是轻罪，期限在五年以内的本地驱逐；

（五）禁止被定罪外国人进入和停留于柬埔寨王国领土，或者永久禁止，或者禁止期限在五年以内；

（六）没收用于或者打算用于实施罪行的任何工具、材料或者物品；

（七）没收涉及犯罪的物品或者资金；

（八）没收犯罪所得的收益或者财产；

（九）没收犯罪发生场所的器具、材料和家具；

（十）没收罪犯拥有的一辆或者多辆机动车；

（十一）禁止拥有或者携带任何武器、爆炸物或者任何种类的弹药；

（十二）关闭用于谋划或者实施犯罪的设施，或者永久禁止，或者禁止期限在五年以内；

（十三）禁止经营向公众开放或者供公众使用的设施，或者永久禁止，或者禁止期限在五年以内；

（十四）公布量刑结果，期限为二个月以内；

（十五）以印刷媒体公布量刑结果；

（十六）通过任何视听传媒公布量刑结果，期限为八天以内。

第二节 以破坏、污损或者损坏财产相威胁的犯罪

第四百二十三条 威胁损坏财产罪

多次或者以书面、图片或者其他物品威胁要对他人财产进行破坏、污损或者损坏的，应当处以一个月至六个月监禁，并处十万瑞尔至一百万瑞尔的罚金。

威胁要进行破坏、污损或者损坏的财产价值不大的，应当处以五千瑞尔至十万瑞尔的罚金。

第四百二十四条 以执行命令威胁损坏罪

以执行或者不执行命令威胁要对他人财产进行破坏、污损或者损坏的，应当处以一年至二年监禁，并处二百万瑞尔至四百万瑞尔的罚金。

第四百二十五条 散发虚假信息罪

为了使人相信他人财产会受到破坏、污损或者损坏，传

播或者散布任何虚假信息的，应当处以一年至二年监禁，并处二百万瑞尔至四百万瑞尔的罚金。

第四百二十六条　附加刑（种类及期限）

对于本节规定的犯罪，可以判处下列附加刑：

（一）剥夺特定权利，或者永久剥夺，或者剥夺期限在五年以内；

（二）禁止从事在从业期间实施了犯罪或者与犯罪有密切关联的职业，或者永久禁止，或者禁止期限在五年以内；

（三）禁止驾驶任何机动车辆，或者永久禁止，或者禁止期限在五年以内；

（四）如是重罪，期限在十年以内的本地驱逐，如是轻罪，期限在五年以内的本地驱逐；

（五）禁止被定罪外国人进入和停留于柬埔寨王国领土，或者永久禁止，或者禁止期限在五年以内；

（六）没收用于或者打算用于实施罪行的任何工具、材料或者物品；

（七）没收涉及犯罪的物品或者资金；

（八）没收犯罪所得的收益或者财产；

（九）没收犯罪发生场所的器具、材料和家具；

（十）没收罪犯拥有的一辆或者多辆机动车；

（十一）禁止拥有或者携带任何武器、爆炸物或者任何种类的弹药；

（十二）关闭用于谋划或者实施犯罪的设施，或者永久禁止，或者禁止期限在五年以内；

(十三）禁止经营向公众开放或者供公众使用的设施，或者永久禁止，或者禁止期限在五年以内；

(十四）公布量刑结果，期限为二个月以内；

(十五）以印刷媒体公布量刑结果；

(十六）通过任何视听传媒公布量刑结果，期限为八天以内。

第二章 与信息技术有关的犯罪

第四百二十七条 擅自进入或者停留于自动数据处理系统罪

以欺骗性手段进入或者停留于自动数据处理系统的，应当处以一个月至一年监禁，并处十万瑞尔至二百万瑞尔的罚金。

行为导致系统数据被破坏或者被修改，或者系统功能的任何改变的，应当处以一年至二年监禁，并处二百万瑞尔至四百万瑞尔的罚金。

第四百二十八条 妨碍自动数据处理系统功能罪

妨碍自动数据处理系统功能的，应当处以一年至二年监禁，并处二百万瑞尔至四百万瑞尔的罚金。

第四百二十九条 擅自输入、删除或者修改数据罪

擅自将数据输入自动数据处理系统，或者擅自删除或者修改自动数据系统中的数据的，应当处以一年至二年监禁，并处二百万瑞尔至四百万瑞尔的罚金。

第四百三十条　有组织地参与或者共谋犯罪

有组织地参与或者以共谋方式计划实施本节规定的一个或者多个犯罪的，应当处以一年至二年监禁，并处二百万瑞尔至四百万瑞尔的罚金。

第四百三十一条　未遂

实施本节规定的轻罪而未遂的，应当处以同样的刑罚。

第四百三十二条　附加刑（种类及期限）

对于本节规定的轻罪，可以判处下列附加刑：

（一）剥夺特定权利，或者永久剥夺，或者剥夺期限在五年以内；

（二）禁止从事在从业期间实施了犯罪或者与犯罪有密切关联的职业，或者永久禁止，或者禁止期限在五年以内；

（三）没收用于或者打算用于实施罪行的任何工具、材料或者物品；

（四）没收涉及犯罪的物品或者资金；

（五）没收犯罪所得的收益或者财产；

（六）没收犯罪发生场所的器具、材料和家具；

（七）没收罪犯拥有的一辆或者多辆机动车；

（八）公布量刑结果，期限为二个月以内；

（九）以印刷媒体公布量刑结果；

（十）通过任何视听传媒公布量刑结果，期限为八天以内。

第四编

危害国家的犯罪

第一部分 侵犯重要国家机构的犯罪

第一章 侵害国王的犯罪

第四百三十三条 杀害国王罪

杀害国王罪即指刺杀国王的行为。

犯刺杀国王罪,应当处以终身监禁。

第四百三十四条 对国王实施酷刑或者虐待罪

对国王实施酷刑或者虐待的,应当处以十年至二十年监禁。

第四百三十五条 暴力侵害国王罪

蓄意对国王实施暴力侵害的,应当处以七年至十五年监禁。

第四百三十六条 加重情节(肢残或者伤残)

蓄意对国王实施暴力侵害,造成国王肢残或者伤残的,应当处以十年至二十年监禁。

第四百三十七条 加重情节(国王死亡)

蓄意对国王实施暴力侵害,意外造成国王死亡的,应当处以二十年至三十年监禁。

第四百三十八条　附加刑（种类及期限）

对于本节规定的犯罪，可以判处下列附加刑：

（一）剥夺特定权利，或者永久剥夺，或者剥夺期限在五年以内；

（二）禁止从事在从业期间实施了犯罪或者与犯罪有密切关联的职业，或者永久禁止，或者禁止期限在五年以内；

（三）如是重罪，期限在十年以内的本地驱逐，如是轻罪，期限在五年以内的本地驱逐；

（四）禁止离开柬埔寨王国领土，期限为五年以内；

（五）禁止被定罪外国人进入和停留于柬埔寨王国领土，或者永久禁止，或者禁止期限在五年以内；

（六）没收用于或者打算用于实施罪行的任何工具、材料或者物品；

（七）禁止拥有或者携带任何种类的任何武器、爆炸物或者弹药；

（八）公布量刑结果，期限为二个月以内；

（九）以印刷媒体公布量刑结果；

（十）通过任何视听传媒公布量刑结果，期限为八天以内。

第二章　危害国家安全的犯罪

第一节　叛国罪和间谍罪

第四百三十九条　叛国罪和间谍罪

柬埔寨公民或者柬埔寨现役军人实施本节规定的罪行的，

构成叛国罪；其他人实施本节规定的罪行的，构成间谍罪。

第四百四十条　向外国交出全部或者部分国家领土罪

向外国或者其代理人交出全部或者部分国家领土的，应当处以终身监禁。

第四百四十一条　向外国交出国家武装力量罪

向外国或者其代理人交出国家武装力量的，应当处以终身监禁。

第四百四十二条　向外国交出国防装备罪

向外国或者其代理人交出用于国防的食品、装备、建筑、设施或者机械设备的，应当处以十五年至三十年监禁。

第四百四十三条　勾结外国势力罪

勾结外国势力罪是与外国或者其代理人达成秘密协议，旨在策动针对柬埔寨王国的战争或者侵略活动的行为。

犯勾结外国势力罪，应当处以十五年至三十年监禁。

第四百四十四条　为外国策动战争或者侵略活动出谋划策罪

为外国或者其代理人策动战争或者实施侵略活动出谋划策的，应当处以十五年至三十年监禁。

第四百四十五条　向外国提供事关国防信息罪

向外国或者其代理人提供事关国防的信息、进展、目标、文件、计算机数据或者文档的，应当处以七年至十五年监禁。

第四百四十六条　收集事关国防信息罪

接受或者收集事关国防的信息、进展、目标、文件、计算机数据或者文档，旨在向外国或者其代理人提供的，应当处以五年至十年监禁。

第四百四十七条　破坏事关国防装备罪

毁坏、污损或者盗用事关国防的任何食品、文件、装备、建筑、设施、机械设备、技术装置、武器、技术备件或者计算机系统，或者使其出现缺陷，应当处以七年至十五年监禁。

第四百四十八条　提供虚假信息罪

为外国谋取利益，向柬埔寨民事机构或者军事机关提供有损于国防的虚假信息的，应当处以二年至五年监禁，并处四百万瑞尔至一千万瑞尔的罚金。

第四百四十九条　未遂

实施第四百四十八条（提供虚假信息罪）规定的轻罪而未遂的，应当处以同样的刑罚。

第四百五十条　附加刑（种类及期限）

对于本节规定的犯罪，可以判处下列附加刑：

（一）剥夺特定权利，或者永久剥夺，或者剥夺期限在五年以内；

（二）禁止从事在从业期间实施了犯罪或者与犯罪有密切关联的职业，或者永久禁止，或者禁止期限在五年以内；

（三）如是重罪，期限在十年以内的本地驱逐，如是轻罪，期限在五年以内的本地驱逐；

（四）禁止离开柬埔寨王国领土，期限为五年以内；

（五）禁止被定罪外国人进入和停留于柬埔寨王国领土，或者永久禁止，或者禁止期限在五年以内；

（六）没收用于或者打算用于实施罪行的任何工具、材料或者物品；

（七）没收罪犯拥有的一辆或者多辆机动车；

（八）禁止拥有或者携带任何武器、爆炸物或者任何种类的弹药；

（九）公布量刑结果，期限为二个月以内；

（十）以印刷媒体公布量刑结果；

（十一）通过任何视听传媒公布量刑结果，期限为八天以内。

第二节　袭扰和策划袭扰的犯罪

第四百五十一条　袭扰罪

袭扰罪包含一项或者多项危及柬埔寨王国制度或者侵犯国家领土完整的暴力行为。

犯袭扰罪，应当处以十五年至三十年监禁。

第四百五十二条　加重情节（犯罪人身份）

掌握公共权力的人员实施袭扰的，应当处以终身监禁。

第四百五十三条　策划袭扰罪

策划袭扰罪是指多人就实施袭扰达成一致并通过一个或者多个实质性举措予以实施的行为。

犯策划袭扰罪，应当处以五年至十年监禁。

掌握公共权力的人员实施本罪的，应当将监禁的刑期提升为十年至二十年。

第四百五十四条 免除刑罚

策划袭扰罪的参与者在被起诉前向有关部门报告策划袭扰的事实并指证其他参与者的,可以免除刑罚。

第四百五十五条 附加刑（种类及期限）

对于本节规定的重罪,可以判处下列附加刑:

(一) 剥夺特定权利,或者永久剥夺,或者剥夺期限在五年以内;

(二) 禁止从事在从业期间实施了犯罪或者与犯罪有密切关联的职业,或者永久禁止,或者禁止期限在五年以内;

(三) 期限在十年以内的本地驱逐;

(四) 禁止离开柬埔寨王国领土,期限为五年以内;

(五) 禁止被定罪外国人进入和停留于柬埔寨王国领土,或者永久禁止,或者禁止期限在五年以内;

(六) 没收用于或者打算用于实施罪行的任何工具、材料或者物品;

(七) 没收罪犯拥有的一辆或者多辆机动车;

(八) 禁止拥有或者携带任何种类的任何武器、爆炸物或者弹药,或者永久禁止,或者禁止期限在五年以内;

(九) 公布量刑结果,期限为二个月以内;

(十) 以印刷媒体公布量刑结果;

(十一) 通过任何视听传媒公布量刑结果,期限为八天以内。

第三节 暴乱活动罪

第四百五十六条 暴乱活动罪的定义

暴乱活动罪是指任何危及柬埔寨王国制度或者侵害国家

领土完整的集体暴力行为。

第四百五十七条 适用的刑罚

以下列方式参与暴乱活动罪的，应当处以七年至十五年监禁：

（一）构筑路障、工事或者任何建筑，旨在阻止或者妨碍公共部队行动的；

（二）以武力或者诡计占据任何建筑物或者设施的；

（三）破坏任何建筑物或者设施的；

（四）为叛乱分子的交通运输或者后勤供应提供保障的；

（五）直接煽动叛乱分子集结的；

（六）个人持有或者携带武器、爆炸物或者弹药的；

（七）篡夺合法权力的。

第四百五十八条 加重情节（叛乱活动）

以下列方式参与叛乱活动的，应当处以十年至二十年监禁：

（一）获取危害人身的武器、弹药、爆炸物或者危险物质；

（二）向叛乱分子提供危害人身的武器、弹药、爆炸物或者危险物质。

第四百五十九条 领导暴乱活动罪

犯领导暴乱活动罪，应当处以二十年至三十年监禁。

第四百六十条 附加刑（种类及期限）

对于本节规定的犯罪，可以判处下列附加刑：

（一）剥夺特定权利，或者永久剥夺，或者剥夺期限在五年以内；

（二）禁止从事在从业期间实施了犯罪或者与犯罪有密切关联的职业，或者永久禁止，或者禁止期限在五年以内；

（三）期限在十年以内的本地驱逐；

（四）禁止离开柬埔寨王国领土，期限为五年以内；

（五）禁止被定罪外国人进入和停留于柬埔寨王国领土，或者永久禁止，或者禁止期限在五年以内；

（六）没收用于或者打算用于实施罪行的任何工具、材料或者物品；

（七）没收罪犯拥有的一辆或者多辆机动车；

（八）禁止拥有或者携带任何种类的任何武器、爆炸物或者弹药，或者永久禁止，或者禁止期限在五年以内；

（九）公布量刑结果，期限为二个月以内；

（十）以印刷媒体公布量刑结果；

（十一）通过任何视听传媒公布量刑结果，期限为八天以内。

第四节　篡夺指挥权和组建武装部队的犯罪

第四百六十一条　篡夺军事指挥权罪

对抗合法当局的命令，非法或者未经授权担任军事指挥官的，应当处以十五年至三十年监禁。

第四百六十二条　非法掌控军事指挥权罪

对抗合法当局的命令，掌控军事指挥权的，应当处以十五年至三十年监禁。

第四百六十三条　非法组建武装部队罪

未经合法当局命令或者授权而组建武装部队的，应当处以十五年至三十年监禁。

第四百六十四条　煽动民众武装对抗国家权力罪

直接煽动民众武装对抗国家权力的，应当处以二年至五年监禁，并处四百万瑞尔至一千万瑞尔的罚金。

煽动产生效果的，刑罚为十五年至三十年监禁。

第四百六十五条　煽动民众武装对抗部分居民罪

直接煽动民众武装对抗部分居民的，应当处以二年至五年监禁，并处四百万瑞尔至一千万瑞尔的罚金。

煽动产生效果的，刑罚为十五年至三十年监禁。

第四百六十六条　未遂

实施本节规定的轻罪而未遂的，应当处以同样的刑罚。

第四百六十七条　附加刑（种类及期限）

对于本节规定的犯罪，可以判处下列附加刑：

（一）剥夺特定权利，或者永久剥夺，或者剥夺期限在五年以内；

（二）禁止从事在从业期间实施了犯罪或者与犯罪有密切关联的职业，或者永久禁止，或者禁止期限在五年以内；

（三）如是重罪，期限在十年以内的本地驱逐，如是轻罪，期限在五年以内的本地驱逐；

（四）禁止离开柬埔寨王国领土，期限为五年以内；

（五）禁止被定罪外国人进入和停留于柬埔寨王国领土，

或者永久禁止，或者禁止期限在五年以内；

（六）没收用于或者打算用于实施罪行的任何工具、材料或者物品；

（七）没收罪犯拥有的一辆或者多辆机动车；

（八）禁止拥有或者携带任何种类的任何武器、爆炸物或者弹药，或者永久禁止，或者禁止期限在五年以内；

（九）公布量刑结果，期限为二个月以内；

（十）以印刷媒体公布量刑结果；

（十一）通过任何视听传媒公布量刑结果，期限为八天以内。

第五节　危害武装部队安全的犯罪

第四百六十八条　唆使军人为外国势力效劳罪

直接唆使隶属于柬埔寨武装力量的军人为外国势力或者其代理人效劳，旨在危害国防的，应当处以五年至十年监禁。

第四百六十九条　妨碍军事装备正常使用罪

妨碍军事装备正常使用，旨在危害国防的，应当处以二年至五年监禁，并处四百万瑞尔至一千万瑞尔的罚金。

第四百七十条　妨碍军事人员或者装备移动罪

妨碍军事人员或者装备移动，旨在危害国防的，应当处以二年至五年监禁，并处四百万瑞尔至一千万瑞尔的罚金。

第四百七十一条　煽动军事人员抗命罪

直接唆使军人违抗命令，旨在危害国防的，应当处以二年至五年监禁，并处四百万瑞尔至一千万瑞尔的罚金。

第四百七十二条 动摇军心罪

参与动摇军心的活动，旨在危害国防的，应当处以二年至五年监禁，并处四百万瑞尔至一千万瑞尔的罚金。

第四百七十三条 混入军事基地罪

未经主管部门授权，混入军事当局使用的或者由其控制的任何土地、建筑物或者任何设施的，应当处以六个月至一年监禁，并处一百万瑞尔至二百万瑞尔的罚金。

第四百七十四条 妨碍国防服务工作罪

妨碍公共机构或者企业的正常运行及其对国防提供重要的公有或者私营服务，旨在危害国防的，应当处以一年至三年监禁，并处二百万瑞尔至六百万瑞尔的罚金。

第四百七十五条 未遂

实施本节规定的轻罪而未遂的，应当处以同样的刑罚。

第四百七十六条 附加刑（种类及期限）

对于本节规定的犯罪，可以判处下列附加刑：

（一）剥夺特定权利，或者永久剥夺，或者剥夺期限在五年以内；

（二）禁止从事在从业期间实施了犯罪或者与犯罪有密切关联的职业，或者永久禁止，或者禁止期限在五年以内；

（三）如是重罪，期限在十年以内的本地驱逐，如是轻罪，期限在五年以内的本地驱逐；

（四）禁止离开柬埔寨王国领土，期限为五年以内；

（五）禁止被定罪外国人进入和停留于柬埔寨王国领土，或者永久禁止，或者禁止期限在五年以内；

（六）没收用于或者打算用于实施罪行的任何工具、材料或者物品；

（七）没收罪犯拥有的一辆或者多辆机动车；

（八）禁止拥有或者携带任何种类的任何武器、爆炸物或者弹药，或者永久禁止，或者禁止期限在五年以内；

（九）公布量刑结果，期限为二个月以内；

（十）以印刷媒体公布量刑结果；

（十一）通过任何视听传媒公布量刑结果，期限为八天以内。

第六节 危害国防秘密的犯罪

第四百七十七条 国防秘密保护原则

披露事关国防安危的信息、流程、物件、文件以及计算机数据或者文档，必须遵守限制其传播的保护令。

王国政府应当规定此类保护措施的制定程序。

第四百七十八条 国防秘密的定义

国防秘密表现为限制传播的信息、流程、物件、文件以及计算机数据或者文档。

第四百七十九条 有意或者无意地泄露国防秘密罪

因其身份而掌握保密信息的任何人将任何属于国防秘密的信息、流程、物件、文件、计算机数据或者文档传播给无权得知的人员的，应当处以二年至五年监禁，并处四百万瑞尔至一千万瑞尔的罚金。

因轻率、大意、疏忽或者违规而发生危害国防秘密的行为，应当处以六个月至二年监禁，并处一百万瑞尔至四百万瑞尔的罚金。

第四百八十条　未经批准持有国防秘密罪

未经授权的个人蓄意获取并持有属于国防秘密的任何信息、流程、物件、文件、计算机数据或者文档的，应当处以二年至五年监禁，并处四百万瑞尔至一千万瑞尔的罚金。

第四百八十一条　毁坏或者复制国防秘密罪

毁坏或者复制属于国防秘密的任何信息、流程、物件、文件、计算机数据或者文档的，应当处以二年至五年监禁，并处四百万瑞尔至一千万瑞尔的罚金。

第四百八十二条　未遂

实施本节规定的轻罪而未遂的，应当处以同样的刑罚。

第四百八十三条　附加刑（种类及期限）

对于本节规定的犯罪，可以判处下列附加刑：

（一）剥夺特定权利，或者永久剥夺，或者剥夺期限在五年以内；

（二）禁止从事在从业期间实施了犯罪或者与犯罪有密切关联的职业，或者永久禁止，或者禁止期限在五年以内；

（三）公布量刑结果，期限为二个月以内；

（四）以印刷媒体公布量刑结果；

（五）通过任何视听传媒公布量刑结果，期限为八天以内。

第三章　危害公共安全的犯罪

第一节　打斗团伙的犯罪

第四百八十四条　打斗团伙的定义

"打斗团伙"是指任何使用武器、组织有序、经常扰乱社会秩序的群体。

第四百八十五条　参与打斗团伙罪

参与打斗团伙的，应当处以一年至三年监禁，并处二百万瑞尔至六百万瑞尔的罚金。

第四百八十六条　组织打斗团伙罪

组织打斗团伙的，应当处以二年至五年监禁，并处四百万瑞尔至一千万瑞尔的罚金。

第四百八十七条　附加刑（种类及期限）

对于本节规定的犯罪，可以判处下列附加刑：

（一）剥夺特定权利，或者永久剥夺，或者剥夺期限在五年以内；

（二）禁止从事在从业期间实施了犯罪或者与犯罪有密切关联的职业，或者永久禁止，或者禁止期限在五年以内；

（三）期限在五年以内的本地驱逐；

（四）没收用于或者打算用于实施罪行的任何工具、材料或者物品；

（五）禁止拥有或者携带任何种类的任何武器、爆炸物或者弹药，或者永久禁止，或者禁止期限在五年以内；

（六）公布量刑结果，期限为二个月以内；

（七）以印刷媒体公布量刑结果；

（八）通过任何视听传媒公布量刑结果，期限为八天以内。

第二节　与武器、爆炸物和弹药有关的犯罪

第四百八十八条　生产或者贩运武器、爆炸物和弹药罪

未经主管部门授权，生产、进口或者出口以及储存任何种类的武器、爆炸物和弹药的，应当处以五年至十年监禁。

武器是指经过生产或者改装的任何可以用于杀人、伤害或者损坏财产的枪支。

弹药和爆炸物是指经过生产或者改装的任何可以用于杀人、伤害或者损坏财产的装置或者材料。

化学武器、生物武器，或者含有化学或者生物物质的弹药，是指经过生产或者改装的任何可以用于危害健康、生命或者财产以及环境的物质。

第四百八十九条　生产或者贩运其他攻击性武器罪

未经主管部门授权，生产、进口或者出口以及储存其他可以用于杀人、伤害的攻击性武器，例如刀、剑、指节铜环等，应当处以二年至五年监禁，并处四百万瑞尔至一千万瑞尔的罚金。

第四百九十条　未经批准持有或者运输武器罪

未经主管部门批准，任何人在其住所外携带或者运输武

器、爆炸物或者弹药的，应当处以六个月至三年监禁，并处一百万瑞尔至六百万瑞尔的罚金。

任何人在其住所外携带或者运输第四百八十九条（生产或者贩运其他攻击性武器罪）规定的武器的，应当处以同样的刑罚。

第四百九十一条 公共场所丢弃武器罪

在公共场所或者公众可以到达的地点丢弃武器或者其他足以危及人身的物体的，应当处以六个月至三年监禁，并处一百万瑞尔至六百万瑞尔的罚金。

第四百九十二条 附加刑（种类及期限）

对于本节规定的犯罪，可以判处下列附加刑：

（一）剥夺特定权利，或者永久剥夺，或者剥夺期限在五年以内；

（二）禁止从事在从业期间实施了犯罪或者与犯罪有密切关联的职业，或者永久禁止，或者禁止期限在五年以内；

（三）如是重罪，期限在十年以内的本地驱逐，如是轻罪，期限在五年以内的本地驱逐；

（四）禁止离开柬埔寨王国领土，期限为五年以内；

（五）禁止被定罪外国人进入和停留于柬埔寨王国领土，或者永久禁止，或者禁止期限在五年以内；

（六）没收用于或者打算用于实施罪行的任何工具、材料或者物品；

（七）没收罪犯拥有的一辆或者多辆机动车；

（八）禁止拥有或者携带任何种类的任何武器、爆炸物或

者弹药,或者永久禁止,或者禁止期限在五年以内;

(九)公布量刑结果,期限为二个月以内;

(十)以印刷媒体公布量刑结果;

(十一)通过任何视听传媒公布量刑结果,期限为八天以内。

第四百九十三条　没收被丢弃在公共场所的武器

对于本法典第四百九十一条(公共场所丢弃武器罪)规定的犯罪,法庭可下令没收该武器或者其他足以危及人身的物体。

第三节　煽动犯罪的犯罪

第四百九十四条　煽动的表现方式

本节所要惩处的煽动行为表现为下列形式:

(一)在公共场所或者会议上发表任何形式的讲话;

(二)向公众展示或者分发任何形式的文字或者图片;

(三)与公众进行任何视听交流。

第四百九十五条　煽动实施重罪罪

采取本法典第四百九十四条(煽动的表现方式)规定的方式之一,直接煽动实施重罪或者扰乱社会秩序,煽动未发生效果的,应当处以六个月至二年监禁,并处一百万瑞尔至四百万瑞尔的罚金。

第四百九十六条　煽动歧视罪

采取本法典第四百九十四条(煽动的表现方式)规定的方式之一,直接煽动针对属于或者不属于特定民族、国籍、种族或者宗教的个人或者群体的恶意或者暴力，煽动未发生效果的，应当处以一年至三年监禁，并处二百万瑞尔至六百万瑞尔的罚金。

第四百九十七条　借助印刷媒体实施的煽动犯罪

借助媒体实施本节规定的犯罪，需同时违反《新闻法》的规定。

第四百九十八条　附加刑（种类及期限）

对于本节规定的犯罪，可以判处下列附加刑：

（一）剥夺特定权利，或者永久剥夺，或者剥夺期限在五年以内；

（二）禁止从事在从业期间实施了犯罪或者与犯罪有密切关联的职业，或者永久禁止，或者禁止期限在五年以内；

（三）公布量刑结果，期限为二个月以内；

（四）以印刷媒体公布量刑结果；

（五）通过任何视听传媒公布量刑结果，期限为八天以内。

第四节　犯罪集团

第四百九十九条　参加犯罪集团罪

参加阴谋实施下列犯罪活动的犯罪集团的，应当处以二年至五年监禁，并处四百万瑞尔至一千万瑞尔的罚金：

（一）共谋一项或者多项本法典第二编（侵犯人身的犯罪）第二部分（侵犯人身的犯罪）第一章（杀人罪）至第六章（侵犯人身自由罪）规定的侵犯人身的重罪；

（二）共谋一项或者多项本法典第三编规定的侵犯财产的重罪。

第五百条　免除刑罚

参加犯罪集团罪的参与者在被起诉前向有关部门报告犯罪组织或者同谋的存在，并指认其他参与者的，可以免除刑罚。

第五百零一条　附加刑（种类及期限）

对于本节规定的轻罪，可以判处下列附加刑：

（一）剥夺特定权利，或者永久剥夺，或者剥夺期限在五年以内；

（二）禁止从事在从业期间实施了犯罪或者与犯罪有密切关联的职业，或者永久禁止，或者禁止期限在五年以内；

（三）期限在五年以内的本地驱逐；

（四）没收用于或者打算用于实施罪行的任何工具、材料或者物品；

（五）禁止拥有或者携带任何种类的任何武器、爆炸物或者弹药，或者永久禁止，或者禁止期限在五年以内；

（六）公布量刑结果，期限为二个月以内；

（七）以印刷媒体公布量刑结果；

（八）通过任何视听传媒公布量刑结果，期限为八天以内。

第四章　危害国家权力的犯罪

第一节　侮辱和妨碍公职人员罪

第五百零二条　侮辱罪

侮辱罪是指用言语、手势、书面文档、图片或者物件贬低他人尊严的行为。

侮辱正在履行职务或者在班的公职人员或者民选公职人员的，应当处以一天至六天的监禁，并处一千瑞尔至十万瑞尔的罚金。

第五百零三条　妨碍公职人员罪

妨碍公职人员罪是指针对公职人员执行法律、政府机关的命令或者司法判决的履职活动实施的暴力抗拒行为。

犯妨碍公职人员罪，应当处以一个月至三个月监禁，并处十万瑞尔至五十万瑞尔的罚金。

第五百零四条　加重情节（妨碍公职人员罪）

下列主体实施妨碍公职人员罪的，应当处以六个月至一年监禁，并处一百万瑞尔至二百万瑞尔的罚金：

（一）多个实行犯、共同实行犯、教唆犯或者帮助犯；

（二）有武装的实行犯。

第五百零五条　煽动妨碍公职人员罪

直接煽动妨碍公职人员的，应当处以一天至一个月监禁，并处一千瑞尔至十万瑞尔的罚金。

第五百零六条　妨碍公共二程罪

以暴力行为妨碍公共工程或者公用设施工程建设的,应当处以一个月至三个月监禁,并处十万瑞尔至五十万瑞尔的罚金。

第五百零七条　附加刑(种类及期限)

对于本节规定的犯罪,可以判处下列附加刑:

(一)禁止拥有或者携带任何种类的任何武器、爆炸物或者弹药,或者永久禁止,或者禁止期限在五年以内;

(二)公布量刑结果,期限为二个月以内;

(三)以印刷媒体公布量刑结果;

(四)通过任何视听传媒公布量刑结果,期限为八天以内。

第五章　侵犯国教的犯罪

第一节　侵犯佛教的犯罪

第五百零八条　未经准许穿着僧袍罪

未经准许当众穿着僧袍的,应当处以六天至三个月监禁,十万瑞尔至五十万瑞尔的罚金。

第五百零九条　窃取佛教圣物罪

在不影响本法典规定的最严厉刑罚的情况下,在宗教场所窃取佛教圣物的,应当处以二年至五年监禁,并处四百万瑞尔至一千万瑞尔的罚金。

第五百一十条　损坏佛教场所或者圣物罪

在不影响本法典规定的最严厉刑罚的情况下，蓄意破坏、污损或者损坏佛教场所或者圣物的，应当处以二年至五年监禁，并处四百万瑞尔至一千万瑞尔的罚金。

第五百一十一条　未遂

实施本节规定的轻罪而未遂的，应当处以同样的刑罚。

第五百一十二条　附加刑（种类及期限）

对于本节规定的轻罪，可以判处下列附加刑：

（一）剥夺特定权利，或者永久剥夺，或者剥夺期限在五年以内；

（二）禁止从事在从业期间实施了犯罪或者与犯罪有密切关联的职业，或者永久禁止，或者禁止期限在五年以内；

（三）禁止拥有或者携带任何种类的任何武器、爆炸物或者弹药，或者永久禁止，或者禁止期限在五年以内；

（四）公布量刑结果，期限为二个月以内；

（五）以印刷媒体公布量刑结果；

（六）通过任何视听传媒公布量刑结果，期限为八天以内。

第二节　侵犯僧人、尼姑和信徒的犯罪

第一分节　施暴罪

第五百一十三条　蓄意施暴罪

蓄意对佛教僧人、尼姑或者信徒实施暴力的，应当处以二年至五年监禁，并处四百万瑞尔至一千万瑞尔的罚金。

第五百一十四条　加重情节（肢残或者伤残）

蓄意对佛教僧人、尼姑或者信徒实施暴力，造成肢残或者伤残的，应当处以七年至十五年监禁。

第五一十五条　加重情节（被害人死亡）

蓄意对佛教僧人、尼姑或者信徒实施暴力，意外造成被害人死亡的，应当处以十至二十年监禁。

第二分节　侮辱罪

第五百一十六条　针对佛教僧人、尼姑和信徒的侮辱罪

如果本法典第五百零二条（侮辱罪）第一款规定的侮辱罪是针对正在进行举行法事或者修行的僧人、尼姑或者信徒的，应当处以一天至六天监禁，一千瑞尔至十万瑞尔的罚金。

第二部分 侵犯司法的犯罪

第一章 危害司法制度的犯罪

第一节 法官的腐败犯罪

第五百一十七条 法官受贿罪

以下列事项作为交换，法官直接或者间接索要或者非法接受礼品、职位、许诺或者利益的，应当处以七年至十五年监禁：

（一）实施与其职务有关的行为；

（二）不实施与其职务有关的行为。

第五百一十八条 对法官行贿罪

以下列事项作为交换，直接或者间接地向法官赠送礼品、职位、许诺或者利益的，应当处以五年至十年监禁：

（一）实施与其职务有关的行为；

（二）不实施与其职务有关的行为。

第五百一十九条 法人刑事责任

根据本法典第四十二条（法人的刑事责任），可以确定法人对本法典第五百一十八条（对法官行贿罪）规定的犯罪承担刑事责任。

应当对法人处以一千万瑞尔至五千万瑞尔的罚金,并处下列附加刑中的一项或者多项:

(一)依照本法典第一百七十条(法人的解散和清算)予以解散;

(二)依照本法典第一百七十一条(置于司法监视)予以司法监视;

(三)依照本法典第一百七十二条(禁止活动的开展),禁止进行一项或者多项活动;

(四)依照本法典第一百七十三条(取消公开招投标的资格),取消公开招投标资格;

(五)依照本法典第一百七十四条(禁止公开上市),禁止公开上市;

(六)依照本法典第一百七十八条(没收物品的所有权、出售和销毁)和第一百七十九条(没收与第三方权利)没收用于或者打算用于实施罪行的任何物品或者资金;

(七)依照本法典第一百七十八条(没收物品的所有权、出售和销毁)和第一百七十九条(没收与第三方权利)没收犯罪产生的收益或者财产;

(八)依照本法典第一百八十条(公布判决),公布量刑结果;

(九)依照本法典第一百八十一条(通过视听传媒播放判决),以印刷媒体公布量刑结果,或者以任何视听传媒播放量刑结果。

第二节　侵犯司法判决罪

第五百二十条　拒不执行司法判决罪

公职人员拒不执行司法机关履行职责作出的判决、裁定或者命令的，应当处以二年至五年监禁，并处四百万瑞尔至一千万瑞尔的罚金。

第五百二十一条　非法发布拘留或者释放命令罪

公职人员或者民选公职人员以任何形式非法发布拘留或者释放被拘留者命令的，应当处以二年至五年监禁，并处四百万瑞尔至一千万瑞尔的罚金。

第五百二十二条　蓄意发表非法胁迫司法权力的评论罪

在终审判决宣布之前发表评论，试图给受理诉讼的法庭施加压力，以期影响终审判决的，应当处以一个月至六个月监禁，并处十万瑞尔至一百万瑞尔的罚金。

第五百二十三条　诋毁司法判决罪

抨击司法文书或者判决，以期扰乱社会秩序或者危害柬埔寨王国制度的，应当处以一个月至六个月监禁，并处十万瑞尔至一百万瑞尔的罚金。

不执行司法判决的，应当处以本条上文第一款规定的同样刑罚。

第五百二十四条　诬告司法机关罪

诬告司法或者行政机关存在犯罪事实，导致不必要调查的，应当处以一个月至六个月监禁，并处十万瑞尔至一百万瑞尔的罚金。

第五百二十五条　未遂

实施本法典第五百二十条（拒不执行司法判决罪）至第五百二十四条（诬告司法机关罪）规定的轻罪而未遂的，应当处以同样的刑罚。

第五百二十六条　附加刑（种类及期限）

对于本节规定的轻罪，可以判处下列附加刑：

（一）剥夺特定权利，或者永久剥夺，或者剥夺期限在五年以内；

（二）禁止从事在从业期间实施了犯罪或者与犯罪有密切关联的职业，或者永久禁止，或者禁止期限在五年以内；

（三）没收用于或者打算用于实施罪行的任何工具、材料或者物品；

（四）禁止拥有或者携带任何种类的任何武器、爆炸物或者弹药，或者永久禁止，或者禁止期限在五年以内；

（五）公布量刑结果，期限为二个月以内；

（六）以印刷媒体公布量刑结果；

（七）通过任何视听传媒公布量刑结果，期限为八天以内。

第二章　侵犯司法程序的犯罪

第一节　向法院起诉的相关犯罪

第五百二十七条　恐吓阻碍起诉罪

以说服被害人不起诉或者撤诉为目的，对被害人进行任何威胁或者恐吓的，应当处以一年至三年监禁，并处二百万瑞尔至六百万瑞尔的罚金。

行为产生效果的，应当处以二年至五年监禁，并处四百万瑞尔至一千万瑞尔的罚金。

第五百二十八条　公职人员对重罪或者轻罪不予报告罪

任何公职人员或者民选公职人员，在行使职责或者在班时发现重罪或者轻罪案件，不告知司法机关或者其他主管部门的，应当处以一年至三年监禁，并处二百万瑞尔至六百万瑞尔的罚金。

第五百二十九条　对重罪或者轻罪不予报告罪及其免责

任何发现重罪但仍有可能阻止或者减少犯罪后果的人，不向司法机关或者其他主管部门报告的，应当处以一个月至一年监禁，并处十万瑞尔至二百万瑞尔的罚金。

但是，下列人员免予处罚：

（一）重罪实行犯、共同实行犯、教唆犯或者帮助犯的上辈亲属和下辈亲属，以及兄弟姐妹；

（二）重罪实行犯、共同实行犯、教唆犯或者帮助犯的配偶；

（三）受职业保密法律义务约束的人。

第五百三十条　对虐待未成年人不报告罪

任何人发现十五岁以下未成年人被虐待或者性侵，不向司法机关或者其他主管部门报告的，应当处以一年至三年监禁，并处二百万瑞尔至六百万瑞尔的罚金。

第二节　有关证据收集的犯罪

第五百三十一条　隐藏尸体罪

隐藏或者掩盖被杀害或者暴力致死的人的尸体的，应当处以六个月至二年监禁，并处一百万瑞尔至四百万瑞尔的罚金。

第五百三十二条　隐藏证据罪

为阻碍发现真相而更动、隐藏或者破坏痕迹或者标记，改变重罪或者轻罪现场的，应当处以一年至三年监禁，并处二百万瑞尔至六百万瑞尔的罚金。

第五百三十三条　破坏现场罪

为阻碍发现真相而破坏、替换或者移动重罪或者轻罪现场存在的物件的，应当处以一年至三年监禁，并处二百万瑞尔至六百万瑞尔的罚金。

第五百三十四条　毁坏文件罪

蓄意毁坏、盗取或者更改有助于查明重罪或者轻罪、辨识或者查获犯罪人的文件或者物件的，应当处以一年至三年监禁，并处二百万瑞尔至六百万瑞尔的罚金。

第五百三十五条　破坏封印罪

破坏主管部门的封印的，应当处以六个月至二年监禁，并处一百万瑞尔至四百万瑞尔的罚金。

第五百三十六条　破坏或者盗用被封禁物品罪

破坏或者盗用主管部门封禁的物品的，应当处以六个月至二年监禁，并处一百万瑞尔至四百万瑞尔的罚金。

第五百三十七条　拒不应答罪

公开声称认识重罪或者轻罪的实行犯、共同实行犯、教唆犯或者帮助犯却拒不回答法官相关询问的，应当处以一个月至一年监禁，并处十万瑞尔至二百万瑞尔的罚金。

第五百三十八条　拒不出庭罪

被传唤到检察机关、调查法官或者刑事法庭作证的任何人无正当理由拒不到场的，应当处以一个月至六个月监禁，并处十万瑞尔至一百万瑞尔的罚金。

第五百三十九条　不提供无罪证据罪及其例外

掌握被指控的人、被告人或者被定罪的人的无罪证据的任何人不向司法机关或者其他主管部门出示证据的，应当处以一年至三年监禁，并处二百万瑞尔至六百万瑞尔的罚金。

但是，下列人员免予刑罚：

（一）被起诉犯罪的实行犯、共同实行犯、教唆犯或者帮助犯；

（二）实行犯、共同实行犯、教唆犯或者帮助犯的前辈或者后辈、兄弟姐妹；

（三）实行犯、共同实行犯、教唆犯或者帮助犯的配偶；

（四）负有职业保密义务的人。

第五百四十条　使用他人身份罪

冒用他人姓名，导致或者可能导致对他人提起刑事诉讼的，应当处以一年至三年监禁，并处二百万瑞尔至六百万瑞尔的罚金。

第五百四十一条　拒不服从警官命令罪

车辆驾驶人拒不服从身着制服或者佩戴标志的警官或者军警为搜查取证发出的停车命令的，应当处以六天至三个月监禁，并处一万瑞尔至五十万瑞尔的罚金。

第五百四十二条　驾驶人拒不接受检查罪

车辆驾驶人拒不接受身着制服或者佩戴标志的警官或者军警为搜查取证对其车辆进行检查的，应当处以六天至三个月监禁，并处一万瑞尔至五十万瑞尔的罚金。

第五百四十三条　逃避罪

道路机动车或者海上航行器的驾驶人明知其刚刚导致了事故或者损害却不停止行驶，企图以此逃避任何民事或者刑事责任的，应当处以六个月至二年监禁，并处一百万瑞尔至四百万瑞尔的罚金。

第五百四十四条　为犯罪人提供帮助罪及其例外

为重罪的实行犯、共同实行犯、教唆犯或者帮助犯提供下列帮助的，应当处以一年至三年监禁，并处二百万瑞尔至六百万瑞尔的罚金：

（一）住处；

（二）隐藏地；

（三）生存手段；或者

（四）逃避搜查或者逮捕的任何其他办法。

但是，下列人员免除刑罚：

（一）重罪的实行犯、共同实行犯、教唆犯或者帮助犯的长辈、后代和兄弟姐妹；

（二）重罪的实行犯、共同实行犯、教唆犯或者帮助犯的配偶。

第五百四十五条　伪证罪及其例外

向任何法庭或者经书面授权的司法警察宣誓又作伪证的，应当处以二年至五年监禁，并处四百万瑞尔至一千万瑞尔的罚金。

但是，如果证人收回其证言，并且在调查或者审理程序终结之前说出真相的，免除刑罚。

第五百四十六条　胁迫证人罪

行为人单独实施或者与第三方共同实施任何胁迫行为，旨在驱使证人不作证或者提供虚假的证言或者证词的，应当处以二年至五年监禁，并处四百万瑞尔至一千万瑞尔的罚金。

第五百四十七条　证人索贿伪证罪

证人直接或者间接索取或者接受礼品、职位、许诺或者利益，以下列事项作为交换的，应当处以五年至十年监禁：

（一）不作证；

（二）提供虚假证明。

第五百四十八条　贿赂证人罪

以下列事项作为交换，直接或者间接给予证人礼品、职位、许诺或者利益的，应当处以五年至十年监禁：

（一）不作证；

（二）提供虚假证明。

第五百四十九条　胁迫发表评论影响证人罪

终审判决宣告之前，胁迫发表旨在影响证人陈述的评论的，应当处以六天至一个月监禁，并处一万瑞尔至十万瑞尔的罚金。

第三节 翻译和专家报告的相关犯罪

第五百五十条 不实翻译罪

翻译人员蓄意歪曲所翻译的言语或者文件的内容的，应当处以二年至五年监禁，并处四百万瑞尔至一千万瑞尔的罚金。

第五百五十一条 专家作假罪

专家在其书面报告或者口头陈述中对任何数据或者调查结果作假的，应当处以二年至五年监禁，并处四百万瑞尔至一千万瑞尔的罚金。

第五百五十二条 恐吓专家或者翻译人员罪

为了影响专家或者翻译人员的履职活动，对其进行恐吓的，应当处以二年至五年监禁，并处四百万瑞尔至一千万瑞尔的罚金。

行为产生效果的，应当处以五年至十年监禁。

第五百五十三条 翻译人员索贿罪

以歪曲所翻译文字或者文件作为交换，翻译人员直接或者间接索要或者接受礼品、职位、许诺或者利益的，应当处以五年至十年监禁。

第五百五十四条 贿赂翻译人员罪

以歪曲所翻译文字或者文件作为交换，直接或者间接给予翻译人员礼品、职位、许诺或者利益的，应当处以五年至十年监禁。

第五百五十五条　专家索贿罪

以对书面或者口头报告的任何数据或者发现作假作为交换，专家直接或者间接索要或者接受礼品、职位、许诺或者利益的，应当处以五年至十年监禁。

第五百五十六条　贿赂专家罪

以对书面或者口头报告的任何数据或者发现作假作为交换，直接或者间接给予专家礼品、职位、许诺或者利益的，应当处以五年至十年监禁。

第四节　未遂和附加刑罚

第五百五十七条　未遂

实施本法典第五百二十七条（恐吓阻碍起诉罪）、第五百三十一条（隐藏尸体罪）、第五百三十六条（破坏或者盗用被封禁物品罪）、第五百四十条（使用他人身份罪）和第五百四十四条（为犯罪人提供帮助罪及其例外）规定的轻罪而未遂的，应当处以同样的刑罚。

第五百五十八条　附加刑（种类及期限）

对于本章规定的犯罪，可以判处下列附加刑：

（一）剥夺特定权利，或者永久剥夺，或者剥夺期限在五年以内；

（二）禁止从事在从业期间实施了犯罪或者与犯罪有密切关联的职业，或者永久禁止，或者禁止期限在五年以内；

（三）如是重罪，期限在十年以内的本地驱逐，如是轻罪，期限在五年以内的本地驱逐；

（四）没收用于或者打算用于实施罪行的任何工具、材料或者物品；

（五）没收涉及犯罪的物品或者资金；

（六）没收犯罪所得的收益或者财产；

（七）没收罪犯拥有的一辆或者多辆机动车；

（八）禁止拥有或者携带任何种类的任何武器、爆炸物或者弹药；

（九）公布量刑结果，期限为二个月以内；

（十）以印刷媒体公布量刑结果；

（十一）通过任何视听传媒公布量刑结果，期限为八天以内。

第五百五十九条　法人的刑事责任

根据本法典第四十二条（法人的刑事责任），可以确定法人对本法典第五百四十八条（贿赂证人罪）、第五百五十四条（贿赂翻译人员罪）和第五百五十六条（贿赂专家罪）规定的犯罪承担刑事责任。

应当对法人处以二千万瑞尔至二亿瑞尔的罚金，并处下列附加刑中的一项或者多项：

（一）依照本法典第一百七十条（法人的解散和清算）予以解散；

（二）依照本法典第一百七十一条（置于司法监视）予以司法监视；

（三）依照本法典第一百七十二条（禁止活动的开展），禁止进行一项或者多项活动；

（四）依照本法典第一百七十三条（取消公开招投标的资格），取消公开招投标资格；

（五）依照本法典第一百七十四条（禁止公开上市），禁止公开上市；

（六）依照本法典第一百七十八条（没收物品的所有权、出售和销毁）和第一百七十九条（没收与第三方权利）没收涉及犯罪的物品或者资金；

（七）依照本法典第一百七十八条（没收物品的所有权、出售和销毁）和第一百七十九条（没收与第三方权利）没收犯罪产生的收益或者财产；

（八）依照本法典第一百八十条（公布判决），公布量刑结果；

（九）依照本法典第一百八十一条（通过视听传媒播放判决），以印刷媒体公布量刑结果，或者以任何视听传媒播放量刑结果。

第三章　有关羁押的犯罪

第一节　脱逃罪

第五百六十条　脱逃罪的定义

"脱逃罪"是被羁押人以任何手段逃离羁押场所的行为。

如果第三方采取了上述手段，也构成脱逃罪。

下列情况下的人员是被羁押人：

（一）被拘留；

（二）因拘留结束、执行命令或者逮捕而正在被送往司法机关；

（三）已经收到羁押令或者逮捕令；

（四）正在监狱服刑或者正在被押解去服刑；

（五）被羁押等待引渡；

（六）依照本法典第一百二十七条（日间释放的适用）正处于日间释放。

第五百六十一条　可适用的刑罚

犯脱逃罪，应当处以一年至三年监禁，并处二百万瑞尔至六百万瑞尔的罚金。

第五百六十二条　等同于脱逃罪的行为

下列行为被视为脱逃罪，应当处以同样的刑罚：

（一）处于医院或者医疗机构，或者法院、警察局、军事警察局等其他场所的被羁押人脱离监管的；

（二）在日间释放、缓刑或者分期服刑，以及经批准离开监狱的期限结束后，罪犯没有返回监狱的。

第二节　有关脱逃的加重情节和配合脱逃的犯罪

第五百六十三条　以武器相威胁或者共同协商行动

存在任何下列情节的脱逃罪，应当处以二年至五年监禁，并处四百万瑞尔至一千万瑞尔的罚金：

（一）威胁使用武器或者爆炸物的；或者

（二）多个被羁押人共同协商行动的。

第五百六十四条　使用武器

使用武器或者爆炸物脱逃的，应当处以五年至十年监禁。

第五百六十五条　帮助脱逃罪

任何人配合或者促成被羁押人脱逃的，应当处以一年至三年监禁，并处二百万瑞尔至六百万瑞尔的罚金。

第五百六十六条　加重情节（促成脱逃的手段）

向被羁押人提供武器、爆燃物质、有毒物质或者酸液，用作脱逃手段或者方便脱逃的，应当处以二年至五年监禁，并处四百万瑞尔至一千万瑞尔的罚金。

第五百六十七条　监管人员配合脱逃罪

任何监管人员配合或者策划被羁押人脱逃，采取有意不作为方式的，应当处以五年至十年监禁。

第五百六十八条　加重情节（监管者帮助脱逃）

任何监管人员向被羁押人提供武器、爆燃物质、有毒物质或者酸液，用作脱逃手段或者方便脱逃的，应当处以七年至十五年监禁。

第五百六十九条　配合脱逃罪（经允许进入监狱的人员）

任何因身份而有权进入监狱的人员配合或者策划被羁押人脱逃，采取有意不作为方式的，应当处以五年至十年监禁。

第五百七十条　加重情节（经允许进入监狱的人员帮助脱逃）

任何因身份而有权进入监狱的人员向被羁押人提供武器、爆燃物质、有毒物质或者酸液，用作脱逃手段或者方便脱逃的，应当处以七年至十五年监禁。

第三节　向被羁押人非法递交钱物的犯罪

第五百七十一条　非法递交罪及其加重情节

任何人向被羁押人递交或者送给钱款、信件、物品或者规章允许范围之外的物质的，应当处以一个月至一年监禁，并处十万瑞尔至二百万瑞尔的罚金。

下列人员实施非法递交罪，应当处以一年至二年监禁，并处二百万瑞尔至四百万瑞尔的罚金：

（一）对被羁押人进行监管的人员；

（二）因身份而有权进入监狱的人。

第五百七十二条　非法接收罪及其加重情节

任何人接收来自被羁押人的任何钱款、信件、物品或者规章允许范围之外的物质的，应当处以一个月至一年监禁，并处十万瑞尔至二百万瑞尔的罚金。

下列人员实施非法接收罪，应当处以一年至二年监禁，并处二百万瑞尔至四百万瑞尔的罚金：

（一）对被羁押人进行监管的人员；

（二）因身份而有权进入监狱的人员。

第四节　未遂和刑罚

第五百七十三条　未遂

实施本章规定的轻罪而未遂的，应当处以同样的刑罚。

第五百七十四条　刑罚的列外

本法典第五百六十一条（可适用的刑罚）和第五百六十

三条（以武器相威胁或者共同协商行动）至第五百七十条加重情节（有权进入监狱的人帮助脱逃）的实行犯、共同实行犯、教唆犯或者帮助犯，如果向有关部门报告后，脱逃被阻止的，可以免除刑罚。

第五百七十五条 附加刑（种类及期限）

对于本章规定的犯罪，可以判处下列附加刑：

（一）剥夺特定权利，或者永久剥夺，或者剥夺期限在五年以内；

（二）禁止从事在从业期间实施了犯罪或者与犯罪有密切关联的职业，或者永久禁止，或者禁止期限在五年以内；

（三）如是重罪，期限在十年以内的本地驱逐，如是轻罪，期限在五年以内的本地驱逐；

（四）没收用于或者打算用于实施罪行的任何工具、材料或者物品；

（五）没收涉及犯罪的物品或者资金；

（六）没收犯罪所得的收益或者财产；

（七）没收罪犯拥有的一辆或者多辆机动车；

（八）禁止拥有或者携带任何种类的任何武器、爆炸物或者弹药，或者永久禁止，或者禁止期限在五年以内；

（九）公布量刑结果，期限为二个月以内；

（十）以印刷媒体公布量刑结果；

（十一）通过任何视听传媒公布量刑结果，期限为八天以内。

第四章　不服从某些司法判决的犯罪

第五百七十六条　不服从本地驱逐罪

任何被处以本地驱逐刑的人在司法机关指定禁止的地方出现的，应当处以一年至二年监禁，并处二百万瑞尔至四百万瑞尔的罚金。

第五百七十七条　不遵守监督措施罪

任何被处以本地驱逐刑的人逃避司法机关确定的监督措施的，应当处以一年至二年监禁，并处二百万瑞尔至四百万瑞尔的罚金。

第五百七十八条　毁弃量刑结果公告罪

判决书要求公布所判处的刑罚，凡毁坏、隐匿或者撕毁此种公告的，应当处以一个月至六个月监禁，并处十万瑞尔至一百万瑞尔的罚金。

第五百七十九条　违反职业禁止令罪

司法机关发出职业禁止令作为刑罚，凡违反禁令的，应当处以一年至二年监禁，并处二百万瑞尔至四百万瑞尔的罚金。

第五百八十条　不服从剥夺特定权利罪

被定罪的人违反因吊销驾驶执照、不得拥有或者携带武器、爆炸物或者弹药、不得签发支票、关闭场所或者取消公开招投标资格产生的义务或者禁例的，应当处以一年至二年监禁，并处二百万瑞尔至四百万瑞尔的罚金。

第五百八十一条 违反没收令罪

毁坏、隐匿或者挪用被没收物品的，应当处以一年至二年监禁，并处二百万瑞尔至四百万瑞尔的罚金。

第五百八十二条 拒不交出驾驶执照罪

不服从终审判决，拒绝向主管部门交出驾驶执照或者被没收物品的，应当处以一年至二年监禁，并处二百万瑞尔至四百万瑞尔的罚金。

第五百八十三条 违反社区服务义务罪

被定罪的人违反因被处以社区服务而产生的义务的，应当处以一年至二年监禁，并处二百万瑞尔至四百万瑞尔的罚金。

第五百八十四条 违反法人义务罪

自然人违反法人因被处罚而产生的义务和禁例的，应当处以一年至二年监禁，并处二百万瑞尔至四百万瑞尔的罚金。

第五百八十五条 附加刑（种类及期限）

对于本章规定的犯罪，可以判处下列附加刑：

（一）剥夺特定权利，或者永久剥夺，或者剥夺期限在五年以内；

（二）公布量刑结果，期限为二个月以内；

（三）以印刷媒体公布量刑结果；

（四）通过任何视听传媒公布量刑结果，期限为八天以内。

第三部分　侵害行政管理的犯罪

第一章　公共代表侵害行政管理的犯罪

第一节　失职罪

第一分节　滥用权力罪

第五百八十六条　设法阻碍执法罪及其加重情节

正在履行职务或者在班的公职人员或者民选公职人员设法阻碍执法的，应当处以二年至五年监禁，并处四百万瑞尔至一千万瑞尔的罚金。

第五百八十七条　非法延续职务罪

公职人员或者民选公职人员收到终止其职务的正式通知后继续履行职务的，应当处以六个月至二年监禁，并处一百万瑞尔至四百万瑞尔的罚金。

第二分节　滥用权力侵犯个人的犯罪

第五百八十八条　侵犯人身自由罪

正在履行职务或者在班的公职人员或者民选公职人员任意侵犯人身自由的，应当处以二年至五年监禁，并处四百万瑞尔至一千万瑞尔的罚金。

第五百八十九条　拒不解除非法羁押罪

正在履行职务或者在班的公职人员或者民选公职人员明知发生了非法剥夺自由的情况，其有权消除这种情况却有意不消除或者有意不让主管部门介入的，应当处以一年至三年监禁，并处二百万瑞尔至六百万瑞尔的罚金。

第五百九十条　非法羁押或者释放罪

监狱管理人员在没有依法制作的令状、判决、羁押令或者释放令的情况下接收或者留置任何人的，应当处以二年至五年监禁，并处四百万瑞尔至一千万瑞尔的罚金。

第五百九十一条　延长非法羁押罪

监狱管理人员非法延长羁押的，应当处以二年至五年监禁，并处四百万瑞尔至一千万瑞尔的罚金。

第二节　贪污及相关犯罪

第一分节　侵吞公款罪

第五百九十二条　侵吞公款罪的定义

侵吞公款罪是公职人员或者民选公职人员实施的下列行为：

（一）要求或者接受任何明知不应当支付或者超过应当支付金额的利税的；

（二）以任何形式和任何理由，非法准予免税的。

第五百九十三条　适用的刑罚

犯侵吞公款罪，应当处以二年至五年监禁，并处四百万瑞尔至一千万瑞尔的罚金。

第二分节 受贿罪

第五百九十四条 受贿罪

公职人员或者民选公职人员未经批准,以下列情形作为交换,直接或者间接索取或者接受礼品、职位、许诺或利益的,应当处以七年至十五年监禁:

(一)实施与职务有关的行为或者职务上方便的行为;

(二)不实施与职务有关的行为或者职务上方便的行为。

第三分节 用影响力做交易罪

第五百九十五条 用影响力做交易受贿罪

"用影响力做交易受贿罪"是公职人员或者民选公职人员未经批准直接或者间接索要或者接受礼品、职位、许诺或者利益而非法利用其实际的或者预期的影响力让行为人从国家机关获得招投标资质或者任何对行为人有利的决定的行为。

第五百九十六条 适用的刑罚

犯用影响力做交易受贿罪,应当处以五年至十年监禁。

第四分节 非法盘剥罪

第五百九十七条 非法盘剥罪的定义

"非法盘剥罪"是公职人员或者民选公职人员实施的直接或者间接地取得、接受或者保存下列情况产生的任何利益的行为:

(一)上述公职人员或者民选公职人员对企业的监督、管理或者清偿负有全部或者部分保证职责的;

（二）上述公职人员或者民选公职人员对实施监督或者清偿负有全部或者部分保证职责的。

第五百九十八条 适用的刑罚

犯非法盘剥罪，应当处以二年至五年监禁，并处四百万瑞尔至一千万瑞尔的罚金。

第五分节 徇私罪

第五百九十九条 徇私罪的定义

"徇私罪"是公职人员或者民选公职人员实施的为他人在公开招投标中获得非法优势的行为。

第六百条 适用的刑罚

犯徇私罪，应当处以六个月至二年监禁，并处一百万瑞尔至四百万瑞尔的罚金。

第三节 毁弃和偷用的犯罪

第六百零一条 蓄意毁弃和偷用罪

公职人员或者民选公职人员蓄意毁弃或者偷用其受托保管的公私资金单证的，应当处以五年至十年监禁。

第六百零二条 非蓄意地毁弃或者丢失罪

公职人员或者民选公职人员非蓄意地毁弃或者丢失其受托保管的公私资金单证的，应当处以一个月至六个月监禁，并处十万瑞尔至一百万瑞尔的罚金。

第四节 未遂和刑罚

第六百零三条 未遂

实施本章规定的轻罪而未遂的,应当处以同样的刑罚,本法典第五百八十九条(拒不解除非法羁押罪)和第六百零二条(非蓄意地毁弃或者丢失罪)规定的轻罪除外。

第六百零四条 附加刑(种类及期限)

对于本章规定的犯罪,可以判处下列附加刑:

(一)剥夺特定权利,或者永久剥夺,或者剥夺期限在五年以内;

(二)禁止从事在从业期间实施了犯罪或者与犯罪有密切关联的职业,或者永久禁止,或者禁止期限在五年以内;

(三)没收用于或者打算用于实施罪行的任何工具、材料或者物品;

(四)没收涉及犯罪的物品或者资金;

(五)没收犯罪所得的收益或者财产;

(六)没收罪犯拥有的一辆或者多辆机动车;

(七)禁止拥有或者携带任何种类的任何武器、爆炸物或者弹药,或者永久禁止,或者禁止期限在五年以内;

(八)公布量刑结果,期限为二个月以内;

(九)以印刷媒体公布量刑结果;

(十)通过任何视听传媒公布量刑结果,期限为八天以内。

第二章 个人侵犯行政管理的犯罪

第一节 贪污和相关犯罪

第一分节 行贿罪

第六百零五条 行贿罪

直接或者间接地非法提供任何礼品、职位、许诺或者利益,旨在诱使公职人员或者民选公职人员做出下列事项的,应当处以五年至十年监禁:

(一)实施与其职务有关或其职务能促成的行为;

(二)不实施与其职务有关或其职务能促成的行为。

第二分节 用影响力做交易的行贿罪

第六百零六条 用影响力做交易行贿罪

直接或者间接地非法提供任何礼品、职位、许诺或者利益,旨在诱使公职人员或者民选公务人员非法利用其实际的或者预期的影响力让行为人从国家机关获得招投标资质或者任何对行为人有利的决定的,应当处以二年至五年监禁,并处四百万瑞尔至一千万瑞尔的罚金。

第三分节 威胁罪

第六百零七条 威胁罪

威胁公职人员或者民选公职人员进行下列事项的,应当处以二年至五年监禁,并处四百万瑞尔至一千万瑞尔的罚金:

（一）实施与其职务有关的行为；

（二）不实施与其职务有关的行为；

（三）利用其实际的或者预期的影响力让行为人从国家机关获得招投标资质或者任何对行为人有利的决定的行为。

第二节　毁弃和偷用的犯罪

第六百零八条　毁弃和偷用罪

毁弃、偷用或者盗取公职人员或者民选公职人员受托保管的公私资金单证或者其他物品的，应当处以二年至五年监禁，并处四百万瑞尔至一千万瑞尔的罚金。

第三节　干涉公共职能和官方职位的犯罪

第六百零九条　非法干涉公共职能履行罪

任何未经授权的人干涉本应当由公职人员行使的职能的，应当处以一年至三年监禁，并处二百万瑞尔至六百万瑞尔的罚金。

第六百一十条　会被误解为执行公务的活动罪

任何人从事足以被公众误解为执行公务的活动的，应当处以一个月至一年监禁，并处十万瑞尔至二百万瑞尔的罚金。

第六百一十一条　使用会造成误解的信件或者文件罪

任何人使用貌似司法文件或者行政文件的书面文件，足以造成公众误解的，应当处以一个月至一年监禁，并处十万瑞尔至二百万瑞尔的罚金。

第六百一十二条　非法使用政府部门制式服装罪

任何人未经授权公开穿戴政府部门的服装、制服或者饰物的，应当处以一个月至一年监禁，并处十万瑞尔至二百万瑞尔的罚金。

第六百一十三条　非法使用职业证书罪

任何人未经授权公开使用由政府部门管理的职业证明文书的，应当处以一个月至一年监禁，并处十万瑞尔至二百万瑞尔的罚金。

第六百一十四条　擅自使用政府部门管理的标志罪

任何人未经授权公开使用政府部门管理的标志的，应当处以一个月至一年监禁，并处十万瑞尔至二百万瑞尔的罚金。

第六百一十五条　擅自使用涂有警用或者军用标志的车辆罪

任何人未经授权使用外表可见警用或者军用标志的车辆的，应当处以一个月至一年监禁，并处十万瑞尔至二百万瑞尔的罚金。

第六百一十六条　使用貌似警服或者军装罪

任何人未经授权公开穿戴貌似警察或者军人的服装、制服、身份卡片、徽章或者车辆，足以造成公众误解的，应当处以一个月至六月监禁，并处十万瑞尔至一百万瑞尔的罚金。

第六百一十七条　加重情节（打算实施重罪或者轻罪）

为准备实施重罪或者轻罪或者为实施重罪或者轻罪创造

条件而实施第六百一十一条（使用会造成误解的信件或者文件罪）至第六百一十六条（使用貌似警服或者军装罪）规定的犯罪的，应当处以一年至三年监禁，并处二百万瑞尔至六百万瑞尔的罚金。

第六百一十八条　擅自使用政府部门管理的官方职业证书罪

擅自使用政府部门管理的官方职业证书的，应当处以一个月至一年监禁，并处十万瑞尔至二百万瑞尔的罚金。

第六百一十九条　擅自使用文凭罪

擅自使用由政府部门确定取得条件的学位或者学历证书的，应当处以一个月至一年监禁，并处十万瑞尔至二百万瑞尔的罚金。

第六百二十条　随意使用头衔罪

企业经理为了企业的利益而在企业的公关广告中使用或者保留王国政府、国民议会、参议院或者法官以及前法官的名称和头衔的，应当处以一个月至一年监禁，并处十万瑞尔至二百万瑞尔的罚金。

第六百二十一条　在公共事务中使用官方身份之外的身份罪

在公共文件或者呈交给政府部门的文件上使用官方身份之外的身份的，应当处以一个月至六个月监禁，并处十万瑞尔至一百万瑞尔的罚金。

第四节 挪移界桩罪

第六百二十二条 挪移界桩罪

拔除或者挪移政府部门竖立的界桩的,应当处以一个月至一年监禁,并处十万瑞尔至二百万瑞尔的罚金。

第五节 未遂和刑罚

第六百二十三条 未遂

实施本章规定的轻罪而未遂的,应当处以同样的刑罚。

第六百二十四条 附加刑(种类及期限)

对于本章规定的犯罪,可以判处下列附加刑:

(一)剥夺特定权利,或者永久剥夺,或者剥夺期限在五年以内;

(二)禁止从事在从业期间实施了犯罪或者与犯罪有密切关联的职业,或者永久禁止,或者禁止期限在五年以内;

(三)没收用于或者打算用于实施罪行的任何工具、材料或者物品;

(四)没收涉及犯罪的物品或者资金;

(五)没收犯罪所得的收益或者财产;

(六)没收罪犯拥有的一辆或者多辆机动车;

(七)禁止拥有或者携带任何种类的任何武器、爆炸物或者弹药,或者永久禁止,或者禁止期限在五年以内;

(八)公布量刑结果,期限为二个月以内;

(九)以印刷媒体公布量刑结果;

（十）通过任何视听传媒公布量刑结果，期限为八天以内。

第六百二十五条　法人的刑事责任

根据本法典第四十二条（法人的刑事责任），可以确定法人对本法典第六百零五条（行贿罪）、第六百零六条（用影响力做交易的行贿罪）和第六百零七条（威胁罪）规定的犯罪承担刑事责任。

应当对法人处以一千万瑞尔至五千万瑞尔的罚金，并处下列附加刑中的一项或者多项：

（一）依照本法典第一百七十条（法人的解散和清算）予以解散；

（二）依照本法典第一百七十一条（置于司法监视）予以司法监视；

（三）依照本法典第一百七十二条（禁止活动的开展），禁止进行一项或者多项活动；

（四）依照本法典第一百七十三条（取消公开招投标的资格），取消公开招投标资格；

（五）依照本法典第一百七十四条（禁止公开上市），禁止公开上市；

（六）依照本法典第一百七十八条（没收物品的所有权、出售和销毁）和第一百七十九条（没收与第三方权利）没收涉及犯罪的物品或者资金；

（七）依照本法典第一百七十八条（没收物品的所有权、出售和销毁）和第一百七十九条（没收与第三方权利）没收犯罪产生的收益或者财产；

（八）依照本法典第一百八十条（公布判决），公布量刑结果；

（九）依照本法典第一百八十一条（通过视听传媒播放判决），以印刷媒体公布量刑结果，或者以任何视听传媒播放量刑结果。

第四部分　损害公众信心的犯罪

第一章　伪造罪

第一节　伪造文件的犯罪

第六百二十六条　伪造罪的定义

伪造罪是指以任何方式在文件或者其他表达媒介中形成的对真相的不实改变，同时符合下列各项条件，足以造成危害的行为：

（一）伪造的目的或者作用是要为承载着法律后果的权利或者行为提供证据；

（二）危害会导致损失。

第六百二十七条　适用的刑罚

犯伪造罪，应当处以一年至三年监禁，并处二百万瑞尔至六百万瑞尔的罚金。

第六百二十八条　使用伪造的文件罪

使用伪造的文件的，应当处以一年至三年监禁，并处二百万瑞尔至六百万瑞尔的罚金。

第六百二十九条　伪造公文罪

对经过认证或者由公共机构签发的旨在证明权利、身份或资格，或者其授权的文件实施伪造行为的，应当处以五年至十年监禁。

第六百三十条　使用伪造的公文罪

对本法典第六百二十九条（伪造公文罪）规定的伪造公文加以使用的，应当处以二年至五年监禁，并处四百万瑞尔至一千万瑞尔的罚金。

第六百三十一条　虚传文件罪

歪曲地向他人传递公共机构签发的旨在证明权利、身份或者资格，或者授权的文件的，应当处以二年至五年监禁，并处四百万瑞尔至一千万瑞尔的罚金。

第六百三十二条　骗取文件罪

为证明权利、身份、资格或者授权，骗取公共机构的任何文件的，应当处以六个月至二年监禁，并处一百万瑞尔至四百万瑞尔的罚金。

第六百三十三条　虚假申报罪

为获得津贴、款项或者任何非法利益，向公共机构提供虚假申报的，应当处以六个月至二年监禁，并处一百万瑞尔至四百万瑞尔的罚金。

第六百三十四条　交予伪造的文件罪

除本节规定的条文之外，制作内容不实的证明或者证书的，应当处以一个月至一年监禁，并处十万瑞尔至二百万瑞尔的罚金。

第六百三十五条　伪造证明罪

伪造证明或者证书的，应当处以一个月至一年监禁，并处十万瑞尔至二百万瑞尔的罚金。

第六百三十六条　使用篡改或者伪造的证明罪

使用篡改或者伪造的证明或者证书的，应当处以一个月至一年监禁，并处十万瑞尔至二百万瑞尔的罚金。

第六百三十七条　经办人员签发虚假证明索贿罪

任何人在职业活动中索取或者接受职位、礼品、许诺或者任何种类的利益，制作内容不实的证明或者证书的，应当处以二年至五年监禁，并处四百万瑞尔至一千万瑞尔的罚金。

第六百三十八条　为使经办人员签发虚假证明行贿罪

任何人为使他人制作内容不实的证明或者证书，提供职位、礼品、许诺或者任何种类的利益的，应当处以一年至三年监禁，并处二百万瑞尔至六百万瑞尔的罚金。

第六百三十九条　医事执业者委员会成员签发虚假证明索贿罪

任何医事执业者或者医事执业者委员会成员索取或者接受职位、礼品、许诺或者任何种类的利益，签发内容不实的证明或者证书的，应当处以二年至五年监禁，并处四百万瑞尔至一千万瑞尔的罚金。

第六百四十条　为使医事执业者委员会成员签发虚假证明行贿罪

任何人为使医事执业者委员会成员制作内容不实的证明或者证书，提供职位、礼品、许诺或者任何种类的利益的，应当处以一年至三年监禁，并处二百万瑞尔至六百万瑞尔的罚金。

第六百四十一条　第六百三十九条和第六百四十条中的轻罪适用于所有医事职业

本法典规定的第六百三十九条（医事执业者委员会成员签发虚假证明索贿罪）和第六百四十条（为使医事执业者委员会成员签发虚假证明行贿罪）适用于所有的医事执业者。

第六百四十二条　未遂

实施本法典第六百三十二条（骗取文件罪）、第六百三十八条（为使经办人员签发虚假证明行贿罪）和第六百四十条（为使医事执业者委员会成员签发虚假证明行贿罪）规定的犯罪而未遂的，应当处以同样的刑罚。

第六百四十三条　附加刑（种类及期限）

对于本节规定的犯罪，可以判处下列附加刑：

（一）剥夺特定权利，或者永久剥夺，或者剥夺期限在五年以内；

（二）禁止从事在从业期间实施了犯罪或者与犯罪有密切关联的职业，或者永久禁止，或者禁止期限在五年以内；

（三）如是重罪，期限在十年以内的本地驱逐，如是轻罪，期限在五年以内的本地驱逐；

（四）没收用于或者打算用于实施罪行的任何工具、材料或者物品；

（五）没收涉及犯罪的物品或者资金；

（六）没收犯罪所得的收益或者财产；

(七) 没收罪犯拥有的一辆或者多辆机动车;

(八) 公布量刑结果,期限为二个月以内;

(九) 以印刷媒体公布量刑结果;

(十) 通过任何视听传媒公布量刑结果,期限为八天以内。

第六百四十四条 法人的刑事责任

根据本法典第四十二条(法人的刑事责任),可以确定法人对本法典第六百三十八条(为使经办人员签发虚假证明行贿罪)和第六百四十条(为使医事执业者委员会成员签发虚假证明行贿罪)规定的犯罪承担刑事责任。

应当对法人处以一千万瑞尔至一亿瑞尔的罚金,并处下列附加刑中的一项或者多项:

(一) 依照本法典第一百七十条(法人的解散和清算)予以解散;

(二) 依照本法典第一百七十一条(置于司法监视)予以司法监视;

(三) 依照本法典第一百七十二条(禁止活动的开展),禁止进行一项或者多项活动;

(四) 依照本法典第一百七十三条(取消公开招投标的资格),取消公开招投标资格;

(五) 依照本法典第一百七十四条(禁止公开上市),禁止公开上市;

(六) 依照本法典第一百七十八条(没收物品的所有权、出售和销毁)和第一百七十九条(没收与第三方权利)没收涉及犯罪的物品或者资金；

（七）依照本法典第一百七十八条（没收物品的所有权、出售和销毁）和第一百七十九条（没收与第三方权利）没收犯罪产生的收益或者财产；

（八）依照本法典第一百八十条（公布判决），公布量刑结果；

（九）依照本法典第一百八十一条（通过视听传媒播放判决），以印刷媒体公布量刑结果，或者以任何视听传媒播放量刑结果。

第二节 伪造货币和钞票的犯罪

第六百四十五条 伪造法定流通货币罪

伪造作为柬埔寨王国法定货币的钞票或者硬币的，应当处以十五年至三十年监禁，或者终身监禁。

第六百四十六条 伪造作为法定货币的钞票罪

伪造国际或者外国有权机构作为法定货币发行的钞票的，应当处以十年至二十年监禁。

第六百四十七条 流通伪造的货币和钞票罪

流通第六百四十五条（伪造法定流通货币罪）和第六百四十六条（伪造作为法定货币的钞票罪）规定的货币或者钞票的，应当处以五年至十年监禁。

有组织犯罪集团实施本罪，应当处以十年至二十年监禁。

第六百四十八条 储存伪造的货币或者钞票罪

为流通本法典第六百四十五条（伪造法定流通货币罪）

和第六百四十六条（伪造作为法定货币的钞票罪）规定的货币或者钞票而进行运输或者储存的，应当处以五年至十年监禁。

有组织犯罪集团实施本罪，应当处以十年至二十年监禁。

第六百四十九条　伪造失去法定货币地位的货币或者钞票罪

伪造失去法定货币地位的货币或者钞票的，应当处以一年至三年监禁，并处二百万瑞尔至六百万瑞尔的罚金。

第六百五十条　非法持有制造货币或者钞票的设备罪

未经批准持有制造货币或者钞票的专用设备或者任何其他物件的，应当处以五年至十年监禁。

第六百五十一条　将伪造的货币和钞票再流通罪

接收了本法典第六百四十五条（伪造法定流通货币罪）和第六百四十六条（伪造作为法定货币的钞票罪）规定的货币或者钞票并误认为是真货币或者真钞票的任何人，再将其投入流通时知道是伪造的，应当处以一天至六天监禁，并处以十万瑞尔至一千万瑞尔的罚金。

第六百五十二条　刑罚的免除

企图实施本节规定的任何一种犯罪的任何人，如果向司法或者行政机关告发，得以阻止犯罪发生，并且指认其他犯罪人的，可以免除刑罚。

第六百五十三条　附加刑（种类及期限）

对于本节规定的犯罪，可以判处下列附加刑：

（一）剥夺特定权利，或者永久剥夺，或者剥夺期限在五年以内；

（二）禁止从事在从业期间实施了犯罪或者与犯罪有密切关联的职业，或者永久禁止，或者禁止期限在五年以内；

（三）如是重罪，期限在十年以内的本地驱逐，如是轻罪，期限在五年以内的本地驱逐；

（四）没收用于或者打算用于实施罪行的任何工具、材料或者物品；

（五）没收涉及犯罪的物品或者资金；

（六）没收犯罪所得的收益或者财产；

（七）没收罪犯拥有的一辆或者多辆机动车；

（八）禁止拥有或者携带任何种类的任何武器、爆炸物或者弹药，或者永久禁止，或者禁止期限在五年以内；

（九）公布量刑结果，期限为二个月以内；

（十）以印刷媒体公布量刑结果；

（十一）通过任何视听传媒公布量刑结果，期限为八天以内。

第二章 伪造政府机关文件的犯罪

第一节 伪造债券和邮票的犯罪

第六百五十四条 伪造柬埔寨王国债券罪

伪造柬埔寨王国债券的，应当处以十年至二十年监禁。

第六百五十五条　伪造外国债券罪

伪造外国债券的，应当处以五年至十年监禁。

第六百五十六条　使用伪造的债券罪

使用伪造的债券的，应当处以二年至五年监禁，并处四百万瑞尔至一千万瑞尔的罚金。

第六百五十七条　伪造邮票罪

伪造柬埔寨王国发行的邮票或者其他邮政信托产品的，应当处以一年至五年监禁，并处五百万瑞尔至二千万瑞尔的罚金。

第六百五十八条　使用伪造的邮票罪

使用伪造的邮票或者其他邮政信托产品的，应当处以一个月至一年监禁，并处一百万瑞尔至五百万瑞尔的罚金。

第六百五十九条　未遂

实施本节规定的轻罪而未遂的，应当处以同样的刑罚。

第六百六十条　附加刑（种类及期限）

对于本节规定的犯罪，可以判处下列附加刑：

（一）剥夺特定权利，或者永久剥夺，或者剥夺期限在五年以内；

（二）禁止从事在从业期间实施了犯罪或者与犯罪有密切关联的职业，或者永久禁止，或者禁止期限在五年以内；

（三）如是重罪，期限在一年以内的本地驱逐，如是轻罪，期限在五年以内的本地驱逐；

（四）没收用于或者打算用于实施罪行的任何工具、材料或者物品；

（五）没收涉及犯罪的物品或者资金；

（六）没收犯罪所得的收益或者财产；

（七）没收罪犯拥有的一辆或者多辆机动车；

（八）禁止拥有或者携带任何种类的任何武器、爆炸物或者弹药，或者永久禁止，或者禁止期限在五年以内；

（九）公布量刑结果，期限为二个月以内；

（十）以印刷媒体公布量刑结果；

（十一）通过任何视听传媒公布量刑结果，期限为八天以内。

第二节　伪造权力标志的犯罪

第六百六十一条　伪造柬埔寨王国官方封印罪

伪造柬埔寨王国官方封印的，应当处以二年至五年监禁，并处四百万瑞尔至一千万瑞尔的罚金。

第六百六十二条　使用伪造的封印罪

使用伪造的柬埔寨王国封印的，应当处以二年至五年监禁，并处四百万瑞尔至一千万瑞尔的罚金。

第六百六十三条　伪造官方信笺罪

伪造政府机构官方专用信笺的，应当处以一个月至一年监禁，并处十万瑞尔至二百万瑞尔的罚金。

第六百六十四条　使用伪造的官方信笺罪

使用伪造的政府机构官方专用信笺的，应当处以一个月至一年监禁，并处十万瑞尔至二百万瑞尔的罚金。

第六百六十五条　制造引起误解的印刷品

制造、销售、分发或者使用与政府机构使用的有标识纸张非常相似的印刷品，足以引起公众误解的，应当处以一个月至一年监禁，并处十万瑞尔至二百万瑞尔的罚金。

第六百六十六条　未遂

实施本节规定的轻罪而未遂的，应当处以同样的刑罚。

第六百六十七条　附加刑（种类及期限）

对于本节规定的犯罪，可以判处下列附加刑：

（一）剥夺特定权利，或者永久剥夺，或者剥夺期限在五年以内；

（二）禁止从事在从业期间实施了犯罪或者与犯罪有密切关联的职业，或者永久禁止，或者禁止期限在五年以内；

（三）如是重罪，期限在十年以内的本地驱逐，如是轻罪，期限在五年以内的本地驱逐；

（四）没收用于或者打算用于实施罪行的任何工具、材料或者物品；

（五）没收涉及犯罪的物品或者资金；

（六）没收犯罪所得的收益或者财产；

（七）没收罪犯拥有的一辆或者多辆机动车；

（八）禁止拥有或者携带任何种类的任何武器、爆炸物或者弹药，或者永久禁止，或者禁止期限在五年以内；

（九）公布量刑结果，期限为二个月以内；

（十）以印刷媒体公布量刑结果；

（十一）通过任何视听传媒公布量刑结果，期限为八天以内。

第五编

衔接性规定

独一章　衔接性规定

第六百六十八条　其他刑事立法的适用

对其他有效刑事法律和刑事条款规定的犯罪，应当适用这些法律和条款。

其他刑事法律和刑事条款与本法典的规定相抵触，应当以本法典第一编（一般规定）的规定为准。

上文第六百六十八第（二）项的规定不适用于特别刑事立法。

第六百六十九条　刑罚时效的期限

《刑事诉讼法》施行后对犯罪宣告的刑罚时效，应当服从本法典的规定。

第六百七十条　本法典第一编（一般规定）的延展适用

所有刑事条款都应当服从本法典第一编（一般规定）的规定，另有规定的除外。

第六编

生效规定

独一章　生效规定

第六百七十一条　原刑事条款的存废

自本法典施行之日起，下列刑事法律和条款即应当失效：

（一）1992年之前的所有刑事条款；

（二）1992年9月10日通过的关于过渡时期柬埔寨王国适用的司法制度、刑法和刑事程序条文中的刑事规定；

（三）2002年1月7日第0102/004号令颁布的关于重罪加重情节的法律。

自本法典施行之日起，其他有效法律的条文中与本法典相抵触的部分，在本法典施行期间不再有效。

但是，上文第六百七十一条第一款和第六百七十一条第二款规定的原刑法条款，除第六百六十八条第二款（其他刑事立法的适用）的规定之外，对本法典施行前实施的犯罪仍然有效。

第六百七十二条　本法典的适用

本法典第一编（一般规定）的一般规定应当在本法典施行后立即适用，其他条款应当在本法典施行一年后适用。

BOOK 1
General Provisions

BOOK 1
General Provisions

Title 1   The Criminal Law

Chapter 1   General Principles

Article 1: scope of application of the criminal law

The criminal law defines offences, determines those who may be found guilty of committing them, sets penalties, and determines how they shall be enforced.

Where necessary, statutory instruments issued by the executive branch may define petty offences that are punishable only by a fine.

Article 2: definition and classification of offences

The law provides that offences are certain acts committed by natural persons or legal entities which cause social disturbance.

Offences are classified pursuant to their seriousness as felonies, misdemeanours and petty offences.

Article 3: principle of legality

Conduct may give rise to criminal conviction only if it constituted an offence at the time it occurred.

A penalty may be imposed only if it was legally applicable at the time the offence was committed.

Article 4: intent

There shall be no offence in the absence of intent to commit it.

However, where so provided by law, an offence may result from recklessness, carelessness, negligence or failure to fulfil a specific obligation.

Article 5: interpretation of criminal law

In criminal matters, the law shall be strictly construed. A judge may neither extend its scope of application nor interpret it by analogy.

Article 6: pronouncement of penalty

No penalty may be enforced unless it was pronounced by a court.

Article 7: application of cambodian criminal law

In criminal matters, the scope of application of cambodian law in space shall be determined by the provisions of this code, subject to international treaties.

Article 8: no impunity for serious violations of international humanitarian law

The provisions of this code may not have the effect of denying justice to the victims of serious offences which, under special legislation, are characterized as violations of international humanitarian law, international custom, or international conventions recognized by the Kingdom of Cambodia.

Chapter 2 Temporal Application of Criminal Law

Article 9: application of less severe laws

A new provision which abolishes an offence shall be applicable immediately. An act committed before the new provision came into force shall no longer be subject to prosecution. Any ongoing prosecutions shall be terminated.

If final judgement has been passed, the resulting penalties shall not enforced or shall cease to be enforced.

Article 10: lighter or heavier penalties

A new provision which prescribes a lighter penalty shall be applicable immediately. However, final judgements shall be enforced regardless of the severity of the relevant penalties.

A new provision which prescribes a heavier penalty shall be applicable only to acts committed after the provision came into force.

Article 11: validity of proceedings

The immediate application of a new provision shall not affect the validity of proceedings taken under a previous provision.

Chapter 3 Territorial Application of Cambodian Criminal Law

Section 1 Offences Committed or Deemed to Have Been Committed in the Territory of the Kingdom of Cambodia

Article 12: meaning of territory of the Kingdom of Cambodia

In criminal matters, Cambodia law is applicable to all offences committed in the territory of the Kingdom of Cambodia.

The territory of the Kingdom of Cambodia includes its corresponding air and maritime spaces.

Article 13: place where offence is committed

An offence shall be deemed to have been committed in the territory of the Kingdom of Cambodia if one of the ingredients of the offence was committed in the territory of the Kingdom of Cambodia.

Article 14: offence committed on board a cambodian vessel

In criminal matters, cambodian law is applicable to offences committed on board vessels flying the cambodian flag, regardless of where they are.

Article 15: offence committed on board a foreign-flagged vessel

In criminal matters, cambodian law is applicable on board

foreign vessels which cambodian authorities are authorized to inspect or board by international agreement.

Article 16: offence committed on board a cambodian registered aircraft

In criminal matters, cambodian law is applicable to offences committed on board an aircraft registered in the Kingdom of Cambodia, regardless of where it is.

Article 17: application of cambodian criminal law to acts initiated in Cambodia

In criminal matters, cambodian law is applicable to any person who, in the territory of the Kingdom of Cambodia, instigates or is an accomplice to a felony or misdemeanor committed abroad, if the following two conditions are met:

The offence is punishable under both the cambodian law and the foreign law; and

The fact that the offence was committed is established by final judgement of a foreign court.

Article 18: characterisation of offences committed by a legal entity

The characterisation of an offences committed by a legal entity as a felony, misdemeanor or the petty offence shall be determined by the penalty incurred by a natural person.

Section 2 Offences Committed Outside the Territory of the Kingdom of Cambodia

Article 19: felony or misdemeanor committed by a cambodian national

In criminal matters, cambodian law is applicable to any felony committed by a cambodian national outside the territory of the Kingdom of Cambodia.

Cambodia law is applicable to misdemeanours committed by cambodian nationals in a foreign country if the conduct is also punishable under the law of that country.

These provisions shall be applicable even if the accused acquired cambodian nationality after the acts which he or she is alleged to have committed.

Article 20: where the victim is a cambodian national

In criminal matters, cambodian law is applicable to any felony committed by a cambodian or foreign national outside the territory of the Kingdom of Cambodia, if the victim is a cambodian national at the time of the offence.

Article 21: initiation of prosecution

In the cases specified in article 19 (felony or misdemeanor committed by a cambodian national) and article 20 (where the victim is a cambodian national), prosecution may only be initiated by the prosecuting authority. It must be preceded either:

By a complaint by the victim or his or her assigns; or

By a formal information by the authorities of the country where the offence was committed.

Article 22: special jurisdiction for specific felonies

In criminal matters, cambodian law is applicable to any felony committed outside the territory of the Kingdom of Cambodia if it is characterized as:

(1) an offence against the security of the Kingdom of Cambodia;

(2) counterfeiting the seal of the Kingdom of Cambodia;

(3) counterfeiting the national currency and banknotes being legal tender in the Kingdom of Cambodia;

(4) an offence against diplomatic or consular agents of the Kingdom of Cambodia;

(5) an offence against diplomatic or consular premises of the Kingdom of Cambodia.

Article 23: prohibition against cumulative charging and convictions

No one may be prosecuted for the same conduct for which he or she has already been finally tried abroad and who, in the event of conviction, establishes that he or she has already served the penalty or that the penalty has been extinguished by statute of limitation.

Title 2   Criminal Responsibility

Chapter 1   General Provisions

Article 24: principle of individual criminal responsibility

No one shall be criminally responsible except for his or her own conduct.

Article 25: definition of perpetrator

The perpetrator of an offence shall be any person who commits the relevant criminally prohibited act.

The definition of perpetrator includes any person who attempts to commit a felony or, in the cases provided for by law, a misdemeanor.

Article 26: definition of co-perpetrator

The co-perpetrators of an offence shall be any persons who, by mutual agreement, attempt to commit a felony or, in the cases provided for by law, a misdemeanor.

Article 27: definition of attempt

An attempt to commit a felony or, in the cases provided for by law, a misdemeanor, shall be punishable if the following conditions are met:

The perpetrator has started to commit the offence, that is, he or she has committed acts which lead directly to the commission of the offence;

The perpetrator did not stop his or her acts voluntarily, but was interrupted solely by circumstances beyond his or her control.

A preparatory act which does not directly lead to the commission of the offence does not constitute a commencement of execution.

An attempt to commit a petty offence shall not be punishable.

Article 28: definition of instigator

An instigator of a felony or a misdemeanor shall be any person who:

(1) gives instructions or orders to commit a felony or misdemeanor;

(2) provokes the commission of a felony or misdemeanor by means of a gift, promise, threat, instigation, persuasion or abuse of authority or power.

An instigator may only be punishable if the felony or misdemeanor was committed or attempted.

An instigator of a felony or misdemeanor shall incur the same penalties as the perpetrator.

Article 29: definition of accomplice

An accomplice shall be any person who knowingly, by aiding

or abetting, facilitates an attempt to commit a felony or a misdemeanor, or its commission.

An accomplice may only be punishable if the felony or misdemeanor was committed or attempted.

An accomplice to a felony or a misdemeanour shall incur the same penalties as the perpetrator.

Article 30: definition of public official and holder of public elected office

"Public official" means:

(a) any person appointed by legal instrument either temporarily or permanently, with or without remuneration and, regardless of his or her status or age, works in a legislative, executive or judicial institution;

(b) any other person who works in the public service, including public agencies or enterprises or other public institutions within the meaning of the laws of the Kingdom of Cambodia.

A holder of public elected office includes senators, members of the national assembly, municipal councilors of the capital, provincial councilors, city councilors, district or khan councilors, and commune or sangkat councilors and any person holding public elected office in any other capacity.

Chapter 2 Exclusion of or Diminished Criminal Responsibility

Article 31: absence of criminal responsibility by reason of mental disorder

A person who, at the time he or she committed an offence, was suffering from a mental disorder which destroyed his or her capacity to reason, shall not be criminally responsible.

A person who, at the time he or she committed an offence, was suffering from a mental disorder which diminished his or her capacity to reason, shall still be criminally responsible. However, the court shall take this into account when it decides the penalty.

A person who, at the time he or she committed an offence, was suffering from a mental disorder resulting from the consumption of alcohol, drugs, or prohibited substances, shall still be criminally responsible.

Article 32: authorization by law or lawful authority

A person shall not be criminally responsible if he or she performs an act prescribed or authorized by law.

A person shall not be criminally responsible if he or she performs an act ordered by a lawful authority, unless the act was manifestly unlawful.

The perpetrator, co-perpetrator, instigator, or accomplice of genocide, or of a crime against humanity, or a war crime shall not, under any circumstances, be excused from criminal responsibility on the ground that:

(1) he or she committed an act prescribed, authorised or not prohibited by the law in force;

(2) he or she acted by order of a lawful authority.

Article 33: self-defence

A person who commits an offence in self-defence shall not be criminally responsible.

Self-defence must meet the following conditions:

The offence was compelled by the necessity to defend oneself or others or to defend property against an unjustified assault;

The offence and the assault must occur at the same time; and

The means used in defence were not disproportionate to the seriousness of the assault.

Article 34: presumption of self-defence

A person shall be presumed to have acted in self-defence if he or she acted:

(1) at night, to repel an entry into a dwelling place committed by forced entry, violence or deception;

(2) to defend himself or herself against the perpetrators of theft or pillaging with violence.

The presumption of self-defence is not absolute. It may be

rebutted by contrary evidence.

Article 35: defence of necessity

A person who commits an offence out of necessity shall not be criminally responsible.

A state of necessity must meet the following conditions:

The commission of the offence was necessary to defend oneself or to protect others or property against a present or imminent danger;

The means used for protection were not disproportionate to the seriousness of the danger.

Article 36: effect of force or compulsion

A person who commits an offence under the influence of an irresistible force or compulsion shall not be criminally responsible.

The force or compulsion can only be the result of circumstances beyond human control. It must be unforeseeable and inevitable.

Article 37: absence of criminal responsibility

A person who is not criminally responsible shall not be liable to criminal punishment.

Chapter 3   Criminal Responsibility of Minors

Article 38: age of criminal responsibility

The age of criminal responsibility shall be eighteen and over.

Article 39: measures applicable to minors

Minors who commit offences shall be subject to supervision, education, protection and assistance.

However, a court may impose a criminal penalty on a minor of fourteen years and over if warranted by the circumstances of the offence or the character of the minor.

Article 40: types of measures

Supervisory, educational, protective and assistance measures shall include:

(1) returning the minor to his or her parents, guardian, custodian, or to another person who is trustworthy;

(2) committing the minor to a social service agency which cares for minors;

(3) committing the minor to a private organization that is qualified to receive minors;

(4) committing the minor to a specialised hospital or institution;

(5) placing the minor under judicial protection.

Article 41: placement under judicial protection

In case of placement under judicial protection, the court shall designate a person to supervise the minor. The supervisor shall report regularly to the prosecutor on the behavior of the minor. The supervisor shall also inform the prosecutor of all events that would entail a variation of the measure.

Chapter 4 Criminal Responsibility of Legal Entities

Article 42: criminal responsibility of legal entities

Where expressly provided by law and statutory instruments, legal entities, with the exception of the state, may be held criminally responsible for offences committed on their behalf by their organs or representatives.

The criminal responsibility of legal entities shall not preclude that of natural persons for the same acts.

Title 3 Penalties

Chapter 1 Categories of Penalties

Section 1 Principal Penalties

Article 43: principal penalties

Principal penalties shall include imprisonment and fines.

Fines shall be expressed in Riels.

Article 44: minimum and maximum principal penalties

If the penalty for an offence is imprisonment, the law shall set the minimum and maximum sentences of imprisonment incurred.

If the penalty for an offence is a fine, the law shall set the minimum and maximum amounts of the fine incurred.

Article 45: aggravated and reduced penalties

The minimum and maximum sentences of imprisonment and fines may be aggravated or reduced as provided for by this code.

Article 46: definition of felony

A felony is an offence which the maximum sentence of imprisonment incurred is:

(1) life imprisonment;

(2) imprisonment for more than five years, but no more than thirty years.

A fine maybe imposed in addition to imprisonment.

Article 47:definition of misdemeanor

A misdemeanor is an offence for which the maximum sentence of imprisonment incurred is more than six days, but no more than five years.

A fine may be imposed in addition to imprisonment.

Article 48:definition of petty offence

A petty offence is an offence:

(1) for which the maximum sentence of imprisonment incurred is six days or less. A fine may be imposed in addition to imprisonment;

(2) punishable solely by a fine.

Article 49: computation of sentence

A term of imprisonment of one day shall mean twenty-four hours.

A term of imprisonment of one month shall mean thirty days.

A term of imprisonment of more than one month shall take into account the actual number of days in the relevant months.

A term of imprisonment of one year shall mean twelve months.

Article 50:calculation of end-date of term of imprisonment

A convicted person whose term of imprisonment would normally end on a Saturday, Sunday or a public holiday within the meaning of the law or legal instruments shall be released on the preceding day.

Article 51: deduction of time spent in pre-trial detention

Time spent in pre-trial detention shall be wholly deducted from the term of imprisonment to be served

Article 52: proceeds from fines

Proceeds from fines shall be paid to the state treasury.

Section 2 Additional Penalties

Article 53: additional penalties

Additional penalties are:

(1) forfeiture of certain rights;

(2) prohibition from practising a profession in the practice of or in connection with which the offence was committed;

(3) prohibition from driving any motor vehicle whatsoever;

(4) suspension of a driving license;

(5) local exclusion;

(6) prohibition from leaving the territory of the Kingdom of Cambodia;

(7) prohibition of a convicted alien from entering and remaining in the territory of the Kingdom of Cambodia;

(8) confiscation of any instruments, materials or items which were used or intended to be used to commit the offence;

(9) confiscation of the items or funds which were the subject

of the offence;

(10) confiscation of the proceeds or property arising out of the offence;

(11) confiscation of the utensils, materials and furnishings in the premises in which the offence was committed;

(12) confiscation of one or more vehicles belonging to the convicted person;

(13) prohibition from possessing or carrying any weapon, explosive or ammunition of any kind;

(14) disqualification from public tenders;

(15) closure of an establishment used to plan or to commit the offence;

(16) prohibition from operating an establishment that is open to or used by the public;

(17) publication of sentencing decision;

(18) publication of sentencing decision in the print media;

(19) broadcasting of sentencing decision by any audio-visual communication.

Other additional penalties may be provided for by specific provision.

Article 54: circumstances under which additional penalties may be pronounced

Additional penalties may be pronounced only if they are specifically provided for in respect of the felony, misdemeanour or petty offence under prosecution.

The pronouncement of additional penalties is optional. However, the pronouncement shall be mandatory if the law expressly so provides.

Article 55: forfeiture of rights

The rights that may be forfeited under article 53(1) (additional penalties) are:

(1) the right to vote;

(2) the right to stand for election;

(3) the right to be a public official;

(4) the right to be appointed as an expert, an arbitrator or to be a judicially appointed official;

(5) the right to receive official decorations and honours;

(6) the right to testify under oath in court.

The penalty of forfeiture of certain rights may be permanent or temporary. In the latter case, the period of forfeiture may not exceed five years.

Article 56: prohibition from practising a profession

The prohibition from practising a profession shall not be applicable to elected office or union stewardship. It shall also not be application in the case of press offences.

The prohibition may be permanent or temporary. In the latter case, the period of prohibition may not exceed five years.

The court shall specify the profession which shall not be

practised.

Article 57: prohibition from driving

The period of prohibition from driving a motor vehicle may not exceed five years.

Article 58: suspension of driving license

The penalty of suspension of a driving license may not exceed five years. The convicted person must surrender his or her license to the greffier of the court. It shall be kept as specified by prakas of the minister of justice.

Article 59: exclusion from certain places in the territory of the Kingdom of Cambodia

The penalty of local exclusion shall mean the prohibition of a convicted person from being in certain places in the territory of the Kingdom of Cambodia. The period of local exclusion may not exceed ten years in the case of a felony, and five years in the case of a misdemeanor.

The court shall list the places where the exclusion applies and the duration of such exclusion.

Local exclusion shall be accompanied by supervision. The convicted person must:

(1) appear when summonsed by the judicial or administrative authorities designated by the court;

(2) report periodically at the offices of the royal police or royal gendarmerie designated by the court.

The court shall determine how the supervision shall be carried out.

The prosecutor shall notify the court decision to the ministry of interior and the ministry of national defence.

Article 60: prohibition from leaving the territory of the Kingdom of Cambodia

The period of prohibition from leaving the territory of Cambodia may not exceed five years.

The convicted person must surrender his or her passport to the greffier of the court. It shall be kept as specified by prakas of the minister of justice.

The convicted person cannot, during the period of the penalty, obtain a passport.

Article 61: prohibition of a convicted alien from entering and remaining in the territory of the Kingdom of Cambodia

Prohibition of a convicted alien from entering and remaining in the territory of the Kingdom of Cambodia may be permanent or temporary. In the latter case, the period of prohibition may not exceed five years. Such prohibition shall entail the expulsion of the convicted person at the end of his or her sentence of imprisonment.

Article 62: confiscation

Confiscation may be ordered in relation to the following items:

(1) any instruments, materials or items which were used or intended to be used to commit the offence;

(2) the items or funds which were the subject of the offence;

(3) the proceeds or property arising out of the offence;

(4) the utensils, materials and furnishings in the premises in which the offence was committed.

However, confiscation shall not be ordered if it affects the rights of third parties.

Article 63: disposition of confiscated items

When confiscation becomes final, the items confiscated shall become the property of the state, except as otherwise specified by specific provision.

The state may sell or destroy the items confiscated as prescribed in the procedures for selling state property.

Article 64: prohibition from possessing or carrying any weapon, explosive or ammunition of any kind

The prohibition from possessing or carrying any weapon, explosive or ammunition of any kind may be permanent or temporary. In the latter case, the period of prohibition may not exceed five years. The prohibition shall apply to weapons, explosives or ammunitions of any kind in the Kingdom of Cambodia.

Article 65: disqualification from public tenders

The penalty of disqualification from public tenders shall entail prohibition from participating, directly or indirectly, in any tender issued by:

(1) the state;

(2) a sub-national entity;

(3) a public establishment; and

(4) a state or sub-national entity concession or a state or sub-national entity-controlled enterprise.

Disqualification from public tenders may be permanent or temporary. In the latter case, the period of disqualification may not exceed five years.

Article 66: closure of establishment

The penalty of closure of an establishment shall entail prohibition from carrying out in the establishment the activity in connection with which the offence was committed.

Closure of an establishment may be permanent or temporary. In the latter case, the period of closure may not exceed five years.

Article 67: prohibition from operating an establishment

The prohibition from operating an establishment that is open to or used by the public may be permanent or temporary. In the latter case, the period of prohibition may not exceed five years.

Article 68: publication of sentencing decision

The penalty of publication of the decision shall be carried out in such places and for such period of time determined by the court. The publication may not extend beyond two months. It may involve all or part of the decision, or mere references thereto. The cost of the publication shall be borne by the convicted person.

If the publication is removed, concealed or torn, a new

publication shall be made at the expense of the person who removed, concealed or tore it.

Article 69: publication of sentencing decision in the print media

The penalty of publishing the decision shall be carried out in the print media in the manner and for the period of time determined by the court.

The cost of publication shall be borne by the convicted person. The convicted person may be subject to imprisonment in default of payment.

A newspaper may not refuse to publish a decision where publication is ordered by the court.

Article 70: broadcast of the sentencing decision by audio-visual communication

The penalty of broadcasting the decision by audio-visual communication shall be carried out in the manner determined by the court. The broadcast may not be carried out for more than eight days. It may involve all or part of the decision, or references thereto. The cost of the broadcast shall be borne by the convicted person.

Article 71: date of enforcement of additional penalties

Unless otherwise decided by the court, additional penalties under articles 53(1), (2), (3), (4), (5), (6) and (7) (additional penalties) shall be enforced upon completion of the sentence of imprisonment.

Section 3   Alternative Penalties

Sub-Section 1   Community Service

Article 72: meaning of community service

If an accused is liable to imprisonment for a maximum period of three years or more, the court may order the convicted person to perform community service.

Community service is an obligation to perform, for a period of thirty to two hundred hours, unpaid service for the benefit of the state, a sub-national entity, or a public corporation, an association or a non-governmental organisation.

Article 73: community service may not benefit a natural person

Community service may not, under any circumstances, be carried out for the benefit of a natural person.

Article 74: provisions pertaining to community service

Community service shall be governed by the provisions of the *Labour Code*, in particular those provisions of the code dealing with night work, occupational health, safety, and women at work.

Community service may be performed in conjunction with a professional activity.

Article 75: reparation for harm caused to third parties

The state shall pay compensation for harm caused to third parties by a convicted person in connection with the performance of community service. The state shall be subrogated by operation of law to the rights of the victim.

Sub-Section 2 Reprimand

Article 76: provisions pertaining to reprimand

A court may reprimand an accused who is liable to a maximum sentence of imprisonment of three years or more if the following three conditions are met:

-the public disturbance caused by the offence has ceased;

-the harm has been repaired;

-the accused provides guarantees of his or her social reintegration.

Chapter 2 Aggravating and Mitigating Circumstances

Section 1 Aggravating Circumstances

Sub-Section 1 Definition of Certain Aggravating Circumstances

Article 77: organised criminal enterprise

An organised criminal enterprise shall be any group or conspiracy established with a view to plan or commit one or more offences.

Article 78: premeditation

Premeditation is the intent, formed prior to the act, to commit an offence.

Article 79: forced entry

Forced entry consists in forcing damaging or destroying any closing device or fence of any kind.

Forced entry includes the following:

(1) the use of false keys;

(2) the use of unlawfully obtained keys;

(3) the use of any instrument which may be employed to operate a closing device without forcing, damaging or destroying it.

Article 80: unlawful entry

Unlawful entry is the act of entering any place, either by climbing over a fence, or by passing through any aperture not designed to be used as an entrance.

Article 81: weapons and items deemed to be weapons

A weapon shall be any item designed to kill or wound.

Weapon includes any other item liable to be dangerous to persons if:

(1) it was used to kill, wound or threaten;

(2) it was intended to be used to kill, wound or threaten.

A weapon includes an animal used to kill, wound or threaten.

Article 82: ambush

An ambush is the act of lying in wait for the victim in any place with a view to committing an offence.

Sub-Section 2 Subsequent Offences

Article 83: subsequent offences: penalties

Committing a subsequent offence shall result in aggravating, in accordance with this sub-section, the maximum sentence of imprisonment incurred for a felony or a misdemeanour.

Article 84: applicability of subsequent offences

A subsequent offence is said to have been committed:

(1) if a person against whom final judgement has already been entered for a felony commits a new felony within ten years;

(2) if a person against whom final judgement has already been entered for a felony commits a misdemeanour within five years;

(3) if a person against whom a final judgement of imprisonment of three years or more has already been entered for a misdemeanor commits a felony within five years;

(4) if a person against whom final judgement has already been entered for a misdemeanor commits the same misdemeanor within five years.

The time limits of ten years and five years shall be computed from the day the conviction for the first offence becomes final.

Article 85: subsequent felonies

If a person against whom final judgement has already been entered for a felony commits a new felony within ten years, the maximum sentence of imprisonment incurred for the new felony shall be aggravated as follows:

(1) if the maximum sentence of imprisonment incurred for the new felony does not exceed twenty years, the maximum sentence of imprisonment shall be doubled;

(2) if the maximum sentence of imprisonment incurred for the new felony is thirty years, the maximum sentence of imprisonment shall be life imprisonment.

Article 86: committing a misdemeanour after sentencing for a felony

If a person against whom final judgement has already been entered for a felony commits a misdemeanour within five years, the maximum sentence of imprisonment incurred for the misdemeanour shall be doubled.

By reason of committing a subsequent offence, the maximum term of imprisonment incurred exceeds five years, the legal qualification of the offence shall remain a misdemeanour despite the aggravation of the penalty.

Article 87: committing a felony after sentencing for a misdemeanour

If a person against whom a final judgement of imprisonment of three years or more has already been entered for a misdemeanour commits a felony within five years, the penalty incurred for the felony shall be aggravated as follows:

(1) if the maximum sentence of imprisonment incurred for the felony does not exceed twenty years, the maximum sentence of

imprisonment shall be doubled;

(2) if the maximum sentence of imprisonment incurred for the felony is thirty years, the maximum sentence of imprisonment shall be life imprisonment.

Article 88: committing a misdemeanour after sentencing for a misdemeanour

If a person against whom final judgement has already been entered for a misdemeanour commits the same misdemeanour within five years, the maximum sentence of imprisonment incurred for the new misdemeanour shall be doubled.

By reason of committing a subsequent offence, the maximum sentence of imprisonment incurred exceeds five years, the legal qualification of the offence shall remain a misdemeanour despite the aggravation of the penalty.

Article 89: deeming

Theft, breach of trust, and fraud shall be deemed to be the same offence for the purposes of the rules pertaining to subsequent offences.

Receiving stolen goods shall be deemed to be the offence by which the goods in question were obtained.

Money laundering shall be deemed to be the offence in connection with which the money laundering occurred.

Article 90: previous offences and prosecution

A court may only consider a previous conviction and use it as grounds for aggravating the sentence of imprisonment if is expressly stated in the indictment.

Article 91: previous offences and final decisions

A decision is considered final where it is no longer subject to appeal.

For the purposes of the rules pertaining to subsequent offences, only final decisions in respect of the criminal prosecution shall be taken into account.

Article 92: specific provisions

A previous conviction may be taken into account not with standing the application of the statute of limitations to the relevant sentence.

A previous conviction may not be taken into account where pardon is granted with respect to the sentence under article 90 new (2)(4) of the constitution of the Kingdom of Cambodia.

Section 2 Mitigating Circumstances

Article 93: definition of mitigating circumstances

The court may grant the accused the benefit of mitigating circumstances if warranted by the nature of the offence or the character of the accused.

The accused may also benefit from mitigating circumstances, notwithstanding that he or she has a previous conviction.

Article 94: effect of mitigating circumstances

If the court grants an accused the benefit of mitigating circumstances, the minimum principal penalty incurred for a felony or a misdemeanour shall be reduced as follows:

(1) if the minimum sentence of imprisonment incurred is ten years or more, it shall be reduced to two years;

(2) if the minimum sentence of imprisonment incurred is five years or more, but less than ten years, it shall be reduced to one year;

(3) if the minimum sentence of imprisonment incurred is two years or more, but less than five years, it shall be reduced to six months;

(4) if the minimum sentence of imprisonment incurred is six days or more, but less than two years, it shall be reduced to one day;

(5) the minimum fine incurred shall be reduced by half.

Article 95: life imprisonment and mitigating circumstances

If the penalty incurred for an offence is life imprisonment, the judge granting the benefit of mitigating circumstances may impose a sentence of between fifteen and thirty years imprisonment.

Chapter 3 Sentencing Principles

Section 1 General Principles

Article 96: principle of individualisation of penalties

In imposing penalties, the court shall take into account the seriousness and circumstances of the offence, the character of the accused, his or her psychological state, his or her means, expenses and motives, as well as his or her behaviour after the offence, especially towards the victim.

Article 97: pronouncement of principal penalties

In all cases where an offence is punished both by a sentence of imprisonment and a fine, the court may impose:

-a sentence of imprisonment and a fine concurrently; or

-a sentence of imprisonment only; or

-a fine only.

Article 98: pronouncement of alternative penalties

Community service may be ordered as an alternative to a principal penalty. If the court orders community service, it may not impose a sentence of imprisonment or a fine.

A reprimand may be issued as an alternative to a principal penalty. If the court issues a reprimand, it may not impose a sentence of imprisonment or a fine.

Article 99: pronouncement of additional penalties in addition to principal penalties

If one or more additional penalties are incurred, such penalties shall be imposed in addition to the principal penalty subject to the provisions of article 100 (pronouncement of additional penalties in lieu of principal penalties) of this code.

Article 100: pronouncement of additional penalties in lieu of principal penalties

The court may decide to substitute one on more additional penalties for principal penalties in the following cases:

(1) if the only principal penalty incurred by the accused is a fine;

(2) if the accused incurs a maximum sentence of imprisonment of three years or less.

If the court decides to substitute one or more additional penalties for principal penalties, it may not impose a sentence of imprisonment or a fine.

Article 101: specific rules applicable to the pronouncement of community service orders

A community service penalty may only be imposed if the accused is present at the hearing and accepts to perform the work. Before issuing its decision or judgement, the court shall inform the accused of his or her right to refuse to perform community service. His or her response shall be recorded in the decision or judgement.

Article 102: duration of community service

If a court orders community service, it shall set its duration and the time within which it shall be performed. This period may not exceed one year.

Article 103: execution of community service penalty

The manner in which a community service penalty shall be executed shall be determined by the prosecutor.

The prosecutor shall designate the legal entity which shall be the beneficiary of the community service.

A community service penalty shall be executed under the supervision of the prosecutor.

Section 2 Suspended Sentence

Sub-Section 1 Common Provisions

Article 104: pronouncement of suspended sentences

The court may suspend the enforcement of a principal penalty as prescribed in this section.

Article 105: rules pertaining to suspended sentences

For the purposes of the provisions pertaining to suspended sentences, only final decisions in respect of a criminal prosecution shall be taken into account.

Sub-Section 2 Prosecution for Felony or Misdemeanour

Article 106: previous convictions

The sentence of an accused charged with a felony or

misdemeanour may be suspended where no final conviction has been entered against him or her within the five years preceding the offence.

Article 107: penalties that may be suspended

The following penalties may be suspended:

(1) sentences of imprisonment of five years or less;

(2) fines.

Article 108: partial suspension

The court may suspend part of a sentence of imprisonment for such period of time as it may determine or suspend part of a fine for such amount as it may determine.

Article 109: revocation of suspended sentences

A suspended sentence imposed upon final conviction for a felony or misdemeanour shall be revoked automatically if a new final conviction for a felony or misdemeanour is entered within five years following the pronouncement of the suspended sentence.

The first penalty shall be executed, but not concurrently with the second penalty.

Article 110: non-revocation of suspended sentences

Notwithstanding the provisions of article 109 (revocation of suspended sentences), the court may, by a specially reasoned decision, decide that the new sentence shall not entail revocation of an existing suspended sentence.

Article 111: suspended sentences deemed never to have been passed

A suspended sentence imposed upon final conviction for a felony or a misdemeanour shall be deemed never to have been passed if no new conviction is entered for a felony or a misdemeanour within five years following the pronouncement of the suspended sentence. The sentence may no longer be enforced.

If part only of a sentence is suspended, the entire sentence shall be deemed never to have been passed. The sentence may no longer be enforced.

Sub-Section 3   Prosecution for Petty Offence

Article 112: previous conviction

The sentence of an accused charged with a petty offence may be suspended if no final conviction to imprisonment has been entered against him or her within the year preceding the offence.

Article 113: penalties that may be suspended

The following penalties for petty offences maybe suspended:

(1) imprisonment;

(2) fines.

Article 114: revocation of suspended sentences

A suspended sentence imposed upon final conviction for a petty offence shall be revoked automatically if a new final conviction for a felony, misdemeanour or petty offence is entered within one year following the pronouncement of the suspended sentence. The first penalty shall be executed, but not concurrently with the second penalty.

Article 115:non-revocation of suspended sentences

Notwithstanding the provisions of article 114 (revocation of suspended sentences), the court may, by a specially reasoned decision, decide that the new sentence shall not entail revocation of an existing suspended sentence.

Article 116: suspended sentences deemed never to have been passed

A suspended sentence imposed upon final conviction for a petty offence shall be deemed never to have been passed if no new conviction is entered for a felony, misdemeanour or petty offence within one year following the pronouncement of the suspended sentence. The sentence may no longer be enforced.

Section 3   Suspended Sentence with Probation

Article 117:meaning of suspended sentence with probation

The court may combine a suspended sentence with probation if the sentence of imprisonment incurred is between six months and five years.

A suspended sentence with probation subjects the convicted person, for a certain period, to probation measures and one or more specific obligations.

Article 118: probationary period

The court shall determine the duration of the probationary period, which may not be less than one year nor more than three years.

Article 119: probation measures

A convicted person shall be subject to the following probation measures:

(1) to appear when summonsed by the prosecutor or his or her designated representative;

(2) to receive visits from any person designated by the prosecutor;

(3) to provide the prosecutor or his or her designated representative with documents establishing his or her social reintegration;

(4) to alert the prosecutor of any change of address;

(5) to alert the prosecutor of any change of employment;

(6) and to obtain prior authorisation from the prosecutor before travelling abroad.

Article 120: specific obligations that may be imposed on a convicted person

The following specific obligations may be imposed on a convicted person:

(1) to remain in employment;

(2) to follow a course of instruction or vocational training;

(3) to take up residence in a specified place;

(4) to undergo medical examination or treatment;

(5) to demonstrate that he or she is contributing to his or her family's expenses;

(6) to repair, pursuant to his or her means, the harm caused by the offence;

(7) to demonstrate that he or she is paying, pursuant to his or her means, the amounts owing to the state as a result of his or her conviction;

(8) not to engage in the professional or social activity—as specified by the court which enabled or facilitated the commission of the offence;

(9) not to be present in such specified by the court;

(10) not to frequent gambling places;

(11) not to frequent drinking establishments;

(12) not to associate with certain persons—as specified by the court, especially the perpetrator, co-perpetrators, instigators, accomplices or victims of the offence;

(13) not to have or carry any weapon, explosive or ammunition of any kind.

The court's decision shall include the specific obligation or obligations imposed on the convicted person.

Article 121: modification of specific obligations by the court

The court may, at any time, modify the specific obligations imposed on a convicted person.

Application therefor shall be made as provided for by the code of criminal procedure.

Article 122: revocation of suspended sentence with probation

A suspended sentence with probation may be revoked by the court:

(1) if, during the probationary period, the convicted person does not comply with the probation measures or specific obligations;

(2) if, during the probationary period, the convicted person is again convicted of a felony or misdemeanour.

The court may order that all or part of the suspended sentence with probation be revoked. In such case, the sentence shall be served in whole or in part.

Application therefor shall be made as provided for by the code of criminal procedure.

Article 123: sentence with probation deemed never to have been passed

A suspended sentence with probation shall be deemed never to have been passed if there has been no request to revoke it, followed by a decision revoking it, prior to the end of the probationary period.

Section 4 Deferment of Sentence

Article 124: circumstances in which sentence may be deferred

In case of prosecution for a misdemeanour, the court may,

after finding the accused guilty, defer passing sentence if the following conditions are met:

-the public disturbance caused by the offence has ceased.

-the accused provides guarantees of his or her social reintegration; and

-the accused requests time to repair the harm.

Article 125: deferment decision

A deferment may only be granted if the accused is present at the hearing.

The court shall, in its decision on judgement, set the date for sentencing.

Sentence must be passed no later than one year following the deferment decision.

Article 126: adjourned hearing

The court shall pass sentence at the adjourned hearing.

Section 5 Day Release

Article 127: availability of day release

If a court imposes a sentence of imprisonment of six months or less, it may decide that the sentence is to be served on day release in order to enable the convicted person to practice a trade or profession, follow a course of instruction or vocational training, undergo medical treatment, or meet the needs of his or her family.

Article 128: day release arrangements

A convicted person placed on day release shall be allowed to leave the penitentiary at prescribed periods.

The court shall, in its decision, set the days and times during which the convicted person shall be allowed to leave the penitentiary.

Article 129: deduction of time spent on day release from penalty

Time spent on day release shall be deducted from the duration of the penalty which is being served.

Article 130: terms and revocation

The court may, at any time, at the request of the prosecutor, set the terms of or revoke a day release arrangement.

Application therefor shall be made as provided for by the code of criminal procedure.

Article 131: arrest and incarceration

The prosecutor may order the arrest and incarceration of a convicted person who fails to return to the penitentiary at the end of a period of day release.

Section 6 Sentence Served in Instalments

Article 132: circumstances in which sentence may be served in instalments

If a court imposes a sentence of imprisonment of one year or less, it may decide that the sentence shall be served in instalments because of serious family, medical, professional or social reasons.

Article 133: service of sentences

None of the instalments of the sentence may be shorter than one month. The total period for serving the sentence, including interruptions, may not exceed two years.

The decision of the court shall set out how the instalments are to be served.

Article 134: terms and revocation

The court may, at any time at the request of the prosecutor, set the terms of or revoke an instalment arrangement.

Application therefor shall be made as provided for by the code of criminal procedure.

Article 135: arrest and incarceration

The prosecutor may order the arrest and incarceration of a convicted person who fails to return to the penitentiary at the end of a period of interruption of his or her sentence.

Chapter 4   Rules Applicable in Case of Concurrent Offences

Section 1   General Rules

Article 136: concurrent offences

Offences are said to be concurrent where an offence is committed by a person who has not yet been finally tried for another offence.

Article 137: single prosecution

If, in the course of a single prosecution, the accused is found guilty of several concurrent offences, each of the penalties incurred may be imposed. However, if several penalties of a similar nature are incurred, only one such penalty not exceeding the highest maximum penalty allowed by law shall be imposed.

Each penalty imposed shall be deemed to be common to the concurrent offences to the extent of the maximum penalty allowed by law that is applicable to each offence.

Article 138: separate prosecutions

If, in the course of separate prosecutions, the accused is found guilty of several concurrent offences, the sentences imposed shall run cumulatively to the extent of the highest maximum penalty allowed by law. However, the last court dealing with the matters may order that all or part of the sentences of a similar nature shall run concurrently.

For the purposes of this article, if an accused is liable to life imprisonment, the highest maximum sentence of imprisonment allowed by law shall be thirty years if the accused has not been sentenced to life imprisonment.

The fact that one of the sentences imposed for concurrent offences is wholly or partially suspended shall not be an impediment to the enforcement of the non-suspended sentences of a similar nature.

Section 2 Special Rules

Article 139: effect of pardon and reduction of penalties

Where pardon is granted in respect of a penalty under article 27 of the constitution of the Kingdom of Cambodia, the resulting penalty shall be taken into account for the purposes of the rules applicable in the case of concurrent offences.

The length of the reduction of the penalty shall be deducted from the penalty to be imposed, if any, following concurrence.

Article 140: cumulative character of fines

Notwithstanding the preceding provisions, fines imposed for petty offences shall be cumulative, including with fines imposed for concurrent felonies or misdemeanours.

Article 141: non-concurrence of sentences for prison escape

Sentences imposed for prison escape shall be cumulated with those sentences imposed for the offence in respect of which the convicted person escaped. They cannot run concurrently.

Chapter 5 General Factors Relevant to The Enforcement of Penalties

Section 1 Statute of Limitations of Penalties

Article 142: effect of statute of limitations

If the statute of limitations for a sentence expires, the sentence may no longer be enforced.

Article 143: non-applicability of statute of limitations for certain crimes.

Penalties imposed for genocide, crimes against humanity and war crimes shall not be subject to any statute of limitations.

Apart from the above crimes, a special law may provide for the non-applicability of statute of limitations to penalties imposed for other crimes.

Article 144: applicability of statute of limitations

The statute of limitations for a felony shall be twenty years.

The statute of limitations misdemeanour shall be five years.

The statute of limitations offence shall be one year.

Article 145: commencement of limitation period

The twenty-year, five-year and one-year limitation periods provided for in article 144 (applicability of statute of limitations) shall start to run from the date when the conviction becomes final.

Article 146: applicability of statute of limitations to civil obligations resulting from a criminal decision

Civil obligations resulting from a final criminal decision are subject to limitation pursuant to the rules set out in the civil code.

Section 2 Pardon

Article 147: effect of pardon

Pardon within the meaning of article 27 of the constitution of the Kingdom of Cambodia shall exempt the offender from serving his or her sentence.

Article 148: effect of pardon on victims' right to reparation

Unless otherwise provided by royal decree, a pardon shall not be an impediment to a victim's right to obtain reparation for the harm he or she suffered.

Section 3 Amnesty

Article 149: effect of amnesty

An amnesty within the meaning of article 90 new (2)(4) of the constitution of the Kingdom of Cambodia, shall expunge the relevant conviction.

Penalties shall not be enforced.

Ongoing enforcement of penalties, if any, shall cease.

However, the state shall not refund any fines and court fees already paid.

Article 150: amnesty and revocation of suspended sentence

If a suspended sentence is revoked by reason of a subsequent conviction, an amnesty in respect of the subsequent conviction shall restore the benefit of the suspension.

Article 151: effect of amnesty on victims' right to reparation

Unless otherwise provided by law, an amnesty shall not be an impediment to a victim's right to obtain reparation for the harm he or she suffered.

Section 4 Adjustment and Removal of Certain Additional Penalties

Article 152: where available

If the court imposes additional penalties under articles 53 (1), (2), (3), (4), (5), (6), (7), (14), (15), and (16), (additional penalties), it may order either an adjustment or removal of one or more penalties if the following conditions are met:

-the public disturbance caused by the offence has ceased;

-the harm has been repaired;

-the decision to adjust or remove the penalties would promote the social reintegration of the offender.

Application therefor shall be made by the prosecuting authority on its own motion or at the request of the convicted person. The court's decision shall be delivered in open court after hearing the views of the representative of the prosecuting authority, the convicted person and his or her lawyer, as the case may be.

Article 153: reinstatement of all or part of rights

In case of forfeiture of rights, the court may reinstate all or part of the rights under article 55 (forfeiture of rights) of this code.

Article 154: adjustment or lifting of prohibition

The court may adjust or lift:

(1) prohibition from carrying on a professional or social activity;

(2) prohibition from driving a motor vehicle.

Article 155: reinstatement of driving license

In case of suspension of a driving license, the court may order that it be reinstated.

Article 156: modification of local exclusion measures

In case of local exclusion, the court may alter the supervision measures.

In case of emergency, the prosecutor may authorise temporary residency for no more than eight days in a prohibited place. The prosecutor shall inform the court of his or her decision.

The decisions of the court and the prosecutor shall be notified to the ministry of interior and the ministry of national defence.

Article 157: modification of prohibition from leaving the territory of the Kingdom of Cambodia

The court may lift prohibition from leaving the territory of the Kingdom of Cambodia. The court may, if it deems necessary, impose certain conditions.

Article 158: modification from entering the territory of the Kingdom of Cambodia

The court may lift the prohibition against a convicted alien from entering and remaining in the territory of the Kingdom of Cambodia. However, the prosecutor must first seek the opinion of the ministry of foreign affairs and international cooperation and notify it to the court.

The court is not bound by the opinion.

Article 159: modification of disqualification from public tenders, closure of an establishment and prohibition from operating an establishment

The court may adjust or terminate the following penalties:

(1) disqualification from public tenders;

(2) closure of an establishment;

(3) prohibition from operating an establishment that is open to or used by the public.

Chapter 6   Penalties Applicable to Minors

Section 1   General Provisions

Article 160: principal penalties applicable to minors over the age of fourteen

If the court decides to impose a criminal sentence on a minor over the age of fourteen, the principal penalties incurred for the offence under prosecution shall be reduced as follows:

(1) the maximum sentence of imprisonment incurred shall be reduced by half;

(2) if the maximum sentence incurred is life imprisonment, it shall be reduced to twenty years imprisonment;

(3) if the minimum sentence incurred is more than one day of imprisonment, it shall be reduced by half;

(4) the minimum and the maximum fines shall be reduced by half.

In case of prosecution for a felony, if by reason of the provisions of this article, the maximum penalty of imprisonment incurred is reduced to five years or less, the offence under prosecution shall remain a felony.

Article 161: additional penalties

Only the following additional penalties shall be applicable to minors:

(1) confiscation of any instruments, materials or items which were used or intended to be used to commit the offence;

(2) confiscation of the items or funds which were the subject of the offence;

(3) confiscation of the proceeds or property arising out of the offence;

(4) confiscation of the utensils, materials and furnishings in the premises in which the offence was committed;

(5) prohibition from possessing or carrying any weapon, explosive or ammunition of any kind.

Article 162: community service penalties

Community service penalties shall be applicable to minors aged sixteen years and over. However, the duration of the community service may not exceed one hundred hours.

The community service must be adapted to minors; it must be

educative and promote social reintegration.

Article 163: minors not subject to provisions pertaining to previous offences

The provisions pertaining to previous offences shall not be applicable to minors.

Article 164: minors may be granted the benefit of mitigating circumstances

The provisions pertaining to mitigating circumstances shall be applicable to minors.

If the court grants a minor the benefit of mitigating circumstances, the minimum principal penalty incurred by the minor for a felony or a misdemeanour shall be reduced as follows:

(1) if the minimum sentence of imprisonment incurred is ten years or more, it shall be reduced to one year;

(2) if the minimum sentence of imprisonment incurred is five years or more, but less than ten years, it shall be reduced to six months;

(3) if the minimum sentence of imprisonment incurred is two years or more, but less than five years, it shall be reduced to three months;

(4) if the minimum sentence of imprisonment incurred is six days or more, but less than two years, it shall be reduced to one day;

(5) the minimum fine incurred shall be reduced by half.

Article 165: specific obligations for minors in case of

suspended sentence with probation

In case of a suspended sentence with probation, only the following specific obligations shall be applicable to minors:

(1) to follow a course of instruction or vocational training;

(2) to take up residence in a specified place;

(3) to undergo medical examination or treatment;

(4) to repair, pursuant to his or her means, the harm caused by the offence;

(5) to demonstrate that he or she is paying, pursuant to his or her means, the amounts owing to the state as a result of the conviction;

(6) not to be present in specified places;

(7) not to frequent drinking establishments;

(8) not to associate with certain persons—as specified by the court—, especially the co-perpetrators, instigators, accomplices or victims of the offence;

(9) not to have or carry any weapon, explosive or ammunition of any kind.

Section 2 Special Provisions

Article 166: separate prison facilities for minors

Minors imprisoned shall be housed in special units separate from adults. They shall be subject to a specific and personalised regime with a large emphasis on education and vocational training.

The detention regime shall be determined by prakas of the minister of justice and relevant ministers.

Chapter 7 Penalties Applicable to Legal Entities

Section 1 General Provisions

Article 167: penalties incurred by legal entities

Specific penalties incurred by legal entities are:

(1) fines as principal penalties;

(2) additional penalties under article 168 (additional penalties applicable to legal entities).

Section 2 Additional Penalties

Article 168: additional penalties applicable to legal entities

Additional penalties applicable to legal entities are:

(1) dissolution;

(2) placement under judicial supervision;

(3) prohibition from undertaking one or more activities;

(4) disqualification from public tenders;

(5) prohibition from making a public offering;

(6) prohibition from issuing cheques other than cheques certified by a bank;

(7) prohibition from using payment cards;

(8) closure of the establishment which was used to plan or to commit the offence;

(9) prohibition from operating an establishment that is open to or used by the public;

(10) confiscation of any instruments, materials or items which were used or intended to be used to commit the offence;

(11) confiscation of the items or funds with which were the subject of the offence;

(12) confiscation of the proceeds or property arising out of the offence;

(13) confiscation of the utensils, materials and furnishings in the premises in which the offence was committed;

(14) publication of sentencing decision, publication of the sentencing decision in the print media or communicating the decision to the public by audio-visual communication.

Specific provisions may institute other additional penalties.

Article 169: where available

The court may only pronounce additional penalties if they are specifically provided for in respect of the alleged offence.

Article 170: dissolution and liquidation of legal entities

The decision ordering the dissolution of a legal entity shall entail the referral of the legal entity before the court having jurisdiction to liquidate it.

Article 171: placement under judicial supervision

The placement under judicial supervision may not exceed a period of five years. The decision to place a legal entity under judicial supervision entails the designation of a judicially appointed official whose remit is determined by the court. At least once every six months, the judicially appointed official shall report to the prosecutor on the fulfilment of his or her remit.

Upon reviewing these reports, the prosecutor may refer the matter to the court which ordered the judicial supervision. The court may then impose a new penalty.

The court shall make its decision in open court after hearing the views of the representative of the prosecuting authority, the judicially appointed official and the lawyer for the legal entity, as the case may be.

Article 172: prohibition from carrying on activities

The prohibition from carrying on an activity may be permanent or temporary. In the latter case, the prohibition may not exceed five years.

The court shall specify the prohibited activity or activities.

Article 173: disqualification from public tenders

Disqualification from public tenders entails the prohibition from participating, directly or indirectly, in any tender issued by:

(1) the state;

(2) a sub-national entity;

(3) a public body;

(4) a state or sub-national entity concession or a state or sub-national entity controlled enterprise;

Disqualification from public tenders may be permanent or temporary. In the latter case, the period of disqualification may not exceed five years.

Article 174: prohibition from making a public offering

The prohibition from making a public offering may be permanent or temporary. In the latter case, the period of prohibition may not exceed five years.

The prohibition from making a public offering shall entail prohibition of the legal entity from using any credit institutions, financial institutions or brokers for the sale of its securities.

It shall also entail prohibition from advertising.

Article 175: prohibition from issuing cheques

The prohibition from issuing cheques may be permanent or temporary. In the latter case, the period of prohibition may not exceed five years.

The same applies in respect of the prohibition from using payment cards.

Article 176: closure of an establishment

The penalty closure of an establishment shall entail prohibition from exercising in the establishment the activity in connection with which the offence was committed.

Closure of an establishment may be permanent or temporary. In the latter case, the period of closure may not exceed five years.

Article 177: prohibition from operating an establishment

The prohibition from operating an establishment that is open to or used by the public may be permanent or temporary. In the latter case, the period of prohibition may not exceed five years.

Article 178: ownership, sale and destruction of items confiscated

When confiscation becomes final, the items confiscated shall become the property of the state, except as otherwise specified by specific provision.

The state may sell or destroy the items confiscated as prescribed in the procedures for selling state property. The law may also provide for the destruction of certain items.

If an item confiscated has not been seized and cannot be produced, the convicted person shall pay its value which shall be set by the court. For the purposes of recovery, the provisions pertaining to imprisonment for default of payment of debts shall apply.

Article 179: confiscation and rights of third parties

Confiscation may be ordered in respect of the following items:

(1) any instruments, materials or items which were used or intended to be used to commit the offence;

(2) the items or funds which were the subject of the offence;

(3) the proceeds or property arising out of the offence;

(4) the utensils, materials and furnishings in the premises in which the offence was committed.

However, confiscation may not be ordered if it affects the rights of third parties.

Article 180: publication of decisions

The penalty of publication of the decision shall be carried out in such places and for such period of time as determined by the court. The publication may not extend beyond two months. It may involve all or part of the decision, or mere references thereto. The cost of the publication shall be borne by the convicted legal entity.

If the publication is removed, concealed or torn, a new publication shall be made at the expense of the person who removed, concealed or tore it.

Article 181: broadcasting of decision by audio-visual communication

The penalty of broadcasting the decision by audio-visual communication shall be carried out in the manner determined by the court. The broadcast may not be carried for more than eight days. It may involve all or part of the decision, or references thereto. The cost of the broadcast shall be borne by the convicted legal entity.

The penalty of publishing the decision shall be carried out in the print media in the manner and for the period of time determined by the court. The cost of publication shall be borne by the convicted legal entity. A newspaper may not refuse to publish a decision where publication is ordered by the court.

Article 182: application of provisions regarding natural persons to legal entities

The provisions of Titles 1, 2 and 3 of Book 1 of this code regarding natural persons shall be applicable to legal entities in so far as they are not inconsistent with the provisions of this chapter.

BOOK 2
Crimes Against Persons

Title 1 Genocide, Crimes Against Humanity, War Crimes

Chapter 1 Genocide

Article 183: definition of genocide

"Genocide" shall mean any of the following acts committed with the intent to destroy, in whole or in part, a national, ethnical, racial or religious group as such:

(1) killing members of the group;

(2) causing serious bodily or mental harm to members of the group;

(3) deliberately inflicting on the group conditions of life calculated to bring about its physical destruction in whole or in part;

(4) imposing forceful measures or voluntary means intended to prevent births within the group;

(5) forcibly transferring children of the group to another group.

Article 184: penalty

Genocide shall be punishable by life imprisonment.

Article 185: planning of genocide

Participation in a group formed or in a conspiracy to plan genocide shall be punishable by imprisonment from twenty to thirty years.

The planning must be characterised by one or more material acts.

Article 186: additional penalties (nature and duration)

The following additional penalties may be imposed in respect of the felonies defined in this chapter:

(1) forfeiture of certain rights, either permanently or for a period not exceeding five years;

(2) prohibition from practising a profession in the practice of or in connection with which the offence was committed, either permanently or for a period not exceeding five years;

(3) local exclusion for a period not exceeding ten years;

(4) prohibition from leaving the territory of the Kingdom of Cambodia for a period not exceeding five years;

(5) prohibition of a convicted alien from entering and remaining in the territory of the Kingdom of Cambodia, either permanently or for a period not exceeding five years;

(6) confiscation of any instruments, materials or items which were used or intended to be used to commit the offence;

(7) prohibition from possessing or carrying any weapon, explosive or ammunition of any kind, either permanently or for a period not exceeding five years;

(8) publication of sentencing decision for a period not exceeding two months;

(9) publication of sentencing decision in the print media;

(10) broadcasting of sentencing decision by any audio-visual communication for a period not exceeding eight days.

Article 187: criminal responsibility of legal entities

Legal entities may be found criminally responsible under article 42 (criminal responsibility of legal entities) of this code for the offences defined in article 183 (genocide) and article 185 (planning of genocide) of this code.

Legal entities shall be punishable by a fine from fifty million to five hundred million Riels and by one or more of the following additional penalties:

(1) dissolution pursuant to article 170 (dissolution and liquidation of legal entities) of this code;

(2) placement under judicial supervision pursuant to article 171 (placement under judicial supervision) of this code;

(3) prohibition from exercising one or more activities pursuant to article 172 (prohibition from carrying on activities) of this code;

(4) disqualification from public tenders pursuant to article 173 (disqualification from public tenders) of this code;

(5) prohibition from making a public offering pursuant to article 174 (prohibition from making a public offering) of this code;

(6) publication of sentencing decision pursuant to article 180 (publication of decisions) of this code;

(7) publication of sentencing decision in the print media or broadcasting of sentencing decision by any audio-visual communication pursuant to article 181 (broadcasting of decision by audio-visual communication) of this code.

Chapter 2   Crimes Against Humanity

Article 188: definition of crimes against humanity

"Crime against humanity" shall mean any of the following acts when committed as part of a widespread or systematic attack directed against any civilian population:

(1) murder;

(2) extermination;

(3) enslavements;

(4) deportation or forcible transfer of population;

(5) imprisonment or other severe deprivation of physical liberty in violation of fundamental rules of international law;

(6) torture;

(7) rape, sexual slavery, enforced prostitution, forced

pregnancy, enforced sterilization, or any other form of sexual violence of comparable gravity;

(8) persecution against any identifiable group or collectivity on political, racial national, ethnic, cultural, religious or gender grounds;

(9) enforced disappearance of persons;

(10) the crime of apartheid;

(11) other inhumane acts intentionally causing great suffering, or serious injury to body.

Article 189: penalty

Crimes against humanity shall be punishable by life imprisonment.

Article 190: planning of crimes against humanity

Participation in a group formed or in a conspiracy to plan crimes against humanity shall be punishable by imprisonment from twenty to thirty years.

The planning must be characterised by one or more material acts.

Article 191: additional penalties (nature and duration)

The following additional penalties may be imposed in respect of the felonies defined in this chapter:

(1) forfeiture of certain rights, either permanently or for a period not exceeding five years;

(2) prohibition from practising a profession in the practice of

or in connection with which the offence was committed, either permanently or for a period not exceeding five years;

(3) local exclusion for a period not exceeding ten years;

(4) prohibition from leaving the territory of the Kingdom of Cambodia for a period not exceeding five years;

(5) prohibition of a convicted alien from entering and remaining in the territory of the Kingdom of Cambodia, either permanently or for a period not exceeding five years;

(6) confiscation of any instruments, materials or items which were used or intended to be used to commit the offence;

(7) prohibition from possessing or carrying any weapon, explosive or ammunition of any kind, either permanently or for a period not exceeding five years;

(8) publication of sentencing decision for a period not exceeding two months;

(9) publication of sentencing decision in the print media;

(10) broadcasting of sentencing decision by any audio-visual communication for a period not exceeding eight days.

Article 192: criminal responsibility of legal entities

Legal entities may be found criminally responsible under article 42 (criminal responsibility of legal entities) of this code for the offences defined in article 188 (crimes against humanity) and article 190 (planning of crimes against humanity) of this code.

Legal entities shall be punishable by a fine from fifty million to five hundred million Riels and by one or more of the following additional penalties:

(1) dissolution pursuant to article 170 (dissolution and liquidation of legal entities) of this code;

(2) placement under judicial supervision pursuant to article 171 (placement under judicial supervision) of this code;

(3) prohibition from exercising one or more activities pursuant to article 172 (prohibition from carrying on activities) of this code;

(4) disqualification from public tenders pursuant to article 173 (disqualification from public tenders) of this code;

(5) prohibition from making a public offering pursuant to article 174 (prohibition from making a public offering) of this code;

(6) publication of sentencing decision pursuant to article 180 (publication of decisions) of this code;

(7) publication of sentencing decision in the print media or broadcasting of sentencing decision by any audio-visual communication pursuant to article 181 (broadcasting of decision by audio-visual communication) of this code.

Chapter 3 War Crimes

Article 193: definition of war crimes

"War crime" shall mean any of the following acts directed

against persons or property protected by the provisions of the Geneva Conventions of 12 August 1949:

(1) murder;

(2) torture or other inhuman treatment including biological experiments;

(3) wilfully causing great suffering, or serious injury to body or health;

(4) extensive destruction or appropriation of property, not justified by military necessity and carried out unlawfully and wantonly;

(5) compelling a prisoner of war or a civilian to serve in the forces of a hostile power;

(6) depriving a prisoner of war or a civilian of the rights of fair and regular trial;

(7) unlawful deportation, transfer or confinement of a civilian;

(8) taking of civilian hostages.

Article 194: other war crimes

Any of the following acts also constitutes a war crime if it is committed during an international or non-international armed conflict:

(1) employing poisonous weapons or other weapons calculated to cause unnecessary suffering;

(2) intentionally attacking or bombarding, by whatever

means, undefended towns, villages, dwellings or buildings which are not military objectives;

(3) intentionally attacking personnel or material involved in a humanitarian mission in accordance with the charter of the United Nations;

(4) intentionally starving civilians by depriving them of objects indispensable to their survival;

(5) utilizing civilians to render certain buildings, areas of the territory or military forces immune from military operations;

(6) intentionally destroying or damaging buildings dedicated to religion, charitable purposes, education, art, science, historic monuments, artistic works or scientific works;

(7) causing widespread, long-term and severe damage to the natural environment which would be clearly excessive in relation to the concrete and direct military advantage anticipated;

(8) plunder of public or private property.

Article 195: penalty

A war crime shall be punishable by life imprisonment.

Article 196: planning of war crimes

Participation in a group formed or in a conspiracy to plan a war crime shall be punishable by imprisonment from twenty to thirty years.

The planning must be characterised by one or more material acts.

Article 197: additional penalties (nature and duration)

The following additional penalties may be imposed in respect of the felonies defined in this chapter.

(1) forfeiture of certain rights, either permanently or for a period not exceeding five years;

(2) prohibition from practising a profession in the practice of or in connection with which the offence was committed, either permanently or for a period not exceeding five years;

(3) local exclusion for a period not exceeding ten years;

(4) prohibition from leaving the territory of the Kingdom of Cambodia for a period not exceeding five years;

(5) prohibition of a convicted alien from entering and remaining in the territory of the Kingdom of Cambodia, either permanently or for a period not exceeding five years;

(6) confiscation of any instruments, materials or items which were used or intended to be used to commit the offence;

(7) prohibition from possessing or carrying any weapon, explosive or ammunition of any kind, either permanently or for a period not exceeding five years;

(8) publication of sentencing decision for a period not exceeding two months;

(9) publication of sentencing decision in the print media;

(10) broadcasting of sentencing decision by any audio-visual communication for a period not exceeding eight days.

Article 198: criminal responsibility of legal entities

Legal entities may be found criminally responsible under article 42 (criminal responsibility of legal entities) of this code for the offences defined in article 193 (war crimes), article 194 (other war crimes) and article 196 (planning of war crimes) of this code.

Legal entities shall be punishable by a fine from fifty million to five hundred million Riels and by one or more of the following additional penalties:

(1) dissolution pursuant to article 170 (dissolution and liquidation of legal entities) of this code;

(2) placement under judicial supervision pursuant to article 171 (placement under judicial supervision) of this code;

(3) prohibition from exercising one or more activities pursuant to article 172 (prohibition from carrying on activities) of this code;

(4) disqualification from public tenders pursuant to article 173 (disqualification from public tenders) of this code;

(5) prohibition from making a public offering pursuant to article 174 (prohibition from making a public offering) of this code;

(6) publication of sentencing decision pursuant to article 180 (publication of decisions) of this code;

(7) publication of sentencing decision in the print media or broadcasting of sentencing decision by any audio-visual communication pursuant to article 181 (broadcasting of decision by audio-visual communication) of this code.

Title 2   Offences Against the Person

Chapter 1   Homicide

Section 1   Intentional Homicide

Article 199: definition of murder

"Murder" shall mean the wilful killing of another person with or without a weapon with no aggravating circumstances within the meaning of article 200 (definition of premeditated murder) to article 205 (murder accompanied by torture, cruelty or rape) of this code.

Murder shall be punishable imprisonment from ten to fifteen years.

Article 200: definition of premeditated murder

"Premeditated murder" shall mean murder committed with premeditation or by ambush.

Premeditation consists of the plan conceived beforehand to make an attempt against the person of the victim.

An ambush consists in the act of laying in wait for another

person with a view to committing acts of violence against the victim.

Premeditated murder shall be punishable by life imprisonment.

Article 201: definition of murder by poisoning

"Murder by poisoning" shall be punishable by imprisonment from fifteen to thirty years.

Article 202: aggravating circumstances (status of the victim)

Murder shall be punishable by imprisonment from fifteen to thirty years if it is committed:

(1) against a person who is particularly vulnerable by reason of his or her age;

(2) against a pregnant woman whose pregnancy is obvious or known to the perpetrator;

(3) against a person who is particularly vulnerable by reason of his or her illness or disability which is obvious or known to the perpetrator;

(4) against a public official in the performance of his or her duties or inconnection therewith.

Article 203: aggravating circumstances (motive)

Murder shall be punishable by imprisonment from fifteen to thirty years if it is committed:

(1) against a victim or a civil party, either to prevent him or her from reporting an offence or seeking reparation for harm;

(2) against a witness, to prevent him or her from testifying at an investigation, a judicial investigation, a trial or in the

proceedings of other complaints;

(3) against a victim or a civil party for reporting an offence or seeking reparation for harm suffered;

(4) against a witness for testifying at an investigation, a judicial investigation, a trial or in the proceedings of other complaints.

Article 204: murder committed by public officials

Murder shall be punishable by imprisonment from fifteen to thirty years if it is committed by a public official in the performance of his or her duties or in connection therewith.

Article 205: murder accompanied by torture, cruelty or rape

Murder preceded or followed by torture, cruelty or rape shall be punishable by life imprisonment.

Article 206: additional penalties (nature and duration)

The following additional penalties may be imposed in respect of the felonies defined in this section:

(1) forfeiture of certain rights, either permanently or for a period nor exceeding five years;

(2) prohibition from practising a profession in the practice of or in connection with which the offence was committed, either permanently or for a period not exceeding five years;

(3) local exclusion, either permanently or for a period not exceeding ten years;

(4) prohibition of a convicted alien from entering and

remaining in the territory of the Kingdom of Cambodia, either permanently or for a period not exceeding five years;

(5) confiscation of any instruments, materials or items which were used or intended to be used to commit the offence;

(6) prohibition from possessing or carrying any weapon, explosive or ammunition of any kind, either permanently or for a period not exceeding five years;

(7) publication of sentencing decision for a period not exceeding two months;

(8) publication of sentencing decision in the print media;

(9) broadcasting of sentencing decision by any audio-visual communication for a period not exceeding eight days.

Section 2   Unintentional Homicide

Article 207: definition of manslaughter

"Manslaughter" shall mean the act of causing the death of another person by:

(1) negligence, recklessness or carelessness;

(2) breach of the safety requirement or due diligence imposed by law.

Manslaughter shall be punishable by imprisonment from one year to three years and a fine from two million to six million riels.

Article 208: additional penalties (nature and duration)

The following additional penalties may be imposed for

manslaughter:

(1) prohibition from practising a profession in the practice of or in connection with which the offence was committed for a period not exceeding five years;

(2) prohibition from driving any motor vehicle for a period not exceeding five years;

(3) suspension of a driving license for a period not exceeding five years;

(4) prohibition from possessing or carrying any weapon, explosive or ammunition of any kind for a period not exceeding five years;

(5) publication of sentencing decision for a period not exceeding two months;

(6) publication of sentencing decision in the print media;

(7) broadcasting of sentencing decision by any audio-visual communication for a period not exceeding eight days.

Article 209: criminal responsibility of legal entities

Legal entities may be found criminally responsible under article 42 (criminal responsibility of legal entities) for offences defined in article 207 (definition of manslaughter) of this code.

Legal entities shall be punishable by a fine from ten million to fifty million riels and by one or more of the following additional penalties:

(1) dissolution pursuant to article 170 (dissolution and

liquidation of legal entities) of this code;

(2) placement under judicial supervision pursuant to article 171 (placement under judicial supervision) of this code;

(3) prohibition from exercising one or more activities pursuant to article 172 (prohibition from carrying on activities) of this code;

(4) disqualification from public tenders pursuant to article 176 (closure of establishment) of this code;

(5) prohibition from making a public offering pursuant to article 177 (prohibition from operating an establishment) of this code;

(6) publication of sentencing decision pursuant to article 180 (publication of decisions) of this code;

(7) publication of sentencing decision in the print media or broadcasting of sentencing decision by any audio-visual communication pursuant to article 181 (broadcasting of decision by audio-visual communication) of this code.

Chapter 2   Violations of Personal Integrity

Section 1   Torture and Acts of Cruelty

Article 210: torture and acts of cruelty

Torture and acts of cruelty committed against another person shall be punishable by imprisonment from seven to fifteen years.

Article 211: aggravating circumstances (status of the victim)

The offences defined in article 210 (torture and acts of cruelty) shall be punishable by imprisonment from ten to twenty years if it is committed:

(1) against a person who is particularly vulnerable by reason of his or her age;

(2) against a pregnant woman whose pregnancy is obvious or known to the perpetrator;

(3) against a person who is particularly vulnerable by reason of illness or disability and whose state is obvious on known to the perpetrator.

Article 212: aggravating circumstances (motive)

The offences defined in article 210 (torture and acts of cruelty) shall be punishable by imprisonment from ten to twenty years if it is committed:

(1) against a victim or a civil party, either to prevent him or her from reporting an offence or seeking reparation for harm suffered;

(2) against a witness, to prevent him or her from testifying at an investigation, a judicial investigation, a trial or in the proceedings of other complaints;

(3) against a victim or a civil party who reported an offence or for seeking reparation for harm suffered;

(4) against a witness for testifying at an investigation, a

judicial investigation, a trial or in the proceeding of other complaints.

Article 213: aggravating circumstances (status of the perpetrator)

The offences defined in article 210 (torture and acts of cruelty) shall be punishable by imprisonment from ten to twenty years if it is committed by a public official in the performance of his or her duties or in connection therewith.

Article 214: aggravating circumstances (mutilation or disability)

The offences defined in article 210 (torture and acts of cruelty) shall be punishable by imprisonment from ten to twenty years if it results in the mutilation or permanent disability of the victim.

Article 215: aggravating circumstances (death of the victim)

The offences defined in article 210 (torture and acts of cruelty) shall be punishable by imprisonment from fifteen to thirty years if, without intent to kill, it results in the death of the victim or if it leads to the suicide of the victim.

Article 216: additional penalties (nature and duration)

The following additional penalties may be imposed in respect of the felonies defined in this section:

(1) forfeiture of certain rights, either permanently or for a period not exceeding five years;

(2) prohibition from practising a profession in the practice of or in connection with which the offence was committed, either permanently or for a period not exceeding five years;

(3) local exclusion for a period not exceeding ten years;

(4) prohibition of a convicted alien from entering and remaining in the territory of the Kingdom of Cambodia, either permanently or for a period not exceeding five years;

(5) confiscation of any instruments, materials or items which were used or intended to be used to commit the offence;

(6) prohibition from possessing or carrying any weapon, explosive or ammunition of any kind, either permanently or for a period not exceeding five years;

(7) publication of sentencing decision for a period not exceeding two months;

(8) publication of sentencing decision in the print media;

(9) broadcasting of sentencing decision by any audio-visual communication for a period not exceeding eight days.

Section 2　Acts of Violence

Article 217: intentional acts of violence

Intentional acts of violence committed against another person shall be punishable by imprisonment from one to three years and a fine from two million to six million riels.

Article 218: aggravating circumstances

Intentional acts of violence shall be punishable by imprisonment from two to five years and a fine from four million to ten million riels if they are committed:

(1) with premeditation;

(2) with the use of or threat to use a weapon;

(3) by several persons acting as perpetrators, co-perpetrators, instigators or accomplices.

Article 219: aggravating circumstances (status of the victim)

Intentional acts of violence shall be punishable by imprisonment from two to five years and a fine from four million to ten million riels if it is committed:

(1) against a person who is particularly vulnerable by reason of his or her age;

(2) against a pregnant woman whose pregnancy is obvious or known to the perpetrator;

(3) against a person who is particularly vulnerable by reason of illness or disability and whose state is obvious or known to the perpetrator.

Article 220: aggravating circumstances (motive)

Intentional acts of violence shall be punishable by imprisonment from two to five years and a fine from four million to ten million riels if they are committed:

(1) against a victim or a civil party, either to prevent him or

her from reporting an offence or seeking reparation for harm suffered;

(2) against a witness, to prevent him or her from testifying at an investigation, a judicial investigation, a trial or in the proceedings of other complaints;

(3) against a victim or a civil party who reported an offence or for seeking reparation for harm suffered;

(4) against a witness for testifying at an investigation, a judicial investigation, a trial or in the proceedings of other complaints.

Article 221: aggravating circumstances (status of the perpetrator)

Intentional acts of violence shall be punishable by imprisonment from two to five years and a fine from four million to ten million riels if it is committed by a public official in the performance of his or her duties or in connection therewith.

Article 222: violence committed by spouse or partner

Intentional acts of violence shall be punishable by imprisonment from two to five years and a fine from four million to ten million riels if they are committed by the spouse or partner of the victim.

Article 223: aggravating circumstances (mutilation or disability)

Intentional acts of violence which result in the mutilation or permanent disability of the victim shall be punishable by imprisonment from five to ten years.

Article 224: aggravating circumstances (death of the victim)

Intentional acts of violence shall be punishable by imprisonment from seven to fifteen years, if, without intent to kill, they cause the death of the victim.

Article 225: toxic substances deemed to be intentional acts of violence

The administration of toxic substances to another person shall be deemed to be intentional acts of violence.

Article 226: toxic food deemed to be intentional acts of violence

Selling, granting or giving food or drinks knowing that the food or drinks are toxic to health are deemed intentional acts of violence.

Article 227: introduction of toxic substances into drinking water deemed to be intentional acts of violence

The introduction of any substance that is toxic to health into public drinking water shall be deemed to be an intentional act of violence.

Article 228: definition of less severe acts of violence

An act, if it is committed with less severe violence against another person and which does not result in any injury, shall be punishable by a fine from five thousand to one hundred thousand riels.

Article 229: additional penalties (nature and duration)

The following additional penalties may be imposed in respect of

the felonies defined in this chapter:

(1) forfeiture of certain rights, either permanently or for a period not exceeding five years;

(2) prohibition from practising a profession in the practice of or in connection with which the offence was committed, either permanently or for a period not exceeding five years;

(3) local exclusion for a period not exceeding ten years for a felony and not exceeding five years for a misdemeanor;

(4) prohibition of a convicted alien from entering and remaining in the territory of the Kingdom of Cambodia, either permanently or for a period not exceeding five years;

(5) confiscation of any instruments, materials or items which were used or intended to be used to commit the offence;

(6) prohibition from possessing or carrying any weapon, explosive or ammunition of any kind, either permanently or for a period not exceeding five years;

(7) publication of sentencing decision for a period not exceeding two months;

(8) publication of sentencing decision in the print media;

(9) broadcasting of sentencing decision by any audio-visual communication for a period not exceeding eight days.

Article 230: criminal responsibility of legal entities

Legal entities may be found criminally responsible under article 42 (criminal responsibility of legal entities) of this code for

the offences defined in article 226 (toxic food deemed to be intentional acts of violence) and article 227 (introduction of toxic substances into drinking water deemed to be intentional acts of violence) of this code.

Legal entities shall be punishable by a fine from ten million to fifty million riels and by one or more of the following additional penalties:

(1) dissolution pursuant to article 170 (dissolution and liquidation of legal entities) of this code;

(2) placement under judicial supervision pursuant to article 171(placement under judicial supervision) of this code;

(3) prohibition from exercising one or more activities pursuant to article 172 (prohibition from carrying on activities) of this code;

(4) disqualification from public tenders pursuant to article 173 (disqualification from public tenders) of this code;

(5) prohibition from making a public offering pursuant to article 174 (prohibition from making a public offering) of this code;

(6) closure of the establishment which was used to commit the offence pursuant to article 176 (closure of an establishment) of this code;

(7) prohibition from operating an establishment that is open to or used by the public pursuant to article 177 (prohibition from operating an establishment) of this code;

(8) confiscation of any instruments, materials or items which were used or intended to be used to commit the offence pursuant to article 178 (ownership, sale and destruction of items confiscated) and article 179 (confiscation and rights of third parties) of this code;

(9) confiscation of the items or funds which were the subject of the offence pursuant to article 178 (ownership, sale and destruction of items confiscated) and article 179 (confiscation and rights of third parties) of this code;

(10) confiscation of the proceeds or property arising out of the offence pursuant to article 178 (ownership, sale and destruction of items confiscated) and article 179 (confiscation and rights of third parties) of this code;

(11) publication of sentencing decision pursuant to article 180 (publication of decisions) of this code;

(12) publication of sentencing decision in the print media or broadcasting of sentencing decision by any audio-visual communication pursuant to article 181 (broadcasting of decision by audio-visual communication) of this code.

Section 3 Threats

Article 231: threats

A threat to commit a felony or a misdemeanour against persons shall be punishable by imprisonment from one to six months and a fine from one hundred thousand to one million riels, if it is repeated, or made by means of a written document, image or any kind of object.

Article 232: threat accompanied by extortion

A threat to commit a felony or a misdemeanour against persons, made by any means whatsoever, shall be punishable by imprisonment from six months to two years and a fine from one million to four million riels if the threat is accompanied by extortion.

Article 233: death threat

A death threat shall be punishable by imprisonment from six months to two years and a fine from one million to four million riels, if it is repeated, or made by means of a written document, image or any kind of object.

Article 234: death threat accompanied by extortion

A death threat made by any means whatsoever shall be punishable by imprisonment from one to three years and a fine from two million to six million riels if the threat is made together with extortion.

Article 235: additional penalties (nature and duration)

The following additional penalties may be imposed in respect of the offences defined in this section:

(1) forfeiture of certain rights, either permanently or for a period not exceeding five years;

(2) prohibition from practising a profession in the practice of or in connection with which the offence was committed, either permanently or for a period not exceeding five years;

(3) local exclusion for a period not exceeding ten years for a felony and not exceeding five years for a misdemeanour;

(4) prohibition of a convicted alien from entering and remaining in the territory of the Kingdom of Cambodia, either permanently or for a period not exceeding five years;

(5) confiscation of any instruments, materials or items which were used or intended to be used to commit the offence;

(6) prohibition from possessing or carrying any weapon, explosive or ammunition of any kind, either permanently or for a period not exceeding five years;

(7) publication of sentencing decision for a period not exceeding two months;

(8) publication of sentencing decision in the print media;

(9) broadcasting of sentencing decision by any audio-visual communication for a period not exceeding eight days.

Section 4 Causing Involuntary Bodily Harm

Article 236: causing involuntary bodily harm

Causing an injury to another person constitutes an offence of causing involuntary bodily harm if it results from:

(1) negligence, recklessness or carelessness causing a

disability to the victim for a period of eight days or more;

(2) breach of the safety requirement or due diligence imposed by law.

Causing involuntary bodily harm shall be punishable by imprisonment from six months to two years and a fine from one million to four million riels.

Article 237: additional penalties (nature and duration)

The following additional penalties may be imposed in respect of the offence of causing involuntary bodily harm:

(1) prohibition from practising a profession in the practice of or in connection with which the offence was committed for a period not exceeding five years;

(2) prohibition from driving any motor vehicle for a period not exceeding five years;

(3) suspension of a driving license for a period not exceeding five years;

(4) prohibition from possessing or carrying any weapon, explosive or ammunition of any kind for a period not exceeding five years;

(5) publication of sentencing decision for a period not exceeding two months;

(6) publication of sentencing decision in the print media;

(7) broadcasting of sentencing decision by any audio-visual communication for a period not exceeding eight days.

Article 238: criminal responsibility of legal entities

Legal entities may be found criminally responsible under article 42 (criminal responsibility of legal entities) for offences defined in article 236 (causing involuntary bodily harm) of this code.

Legal entities shall be punishable by a fine from five million to twenty million riels and by one or more of the following additional penalties:

(1) dissolution pursuant to article 170 (dissolution and liquidation of legal entities) of this code;

(2) placement under judicial supervision pursuant to article 171 (placement under judicial supervision) of this code;

(3) prohibition from exercising one or more activities pursuant to article 172 (prohibition from carrying on activities) of this code;

(4) closure of the establishment which was used to commit the offence pursuant to article 176 (closure of an establishment) of this code;

(5) prohibition from making a public offering pursuant to article 177 (prohibition from operating an establishment) of this code;

(6) publication of sentencing decision pursuant to article 180 (publication of decisions) of this code;

(7) publication of sentencing decision in the print media or broadcasting of sentencing decision by any audio-visual communication

pursuant to article 181 (broadcasting of decision by audio-visual communication) of this code.

Chapter 3 Sexual Assaults

Section 1 Rape

Article 239: definition of rape

"Rape" shall mean any act of sexual penetration with a sexual organ or an object committed against another person of either sex by violence, coercion, threat or by being opportunistic.

Rape shall be punishable by imprisonment from five to ten years.

The age for sexual majority shall be fifteen years of age.

Article 240: aggravating circumstances (means used or status of the perpetrator)

Rape shall be punishable by imprisonment from seven to fifteen years if it is committed:

(1) with the use or threatened use of a weapon;

(2) with the use of a narcotic or any means liable to overcome or weaken the victim's resistance;

(3) by any person having authority over the victim;

(4) by any person abusing the authority vested in him or her by his or her duties;

(5) by several persons acting as perpetrators, co-perpetrators, instigators or accomplices.

Article 241: aggravating circumstances (status of the victim)

Rape shall be punishable by imprisonment from seven to fifteen years if it is committed:

(1) against a person who is particularly vulnerable by reason of his or her age;

(2) against a pregnant woman whose pregnancy is obvious or known to the perpetrator;

(3) against a person who is particularly vulnerable by reason of illness or disability and whose state is obvious or known to the perpetrator.

Article 242: aggravating circumstances (mutilation or disability)

Rape shall be punishable by imprisonment from ten to twenty years if it results in the mutilation or permanent disability of the victim.

Article 243: aggravating circumstances (torture or acts of cruelty)

Rape shall be punishable by imprisonment from ten to thirty years if it is preceded, accompanied or followed by torture or acts of cruelty.

Article 244: aggravating circumstances (death of the victim)

Rape shall be punishable by imprisonment from fifteen to thirty years if, without intent to kill, it results in the death of the victim or it leads to the suicide of the victim.

Article 245: additional penalties (nature and duration)

The following additional penalties may be imposed in respect of the felonies defined in this section:

(1) forfeiture of certain rights, either permanently or for a period not exceeding five years;

(2) prohibition from practising a profession in the practice of or in connection with which the offence was committed, either permanently or for a period not exceeding five years;

(3) local exclusion for a period not exceeding ten years;

(4) prohibition of a convicted alien from entering and remaining in the territory of the Kingdom of Cambodia, either permanently or for a period not exceeding five years;

(5) confiscation of any instruments, materials or items which were used or intended to be used to commit the offence;

(6) publication of sentencing decision for a period not exceeding two months;

(7) publication of sentencing decision in the print media;

(8) broadcasting of sentencing decision by any audio-visual communication for a period not exceeding eight days.

Section 2   Other Sexual Assaults

Article 246: definition of indecent assault

Touching, fondling or caressing the sexual organs or other part of a person without that person's consent or coercing another person to perform such acts on the perpetrator himself or herself or a third person for the purpose of arousing the perpetrator or providing sexual pleasure to the perpetrator constitutes indecent assault.

Indecent assault shall be punishable by imprisonment from one to three years and a fine from two million to six million riels.

Article 247: aggravating circumstances (means used or status of the perpetrator)

The offence defined in article 246 (definition of indecent assault) of this code shall be punishable by imprisonment from two to five years and a fine from four million to ten million riels if it is committed:

(1) with the use or threatened use of a weapon;

(2) with the use of a narcotic or any means liable to overcome or weaken the victim's resistance;

(3) by any person having authority over the victim;

(4) by any person abusing the authority vested in him or her by his or her duties;

(5) by several persons acting as perpetrators, co-perpetrators, instigators or accomplices.

Article 248: aggravating circumstances (status of the victim)

The offence defined in article 246 (definition of indecent assault) of this code shall be punishable by imprisonment from two to five years and a fine from four million to ten million riels if it is committed:

(1) against a person who is particularly vulnerable by reason of his or her age;

(2) against a pregnant woman whose pregnancy is obvious or known to the perpetrator;

(3) against a person who is particularly vulnerable by reason of illness or disability and whose state is obvious or known to the perpetrator.

Article 249: indecent exposure

Any indecent exposure to others in a public place shall be punishable by imprisonment from six days to three months and a fine from one hundred thousand to five hundred thousand riels.

Article 250: definition of sexual harassment

"Sexual harassment" shall mean the abuse by one person of the authority conferred by his or her functions against another person for the purpose of applying pressure repeatedly in order to obtain sexual favours.

Sexual harassment shall be punishable by imprisonment from six days to three months and a fine from one hundred thousand to five hundred thousand riels.

Article 251: attempt

An attempt to commit the misdemeanours defined in this section shall be punishable by the same penalties.

Article 252: additional penalties (nature and duration)

The following additional penalties may be imposed in respect of

the offences defined in this section:

(1) forfeiture of certain rights, either permanently or for a period not exceeding five years;

(2) prohibition from practising a profession in the practice of or in connection with which the offence was committed, either permanently or for a period not exceeding five years;

(3) local exclusion for a period not exceeding five years;

(4) prohibition of a convicted alien from entering and remaining in the territory of the Kingdom of Cambodia, either permanently or for a period not exceeding five years;

(5) prohibition from possessing or carrying any weapon, explosive or ammunition of any kind, either permanently or for a period not exceeding five years;

(6) publication of sentencing decision for a period not exceeding two months;

(7) publication of sentencing decision in the print media;

(8) broadcasting of sentencing decision by any audio-visual communication for a period not exceeding eight days.

Chapter 4 Unlawful Deprivation of Liberty

Section 1 Arrest, Detention and Unlawful Confinement

Article 253: arrest, detention and unlawful confinement

Anyone who, without judicial authorization, or who unlawfully arrests, detains or unlawfully confines another person shall be punishable by imprisonment:

(1) from one to three years if the arrest, detention or unlawful confinement is for less than forty eight hours;

(2) from three to five years if the arrest, detention or unlawful confinement is for more than forty eight hours but less than one month;

(3) from five to ten years if the arrest, detention or unlawful confinement is for one month or more.

Article 254: aggravating circumstances

Anyone who, without judicial authorisation, or who unlawfully arrests, detains or unlawfully confines another person shall be punishable by imprisonment from fifteen to thirty years in the following cases:

(1) the arrest, detention or unlawful confinement is accompanied by torture or acts of cruelty;

(2) the arrest, detention or unlawful confinement is followed by the unintentional death of the person;

(3) if the arrest, detention or unlawful confinement is committed to secure the payment of a ransom or to demand fulfilment of a condition.

Article 255: additional penalties (nature and duration)

The following additional penalties may be imposed in respect of the offences defined in this section:

(1) forfeiture of certain rights, either permanently or for a period not exceeding five years;

(2) prohibition from practising a profession in the practice of or in connection with which the offence was committed, either permanently or for a period not exceeding five years;

(3) local exclusion for a period not exceeding ten years for a felony or for a period not exceeding five years for a misdemeanour;

(4) prohibition of a convicted alien from entering and remaining in the territory of the Kingdom of Cambodia, either permanently or for a period not exceeding five years;

(5) confiscation of any instruments, materials or items which were used or intended to be used to commit the offence;

(6) confiscation of the proceeds or property arising out of the offence;

(7) confiscation of one or more vehicles belonging to the convicted person;

(8) prohibition from possessing or carrying any weapon, explosive or ammunition of any kind, either permanently or for a period not exceeding five years;

(9) publication of sentencing decision for a period not exceeding two months;

(10) publication of sentencing decision in the print media;

(11) broadcasting of sentencing decision by any audio-visual communication for a period not exceeding eight days.

Section 2　Other Deprivation of Liberty

Article 256: hijacking of a means of transport

Seizing or taking control, by violence or threat of violence, of any means of transportation carrying people, shall be punishable by imprisonment from five to ten years.

Article 257: aggravating circumstances (mutilation or disability)

The offence defined in article 256 (hijacking of a means of transport) of this code shall be punishable by imprisonment from ten to twenty years if it results in the mutilation or permanent disability of a victim.

Article 258: aggravating circumstances (torture or acts of cruelty)

The offence defined in article 256 (hijacking of a means of transport) of this code shall be punishable by imprisonment from fifteen to thirty years if it is preceded, accompanied or followed by torture or acts of cruelty.

Article 259: aggravating circumstances (death of the victim)

The offence defined in article 256 (hijacking of a means of transport) of this code shall be punishable by imprisonment from fifteen to thirty years if it results in the death of one or more persons.

Article 260: additional penalties (nature and duration)

The following additional penalties may be imposed in respect of the offences defined in this section:

(1) forfeiture of certain rights, either permanently or for a period not exceeding five years;

(2) prohibition from practising a profession in the practice of or in connection with which the offence was committed, either permanently or for a period nor exceeding five years;

(3) local exclusion for a period not exceeding ten years;

(4) prohibition of a convicted alien from entering and remaining in the territory of the Kingdom of Cambodia, either permanently or for a period not exceeding five years;

(5) confiscation of any instruments, materials or items which were used or intended to be used to commit the offence;

(6) confiscation of the proceeds or property arising out of the offence;

(7) confiscation of one or more vehicles belonging to the convicted person;

(8) prohibition from possessing or carrying any weapon, explosive or ammunition of any kind, either permanently or for a period not exceeding five years;

(9) publication of sentencing decision for a period not exceeding two months;

(10) publication of sentencing decision in the print media;

(11) broadcasting of sentencing decision by any audio-visual communication for a period not exceeding eight days.

Chapter 5   Violation of Personal Dignity

Section 1   Violation of Respect for The Dead

Article 261: violation of physical integrity of a corpse

Violating the physical integrity of a corpse shall be punishable by imprisonment from one month to one year and a fine from one hundred thousand to two million riels.

Article 262: desecrating burial grounds

Desecrating tombs, burial grounds, stupa or monuments erected in the memory of the dead by any means whatsoever, shall be punishable by imprisonment from one month to one year and a fine from one hundred thousand to two million riels.

Article 263: attempt

An attempt to commit the misdemeanours defined in this section shall be punishable by the same penalties.

Article 264: additional penalties (nature and duration)

The following additional penalties may be imposed in respect of the offences defined in this section:

(1) forfeiture of certain rights, either permanently or for a

period not exceeding five years;

(2) prohibition from practising a profession in the practice of or in connection with which the offence was committed, either permanently or for a period not exceeding five years;

(3) publication of sentencing decision for a period not exceeding two months;

(4) publication of sentencing decision in the print media;

(5) broadcasting of sentencing decision by any audio-visual communication for a period not exceeding eight days.

Section 2 Discrimination

Article 265: refusal to supply goods or services

Refusing to supply goods or services to another person shall be punishable by imprisonment from one month to one year and a fine from ten thousand to two million riels if the refusal is based on any of the following grounds:

(1) membership or non-membership of a given ethnic group, nationality or race;

(2) membership or non-membership of a given religion;

(3) political affiliation;

(4) union activities;

(5) family situation;

(6) gender;

(7) state of health;

(8) disability.

Article 266: subjecting the supply of goods or services to conditions

Subjecting the supply of goods or services to another person to any of the following conditions shall be punishable by imprisonment from one month to one year and a fine from ten thousand to two million riels:

(1) membership or non-membership of a given ethnic group, nationality or race;

(2) membership or non-membership of a given religion;

(3) political affiliation;

(4) union activities;

(5) family situation;

(6) gender;

(7) state of health;

(8) disability.

Article 267: refusal to hire

Refusing to hire a person shall be punishable by imprisonment from one month to one year and a fine from ten thousand to two million riels if it is based on any of the grounds set out in paragraphs 265(1) to (8) (refusal to supply goods or services) of this code.

Article 268: subjecting offer of employment to conditions

Subjecting an offer of employment to any of the conditions set out in paragraphs 266(1) to (8) (subjecting the supply of goods or services to conditions) of this code shall be punishable by imprisonment from one month to one year and a fine from ten thousand to two million riels.

Article 269: termination of employment or removal from office on discriminatory grounds

Terminating employment or removing a person from office shall be punishable by imprisonment from one month to one year and a fine from ten thousand to two million riels if it is based on any of the grounds set out in paragraphs 265(1) to (8) (refusal to supply goods or services) of this code.

Article 270: denial of rights by public officials on discriminatory grounds

Refusal by a public official in the performance of his or her duties or in connection therewith of the rights of another person shall be punishable by imprisonment from six months to two years and a fine from one million to four million riels if it is based on any of the grounds set out in paragraphs 265(1) to (8) (refusal to supply goods or services) of this code.

Article 271: discrimination authorised by law

No offence shall be committed under this section if the discrimination is authorised by law.

The provisions in this section shall not apply if the discrimination:

(1) is based on the state of health and its aim is to prevent the risk to physical integrity, incapacity to work or disability;

(2) is based on the state of health or disability and the refusal to hire or the termination of employment is based on a medically established incapacity;

(3) in hiring is based on gender if the fact of being male or female is the determining factor in the practice of an employment or a profession.

Article 272: additional penalties (nature and duration)

The following additional penalties may be imposed in respect of the offences defined in this section:

(1) forfeiture of certain rights, either permanently or for a period not exceeding five years;

(2) prohibition from practising a profession in the practice of or in connection with which the offence was committed, either permanently or for a period not exceeding five years;

(3) publication of sentencing decision for a period not exceeding two months;

(4) publication of sentencing decision in the print media;

(5) broadcasting of sentencing decision by any audio-visual communication for a period not exceeding eight days.

Article 273: criminal responsibility of legal entities

Legal entities may be found criminally responsible under article 42 (criminal responsibility of legal entities) of this code for

the offences defined in article 265 (refusal to supply goods or services) and article 269 (termination of employment or removal from office on discriminatory grounds) of this code.

Legal entities shall be punishable by a fine from one million to ten million riels and by one or more of the following additional penalties:

(1) placement under judicial supervision pursuant to article 171 (placement under judicial supervision) of this code;

(2) prohibition from exercising one or more activities pursuant to article 172 (prohibition from carrying on activities) of this code;

(3) publication of sentencing decision pursuant to article 180 (publication of decisions) of this code;

(4) publication of sentencing decision in the print media or broadcasting of sentencing decision by any audio-visual communication pursuant to article 181 (broadcasting of decision by audio-visual communication) of this code.

Section 3 Working Conditions Incompatible with Human Dignity

Article 274: subjecting to working conditions incompatible with human dignity

Subjecting a person, by exploiting his or her vulnerability or dependence, to working conditions incompatible with human dignity shall be punishable by imprisonment from one month to one year and a fine from one hundred thousand to two million riels.

Article 275: attempt

An attempt to commit the misdemeanour defined in article 274 (subjecting to working conditions incompatible with human dignity) of this code shall be punishable by the same penalties.

Article 276: additional penalties (nature and duration)

The following additional penalties may be imposed in respect of the offences defined in this section:

(1) forfeiture of certain rights, either permanently or for a period not exceeding five years;

(2) prohibition from practising a profession in the practice of or in connection with which the offence was committed, either permanently or for a period not exceeding five years;

(3) publication of sentencing decision for a period not exceeding two months;

(4) publication of sentencing decision in the print media;

(5) broadcasting of sentencing decision by any audio-visual communication for a period not exceeding eight days.

Article 277: criminal responsibility of legal entities

Legal entities may be found criminally responsible under article 42 (criminal responsibility of legal entities) of this code for the offences defined in article 274 (subjecting to working conditions incompatible with human dignity) of this code.

Legal entities shall be punishable by a fine from one million to ten million riels and by one or more of the following additional penalties:

(1) dissolution pursuant to article 170 (dissolution and liquidation of legal entities) of this code;

(2) placement under judicial supervision pursuant to article 171 (placement under judicial supervision) of this code;

(3) prohibition from exercising one or more activities pursuant to article 172 (prohibition from carrying on activities) of this code;

(4) disqualification from public tenders pursuant to article 173 (disqualification from public tenders) of this code;

(5) prohibition from making a public offering pursuant to article 174 (prohibition from making a public offering) of this code;

(6) closure of the establishment which was used to commit the offence pursuant to article 176 (closure of an establishment) of this code;

(7) prohibition from operating an establishment that is open to or used by the public pursuant to article 177 (prohibition from operating an establishment) of this code;

(8) confiscation of any instruments, materials or items which were used or intended to be used to commit the offence pursuant to article 178 (ownership, sale and destruction of items confiscated) and article 179 (confiscation and rights of third parties) of this code;

(9) confiscation of the items or funds which were the subject of the offence pursuant to article 178 (ownership, sale and destruction of items confiscated) and article 179 (confiscation and rights of third parties) of this code;

(10) confiscation of the proceeds or property arising out of the offence pursuant to article 178 (ownership, sale and destruction of items confiscated) and article 179 (confiscation and rights of third parties) of this code;

(11) publication of sentencing decision pursuant to article 180 (publication of decisions) of this code;

(12) publication of sentencing decision in the print media or broadcasting of sentencing decision by any audio-visual communication pursuant to article 181 (broadcasting of decision by audio-visual communication) of this code.

Section 4   Corruption by Employees and Administrators

Article 278: requesting or accepting bribes by employees

An employee who requests or accepts, unknown to his or her employer or without his or her authorization, any donation, gift, promise, or reward for performing or refraining from performing an act pertaining to his or her duties, shall be punishable by imprisonment from six months to two years and a fine from one million to four million riels.

Article 279: giving bribes to employees

Any person who offers any donation, gift, promise, or reward to an employee, unknown to his or her employer or without his or her authorization, to perform or refrain from performing an act pertaining to his or her duties shall be punishable by imprisonment from six months to two years and a fine from one million to four million riels.

Article 280: bribery by administrators

(1) if any person referred to in paragraphs 393(1) and (2) (breach of trust specifically by administrators or other persons) of this code or an inspector accepting an unlawful request receives a material benefit or demands or promises to receive benefits from illegal request shall be punishable by imprisonment from five to ten years.

(2) the same penalty is applicable to anyone who furnishes, offers or promises a benefit within the meaning of paragraph (1).

(3) any material benefit within the meaning of paragraph (1) shall be confiscated. If the benefit cannot be confiscated in whole or in part, the shortfall shall be paid by the recipient.

Article 281: attempt

An attempt to commit the misdemeanour defined in article 278 (requesting or accepting bribes by employees) and article 279 (giving bribes to employees) of this code shall be punishable by the same penalties.

Article 282: additional penalties (nature and duration)

The following additional penalties may be imposed in respect of the offences defined in this section:

(1) forfeiture of certain rights, either permanently or for a period not exceeding five years;

(2) prohibition from practising a profession in the practice of or in connection with which the offence was committed, either permanently or for a period not exceeding five years;

(3) publication of sentencing decision for a period not exceeding two months;

(4) publication of sentencing decision in the print media;

(5) broadcasting of sentencing decision by any audio-visual communication for a period not exceeding eight days.

Article 283: criminal responsibility of legal entities

Legal entities may be found criminally responsible under article 42 (criminal responsibility of legal entities) of this code for the offences defined in article 279 (giving bribes to employees) of this code.

Legal entities shall be punishable by a fine from five million to twenty million riels and by one or more of the following additional penalties:

(1) dissolution pursuant to article 170 (dissolution and liquidation of legal entities) of this code;

(2) placement under judicial supervision pursuant to article

171 (placement under judicial supervision) of this code;

(3) prohibition from exercising one or more activities pursuant to article 172 (prohibition from carrying on activities) of this code;

(4) disqualification from public tenders pursuant to article 173 (disqualification from public tenders) of this code;

(5) prohibition from making a public offering pursuant to article 174 (prohibition from making a public offering) of this code;

(6) confiscation of any instruments, materials or items which were used or intended to be used to commit the offence pursuant to article 178 (ownership, sale and destruction of items confiscated) and article 179 (confiscation and rights of third parties) of this code;

(7) publication of sentencing decision pursuant to article 180 (publication of decisions) of this code;

(8) publication of sentencing decision in the print media or broadcasting of sentencing decision by any audio-visual communication pursuant to article 181 (broadcasting of decision by audio-visual communication) of this code.

Section 5　Procuring

Article 284: procuring

"Procuring" shall mean:

(1) making a financial gain out of the prostitution of others;

(2) aiding in or protecting the prostitution of others or organising, in whatever manner, prostitution;

(3) recruiting, abducting or inducing a person into prostitution;

(4) exercising pressure on any person to become a prostitute.

Procuring shall be punishable by imprisonment from two to five years and a fine from four million to ten million riels.

Article 285: acting as intermediary between prostitute and procurer

Acting as an intermediary between a prostitute and a procurer shall be punishable by imprisonment from two to five years and a fine from four million to ten million riels.

Article 286: justification of resources from procuring

Facilitating the justification or concealment of a procurer's fictitious resources shall be punishable by imprisonment from two to five years and a fine from four million to ten million riels.

The same penalty is applicable for anyone who cannot account for an income compatible with his or her lifestyle while living with a person habitually engaging in prostitution or while entertaining a habitual relationship with one or more persons engaging in prostitution.

Article 287: obstructing measures designed to prevent prostitution

Any act of obstructing the prevention assistance or re-education initiatives undertaken by public service agencies or competent private institutions in favour of persons or engaging in or in danger of engaging in prostitution shall be punishable by imprisonment from two to five years and a fine from four million to ten million riels.

Article 288: aggravating circumstances (status of the perpetrator)

Procuring shall be punishable imprisonment from five to ten years if:

(1) the procurer or pimp is an ascendant or a descendent of the person engaging in prostitution;

(2) the procurer or pimp abuses his or her authority by reason of his or her duties over the person engaging in prostitution;

(3) the procurer or pimp uses coercion or violence against the person engaging in prostitution;

(4) it is committed by an organised criminal enterprise;

(5) several persons engage in prostitution.

Article 289: aggravating circumstances (status of the victim)

Procuring shall be punishable by imprisonment from seven to fifteen years if the person engaging in prostitution is a minor.

Article 290: aggravating circumstances (torture or acts of cruelty)

Procuring shall be punishable by imprisonment from ten to twenty years if the procurer inflicts torture or acts of cruelty on the person engaging in prostitution.

Article 291: operating a place of prostitution

Managing, exploiting, directing, operating or financing a

place of prostitution, directly or through an intermediary, shall be punishable by imprisonment from two to five years and a fine from four million to ten million riels.

Article 292: consent for activities involving prostitution in an establishment

A penalty of imprisonment from two to five years and a fine from four million to ten million riels shall be imposed on anyone who manages, exploits, directs, or operates an establishment open to the public, acting directly or through an intermediary, and accepts or habitually tolerates any person:

(1) to engage in prostitution within the premises or their annexes;

(2) to regularly solicit clients in such premises with a view to prostitution within the premises or their annexes.

Article 293: making premises available for prostitution

A penalty of imprisonment from two to five years, and a fine from four million to ten million riels shall be imposed on anyone who sells or makes available to any person any premises or places not open to the public, in the knowledge that they will there engage in prostitution.

Article 294: attempt

An attempt to commit the misdemeanours defined in this section shall be punishable by the same penalties.

Article 295: additional penalties (nature and duration)

The following additional penalties may be imposed in respect of

the offences defined in this section:

(1) forfeiture of certain rights either permanently or for a period not exceeding five years;

(2) prohibition from practising a profession in the practice of or in connection with which the offence was committed, either permanently or for a period not exceeding five years;

(3) local exclusion for a period not exceeding ten years for a felony or not exceeding five years for a misdemeanour;

(4) prohibition of a convicted alien from entering and remaining in the territory of the Kingdom of Cambodia, either permanently or for a period not exceeding five years;

(5) confiscation of any instruments, materials or items which were used or intended to be used to commit the offence;

(6) confiscation of the items or funds which were the subject of the offence;

(7) confiscation of the proceeds or property arising out of the offence;

(8) confiscation of the utensils, materials and furnishings in the premises in which the offence was committed;

(9) confiscation of one or more vehicles belonging to the convicted person;

(10) prohibition from possessing or carrying any weapon, explosive or ammunition of any kind, either permanently or for a period not exceeding five years;

(11) closure of an establishment used to plan or to commit the offence, either permanently or for a period not exceeding five years;

(12) prohibition from operating an establishment that is open to or used by the public, either permanently or for a period not exceeding five years;

(13) publication of sentencing decision for a period not exceeding two months;

(14) publication of sentencing decision in the print media;

(15) broadcasting of sentencing decision by any audio-visual communication for a period not exceeding eight days.

Article 296: criminal responsibility of legal entities

Legal entities may be held criminally responsible under article 42 (criminal responsibility of legal entities) of this code for offences defined in this section.

Legal entities shall be punishable by a fine from ten million to fifty million riels and by one or more of the following additional penalties:

(1) dissolution pursuant to article 170 (dissolution and liquidation of legal entities) of this code;

(2) placement under judicial supervision pursuant to article 171 (placement under judicial supervision) of this code;

(3) prohibition from exercising one or more activities pursuant to article 172 (prohibition from carrying on activities) of this code;

(4) closure of the establishment which was used to commit the offence pursuant to article 176 (closure of an establishment) of this code;

(5) prohibition from operating an establishment that is open to or used by the public pursuant to article 177 (prohibition from operating an establishment) of this code;

(6) confiscation of any instruments, materials or items which were used or intended to be used to commit the offence pursuant to article 178 (ownership, sale and destruction of items confiscated) and in article 179 (confiscation and rights of third parties) of this code;

(7) confiscation of the items or funds which were the subject of the offence pursuant to article 178 (ownership, sale and destruction of items confiscated) and article 179 (confiscation and rights of third parties) of this code;

(8) confiscation of the proceeds or property arising out of the offence pursuant to article 178 (ownership, sale and destruction of items confiscated) and article 179 (confiscation and rights of third parties) of this code;

(9) publication of sentencing decision pursuant to article 180 (publication of decisions) of this code;

(10) publication of sentencing decision in the print media or broadcasting of sentencing decision by any audio-visual communication pursuant to article 181 (broadcasting of decision by audio-visual

communication) of this code.

Section 6   Other Violations of Dignity

Article 297: intoxication

Any person who is manifestly drunk on a public thoroughfare shall be punishable by a fine from five thousand to ten thousand riels.

Article 298: soliciting in public places

Publicly soliciting another person with a view to inciting them to engage in sexual relations shall be punishable by a fine from five thousand to fifty thousand riels.

Chapter 6   Violations of Personal Liberty

Section 1   Violations of Privacy

Article 299: breaking and entering into dwelling place

Entering the dwelling place of another person by acts of violence, or by coercion, threats or manoeuvres, except where authorised by law, shall be punishable by imprisonment from one month to one year and a fine from ten thousand to two million riels.

Article 300: aggravating circumstances (status of the perpetrator)

Entering the dwelling place of another person against the person's will by a public official in the performance of his or her duties or in connection therewith, except where authorised by law, shall be punishable by imprisonment from one year to two years and a fine from two million to four million riels.

Article 301: intercepting or recording private conversation

Intercepting or recording words uttered in private or confidential circumstances without the consent of the person concerned, except where authorised by law, shall be punishable by imprisonment from one month to one year and a fine from one hundred thousand to two million riels.

Consent shall be presumed if the person concerned was notified of the interception or recording, but did not object to it.

Article 302: violation of privacy (recording of a person's image)

Recording the image of a person who is in a private place, without the person's consent of the person concerned, except where authorised by law, shall be punishable by imprisonment from one month to one year and a fine from one hundred thousand to two million riels.

Consent shall be presumed if the person concerned was notified of the recording, but did not object to it.

Article 303: attempt

An attempt to commit the misdemeanours defined in this section shall be punishable by the same penalties.

Article 304: additional penalties (nature and duration)

The following additional penalties may be imposed in respect of the offences defined in this section:

(1) forfeiture of certain rights, either permanently or for a period not exceeding five years;

(2) prohibition from practising a profession in the practice of or in connection with which the offence was committed, either permanently or for a period not exceeding five years;

(3) publication of sentencing decision for a period not exceeding two months;

(4) publication of sentencing decision in the print media;

(5) broadcasting of sentencing decision by any audio-visual communication for a period not exceeding eight days.

Section 2 Defamation and Public Insult

Article 305: definition of defamation

"Defamation" shall mean any allegation or charge made in bad faith which tends to injure the honour or reputation of a person or an institution.

Defamation shall be punishable by a fine from one hundred thousand to ten million riels if it is committed by any of the following means:

(1) any words whatsoever uttered in a public place or in a public meeting;

(2) written documents or pictures of any type released or displayed to the public;

(3) any audio-visual communication intended for the public.

Article 306: defamation through the media

Defamation committed through the media shall be subject to the provisions of the press law.

Article 307: definition of public insult

"Insult" shall mean outrageous expression, term of contempt or any invective that does not involve any imputation of fact.

An insult committed by any of the following means shall be punishable by a fine from one hundred thousand to ten million riels:

(1) any words whatsoever uttered in a public place or in a public meeting;

(2) written documents or pictures of any type released or displayed to the public;

(3) any audio-visual communication intended for the public.

Article 308: insult through the media

An insult committed through the media shall be subject to the provisions of the press law.

Article 309: court proceeding with regard to defamation and public insult

In case of defamation or insult of members of the royal government, public officials or any citizen perform public mission or public mandate, the prosecution shall be undertaken either following their complaint or *proprio motu* following a complaint filed by the person concerned or by the head of the institution concerned.

In case of defamation or insult against private individual, the charge shall be filed by the person who suffered from defamation or insult.

The complaint by the individual or the head of the institution as stipulated in article 309(1)(2) above is the required condition for the prosecuting authority to initiate criminal prosecution and the withdrawal of such complaint shall extinguish the criminal complaint.

However, the charge may be automatically filed by a prosecutor if the defamation or insulting is committed against a person or a group of persons based on the origin, ethnicity, race, nationality or religion of the person. In such case, the procedures for forwarding the case for trial shall be in compliance with the provisions of the criminal code of procedure.

Article 310: additional penalties (nature and duration)

The following additional penalties may be imposed in respect of the offences defined in this section:

(1) publication of sentencing decision;

(2) publication of sentencing decision in the print media;

(3) broadcasting of sentencing decision by any audio-visual communication for a period not exceeding eight days.

Section 3 Malicious Denunciation

Article 311: definition of malicious denunciation

"Malicious denunciation" is a denunciation of a fact, which is known to be false and liable to causing criminal or disciplinary sanctions, if it is sent to:

—a competent authority to take action, including judges, judicial police officers, or an employer; or

—any person having the power to refer it to the competent authority.

Article 312: applicable penalty and conditions for prosecution

Malicious denunciation shall be punishable by imprisonment from one month to one year and a fine from one hundred thousand to two million riels.

The statute of limitation of this criminal action is one year.

The limitation period for the offence shall start to run from the day the malicious denunciation became known or referred to the competent authority.

In case where the subject-matter of the denunciation has led to criminal prosecution, the action for malicious denunciation shall be suspended until the prosecution is completed.

Article 313: additional penalties (nature and duration)

The following additional penalties may be imposed in respect of the misdemeanour defined in this section:

(1) publication of sentencing decision for a period not exceeding two months;

(2) publication of sentencing decision in the print media;

(3) broadcasting of sentencing decision by any audio-visual communication for a period not exceeding eight days.

Section 4 Breach of Professional Secrecy

Article 314: breaches of professional secrecy

Any person who, by reason of his or her position or profession, or his or her duties or mission, is entrusted with secret information, shall be punishable by imprisonment from one month to one year and a fine from one hundred thousand to two million riels, if he or she discloses such information to a person not qualified to receive the information.

There shall be no offence if the law authorises or imposes the disclosure of the secret.

Article 315: inapplicability of article 314

The offence defined in article 314 (breaches of professional secrecy) of this code shall be deemed not to have been committed if a person discloses to any judicial, medical or administrative authority mistreatment inflicted on a minor under the age of fifteen which came to his or her knowledge in the performance of his or her profession.

Article 316: additional penalties (nature and duration)

The following additional penalties may be imposed in respect of

the misdemeanour defined in this section:

(1) prohibition from practising a profession in the practice of or in connection with which the offence was committed, either permanently or for a period not exceeding five years;

(2) publication of sentencing decision for a period not exceeding two months;

(3) publication of sentencing decision in the print media;

(4) broadcasting of sentencing decision by any audio-visual communication for a period not exceeding eight days.

Section 5   Breach of Privacy of Correspondence and Telecommunication

Article 317: breaches of correspondence

Maliciously opening, destroying, delaying or diverting correspondence sent to a third party, shall be punishable by imprisonment from one month to one year and a fine from one hundred thousand to two million riels.

The same penalty shall apply to the malicious interception of correspondence sent to a third party.

Article 318: breaches of privacy of telephone conversation

Maliciously listening to or interfering with telephone conversations shall be punishable by imprisonment from one month to one year and a fine from one hundred thousand to two million riels.

The same penalties shall be applicable to the malicious interception of or interference with, or viewing or listening to messages transmitted by means of telecommunication.

Article 319: attempt

An attempt to commit the misdemeanours defined in this section shall be punishable by the same penalties.

Article 320: additional penalties (nature and duration)

The following additional penalties may be imposed in respect of the offences defined in this section:

(1) prohibition from practising a profession in the practice of or in connection with which the offence was committed, either permanently or for a period not exceeding five years;

(2) confiscation of any instruments, materials or items which were used or intended to be used to commit the offence;

(3) publication of sentencing decision for a period not exceeding two months;

(4) publication of sentencing decision in the print media;

(5) broadcasting of sentencing decision by any audio-visual communication for a period not exceeding eight days.

Title 3   Offences Against Minors and The Family

Chapter 1   Abandonment of Minors

Article 321: penalty for abandonment of minors

The abandonment of a minor under fifteen years of age by a legal custodian shall be punishable by imprisonment from one to five years and a fine from two million to ten million riels where the circumstance of the abandonment endangers the health or safety of the minor.

Article 322: attempt

An attempt to commit the misdemeanour defined in this chapter shall be punishable by the same penalties.

Article 323: additional penalties (nature and duration)

With respect to the misdemeanour defined in this chapter. The following additional penalties may be imposed:

(1) forfeiture of certain rights for a period not exceeding five years;

(2) publication of sentencing decision for a period not exceeding two months;

(3) publication of sentencing decision in the print media;

(4) broadcasting of sentencing decision by any audio-visual communication for a period not exceeding eight days.

Chapter 2   Abandonment of Family

Article 324: abandonment of family

Failure to comply with a final court decision to pay alimony support to one's spouse or ex-spouse, to a minor, or to a descendant, an ascendant or other relatives for more than two months shall be punishable by imprisonment from one month to one year and a fine from one hundred thousand to two million riels.

Article 325: additional penalties (nature and duration)

With respect to the misdemeanours defined in this chapter, the following additional penalties may be imposed:

(1) forfeiture of certain rights for a period not exceeding five years;

(2) publication of sentencing decision for a period not exceeding two months;

(3) publication of sentencing decision in the print media;

(4) broadcasting of sentencing decision by any audio-visual communication for a period not exceeding eight days.

Chapter 3   Interference with The Custody of Minors

Article 326: failure to hand over minors

Maliciously failing to hand over a minor to the person who has the right to claim shall be punishable by imprisonment from one month to one year and a fine from one hundred thousand to two million riels.

Article 327: taking away of minors

Taking away a minor from the person who has legal custody shall be punishable by imprisonment from one month to one year and a fine from one hundred thousand to two million riels.

The offence shall be punishable by imprisonment from one year to three years and a fine from two million to six million riels if the minor is kept outside the territory of the Kingdom of Cambodia.

Article 328: attempt

An attempt to commit the misdemeanours defined in this chapter shall be punishable by the same penalties.

Article 329: additional penalties (nature and duration)

The following additional penalties may be imposed in respect of the offences defined in this chapter:

(1) forfeiture of certain rights for a period not exceeding five years;

(2) publication of sentencing decision for a period not

exceeding two months;

(3) publication of sentencing decision in the print media;

(4) broadcasting of sentencing decision by any audio-visual communication for a period not exceeding eight days.

Chapter 4   Offences Against Familial Relationships

Article 330: incitement to abandon a child

The direct incitement for pecuniary gain of one or both parents to abandon a child, born or to be born, shall be punishable by imprisonment from one month to six months and a fine from one hundred thousand to one million riels.

Article 331: acting as an intermediary in case of adoption or abandonment

Acting as an intermediary for pecuniary gain between a person or a couple desiring to adopt a child and a parent desiring to abandon its born or unborn child shall be punishable by imprisonment from one month to six months and a fine from one hundred thousand to one million riels.

Article 332: intermediary between an adoptive parent and a pregnant woman

Acting as an intermediary for pecuniary gain between a person or a couple desiring to adopt a child and a woman agreeing to bear the child with the intent to give up the child to them shall be punishable by imprisonment from one month to six months and a fine from one hundred thousand to one million riels.

Article 333: acts of substitution, false representation or concealment of a child existence

Substitution, false representation or concealment of the existence of a child which infringes his or her civil status shall be punishable by imprisonment from one month to one year and a fine from one hundred thousand to two million riels.

Article 334: attempt

An attempt to commit the misdemeanours defined in this chapter shall be punishable by the same penalties.

Article 335: additional penalties (nature and duration)

The following additional penalties may be imposed in respect of the offences defined in this chapter:

(1) forfeiture of certain rights for a period not exceeding five years;

(2) publication of sentencing decision for a period not exceeding two months;

(3) publication of sentencing decision in the print media;

(4) broadcasting of sentencing decision by any audio-visual communication for a period not exceeding eight days.

Article 336: criminal responsibility of legal entities

Legal entities may be found criminally responsible under article 42 (criminal responsibility of legal entities) of this code for

the offences defined in article 330 (incitement to abandon a child), article 331 (acting as an intermediary in case of adoption or abandonment) and article 332 (intermediary between an adoptive parent and a pregnant woman) of this code.

Legal entities shall be punishable by a fine from one million to five million riels and by one or more of the following additional penalties:

(1) placement under judicial supervision pursuant to article 171 (placement under judicial supervision) of this code;

(2) prohibition from exercising one or more activities pursuant to article 172 (prohibition from carrying on activities) of this code;

(3) closure of the establishment which was used to commit the offence pursuant to article 176 (closure of an establishment) of this code;

(4) confiscation of the items or funds which were the subject of the offence pursuant to article 178 (ownership, sale and destruction of items confiscated) and article 179 (confiscation and rights of third parties) of this code;

(5) publication of sentencing decision pursuant to article 180 (publication of decisions) of this code;

(6) publication of sentencing decision in the print media or broadcasting of sentencing decision by any audio-visual communication pursuant to article 181 (broadcasting of decision by audio-visual communication) of this code.

Chapter 5 Endangerment of Minors

Section 1 Threat to Physical and Mental Health

Article 337: depriving minor under the age of 15 years of food or care

Depriving a minor under the age of 15 years of food or care to the point of endangering his or her health, inflicted by any person having authority over him or her, shall be punishable by imprisonment from two to five years and a fine from four million to ten million riels.

Article 338: aggravating circumstances (death of the victim)

The offence defined in article 337 (depriving minor under the age of 15 years of food or care) of this code shall be punishable by imprisonment from seven to fifteen years if it results in the death of the victim.

Article 339: subjecting minor to working conditions harmful to his or her health

Subjecting a minor to working conditions harmful to his or her health or physical development shall be punishable by imprisonment from two to five years and a fine from four million to ten million riels.

Article 340: aggravating circumstances as a consequence of the death of the minor

The offences defined in article 339 (subjecting minor to working conditions harmful to his or her health) of this code shall be punishable by imprisonment from seven to fifteen years if it results in the death of the victim.

Article 341: indecent assault of minor under 15 years of age

An indecent assault is the act of touching or exposing the sexual organs or other parts of another person's body, or of letting another person to touch the sexual organs or other parts of the perpetrator's body or that of a third person for the purpose of sexual arousal or satisfaction of the perpetrator.

Where an indecent assault is committed upon a minor under fifteen years of age the perpetrator shall be punishable by imprisonment from one year to three years and a fine from two million to six million riels.

Article 342: aggravating circumstances

The offence defined in article 341 (indecent assault of minor under 15 years of age) of this code shall be punishable by imprisonment from two to five years and a fine from four million to ten million riels, if:

(1) it is committed by an ascendant;

(2) it is committed by a person having authority over the minor;

(3) it is committed by several persons acting as perpetrators, co-perpetrators, instigators, or accomplices;

(4) it involves the payment of remunerations.

Section 2　Inciting Minors to Commit Unlawful or Dangerous Acts

Article 343: inciting minor to consume narcotics

The direct incitement of a minor to unlawfully and regularly consume large quantities of narcotics shall be punishable by imprisonment from six months to two years and a fine from one million to four million riels.

Article 344: inciting minor to beg

The direct incitement of a minor to beg shall be punishable by imprisonment from one month to one year and a fine from one hundred thousand to two million riels.

Article 345: inciting minor to commit felony or misdemeanour

The direct incitement of a minor to commit a felony or a misdemeanour shall be punishable by imprisonment from two to five years and a fine from four million to ten million riels.

Article 346: arrangement by an adult of indecent exposure or sexual relations involving minors

The arrangement, by an adult, of meetings involving indecent exposure or sexual relations at which minors are present or participate shall be punishable by imprisonment from one to five years and a fine from two million to ten million riels.

Section 3 Abuse of Parental Authority

Article 347: abuse of parental authority

The abuse of parental authority by a legal, natural or adoptive ascendant of his or her authority over a minor to the point of depriving the minor of his or her freedom shall be punishable by imprisonment from one month to one year and a fine from one hundred thousand to two million riels, if, by reason of the abuse, the health, safety or mental condition of the minor is endangered.

Section 4 Attempt and Penalties

Article 348: attempt

An attempt to commit the misdemeanours defined in this chapter shall be punishable by the same penalties.

Article 349: additional penalties (nature and duration)

The following additional penalties may be imposed in respect of the offences defined in this chapter:

(1) forfeiture of certain rights for a period not exceeding five years;

(2) prohibition from practising a profession in the practice of or in connection with which the offence was committed, ether permanently, or for a period not exceeding five years;

(3) local exclusion for a period not exceeding ten years for a felony or not exceeding five years for a misdemeanour;

(4) publication of sentencing decision for a period not exceeding two months;

(5) publication of sentencing decision in the print media;

(6) broadcasting of sentencing decision by any audio-visual communication for a period not exceeding eight days.

Chapter 6   Other Offences Against the Family

Article 350: bigamy

Contracting a second marriage before the dissolution of a previous marriage shall be punishable by imprisonment from one month to one year and a fine from one hundred thousand to two million riels.

The same punishment shall be applied to a civil status registration officer who is aware of the fact, but still authorizes or registers a marriage before the dissolution of a previous marriage.

Article 351: sexual assault of minor by ascendant

Sexual intercourse by an ascendant with a minor under eighteen years of age shall be punishable by imprisonment from five to ten year if the perpetrator is an ascendant of the minor.

Article 352: sexual assault by consanguinity or affinity

Having sexual intercourse among consanguinity or affinity of the three levels shall be punishable by imprisonment from one month to one year and a fine from one hundred thousand to two million riels.

BOOK 3
Offences Against Properties

Title 1　　Fraudulent Appropriation

Chapter 1　　*Theft and Related Offences*

Section 1　Theft

Article 353: definition of theft

Theft is the fraudulent taking by any means of property belonging to another person with intent to keep it.

Article 354: theft of energy

The fraudulent use of energy to the prejudice of another person shall be deemed to be theft.

Article 355: family immunity

Theft shall not be criminally prosecuted if it is committed by a person:

(1) to the prejudice of his or her ascendant or his or her descendant;

(2) to the prejudice of a spouse.

Article 356: applicable penalty

Theft shall be punishable by imprisonment from six months to three years and a fine from one million to six million riels.

Article 357: aggravating circumstances (violence)

Theft shall be punishable by imprisonment from three to ten years:

(1) if it is preceded, accompanied or followed by acts of violence;

(2) if it is committed by breaking and entering.

Article 358: aggravating circumstances (mutilation or disability)

Theft shall be punishable by imprisonment from ten to twenty years if it is preceded, accompanied or followed by acts of violence causing mutilation or permanent disability.

Article 359: aggravating circumstances (torture or acts of cruelty)

Theft shall be punishable by imprisonment from fifteen to thirty years if it is preceded, accompanied or followed by torture or acts of cruelty.

Article 360: aggravating circumstances (death of the victim)

Theft shall be punishable by imprisonment from fifteen to thirty years if it is preceded, accompanied or followed by violence unintentionally causing the death of the victim.

Article 361: attempt

An attempt to commit the misdemeanours defined in this

section shall be punishable by the same penalties.

Article 362: additional penalties (nature and duration)

The following additional penalties may be imposed in respect of the offences defined in this section:

(1) forfeiture of certain rights, either permanently or for a period not exceeding five years;

(2) prohibition from practising a profession in the practice of or in connection with which the offence was committed, either permanently or for a period not exceeding five years;

(3) prohibition from driving any motor vehicle permanently or for a period not exceeding five years;

(4) local exclusion for a period not exceeding ten years for a felony or not exceeding five years for a misdemeanour;

(5) prohibition from entering and residing in the territory of the Kingdom of Cambodia for a convicted foreigner, either permanently or for a period not exceeding five years;

(6) confiscation of any instruments, materials or items which were used or intended to be used to commit the offence;

(7) confiscation of the items or funds which were the subject of the offence;

(8) confiscation of the proceeds or property arising out of the offence;

(9) confiscation of the utensils, materials and furnishings in the premises in which the offence was committed;

(10) confiscation of one or more vehicles belonging to the convicted person;

(11) prohibition from possessing or carrying any weapon, explosive or ammunition of any kind;

(12) closure of an establishment used to plan or to commit the offence, either permanently or for a period not exceeding five years;

(13) prohibition from operating an establishment that is open to or used by the public, either permanently or for a period not exceeding five years;

(14) publication of sentencing decision for a period not exceeding two months;

(15) publication of sentencing decision in the print media;

(16) broadcasting of sentencing decision by any audio-visual communication for a period not exceeding eight days.

Section 2　Extortion

Article 363: definition of extortion

Extortion is the act of obtaining by violence, threat of violence or coercion:

(1) a signature or fingerprint;

(2) a commitment or an abandonment;

(3) the disclosure of a secret;

(4) the handing over of funds, valuables or of any asset.

Article 364: applicable penalty

Extortion shall be punishable by imprisonment from two to five years and a fine from four million to ten million riels.

Article 365: aggravating circumstances (status of the victim)

Extortion shall be punishable by imprisonment from five to ten years if it is committed:

(1) against a person who is particularly vulnerable by reason of his or her age;

(2) against a pregnant woman whose pregnancy is obvious or known to the perpetrator;

(3) against a person who is particularly vulnerable by reason of illness or disability and whose state is obvious or known to the perpetrator.

Article 366: aggravating circumstances (use of a weapon)

Extortion shall be punishable by imprisonment from seven to fifteen years if it is committed either with the use or threatened use of a weapon.

Article 367: aggravating circumstances (mutilation or disability)

Extortion shall be punishable by imprisonment from ten to twenty years if it is preceded, accompanied or followed by acts of violence causing mutilation or permanent disability.

Article 368: aggravating circumstances (torture or acts of cruelty)

Extortion shall be punishable by imprisonment from fifteen to thirty years if it is preceded, accompanied or followed by acts of torture or cruelty.

Article 369: aggravating circumstances (death of the victim)

Extortion shall be punishable by imprisonment from fifteen to thirty years if it is preceded, accompanied or followed by acts of violence unintentionally causing the death of the victim.

Article 370: attempt

An attempt to commit the misdemeanours defined in this section shall be punishable by the same penalties.

Article 371: additional penalties (nature and duration)

The following additional penalties may be imposed in respect of the offences defined in this section:

(1) forfeiture of certain rights, either permanently or for a period not exceeding five years;

(2) prohibition from practising a profession in the practice of or in connection with which the offence was committed, either permanently or for a period not exceeding five years;

(3) local exclusion for a period not exceeding ten years for a felony or not exceeding five years for a misdemeanour;

(4) prohibition of a convicted alien from entering and remaining in the territory of the Kingdom of Cambodia, either permanently or for a period not exceeding five years;

(5) confiscation of any instruments, materials or items which were used or intended to be used to commit the offence;

(6) confiscation of the items or funds which were the subject of the offence;

(7) confiscation of the proceeds or property arising out of the offence;

(8) confiscation of the utensils, materials and furnishings in the premises in which the offence was committed;

(9) confiscation of one or more vehicles belonging to the convicted person;

(10) prohibition from possessing or carrying any weapon, explosive or ammunition of any kind, either permanently or for a period not exceeding five years;

(11) publication of sentencing decision for a period not exceeding two months;

(12) publication of sentencing decision in the print media;

(13) broadcasting of sentencing decision by any audio-visual communication for a period not exceeding eight days.

Section 3 Blackmail

Article 372: definition of blackmail

Blackmail is the act of obtaining by threatening to disclose or to impute facts liable to harm a person's honour or reputation:

(1) a signature or a fingerprint;

(2) a commitment or an abandonment;

(3) the disclosure of a secret; or

(4) the handing over of funds, valuables or of any asset.

Article 373: applicable penalty

Blackmail shall be punishable by imprisonment from two to five years and a fine from four million to ten million riels.

Article 374: aggravating circumstances by reason of carrying out the threat

If the threat to disclose or impute facts liable to harm a person's honour or reputation has been carried out, the perpetrator shall be punishable by imprisonment from five to ten years.

Article 375: attempt

An attempt to commit the misdemeanours defined in this section shall be punishable by the same penalties.

Article 376: additional penalties (nature and duration)

The following additional penalties may be imposed in respect of the offences defined in this section:

(1) forfeiture of certain rights, either permanently or for a period not exceeding five years;

(2) prohibition from practising a profession in the practice of or in connection with which the offence was committed, either permanently or for a period not exceeding five years;

(3) local exclusion for a period not exceeding ten years for a felony or not exceeding five years for a misdemeanour;

(4) prohibition of a convicted alien from entering and remaining in the territory of the Kingdom of Cambodia, either permanently or for a period not exceeding five years;

(5) confiscation of any instruments, materials or items which were used or intended to be used to commit the offence;

(6) confiscation of the items or funds which were the subject of the offence;

(7) confiscation of the proceeds or property arising out of the offence;

(8) confiscation of the utensils, materials and furnishings in the premises in which the offence was committed;

(9) confiscation of one or more vehicles belonging to the convicted person;

(10) prohibition from possessing or carrying any weapon, explosive or ammunition of any kind, either permanently or for a period not exceeding five years;

(11) publication of sentencing decision for a period not exceeding two months;

(12) publication of sentencing decision in the print media;

(13) broadcasting of sentencing decision by any audio-visual communication for a period not exceeding eight days.

Chapter 2   Fraud and Related Offences

Section 1   Fraud

Article 377: definition of fraud

"Fraud" is the act of deceiving a natural or legal person by the use of a false name or a fictitious capacity, by the abuse of a genuine capacity, or by means of unlawful manoeuvres, in order to obtain from that person to his or her prejudice or to the prejudice of a third party:

(1) the transfer of funds, valuables or any property;

(2) the provision of a service; or

(3) the making of a document incurring or discharging an obligation.

Article 378: applicable penalty

Fraud shall be punishable by imprisonment from six months to three years and a fine from one million to six million riels.

Article 379: aggravating circumstances (status of the victim)

Fraud shall be punishable by imprisonment from two to five years if it is committed:

(1) against a person who is particularly vulnerable by reason of his or her age;

(2) against a pregnant woman whose pregnancy is obvious or known to the perpetrator;

(3) against a person who is particularly vulnerable by reason of illness or disability and whose state is obvious or known to the perpetrator.

Article 380: other aggravating circumstances

Fraud shall be punishable by imprisonment from two to five years if it is committed:

(1) by a civilian or military public official in the performance of his or her duties or in connection therewith;

(2) by a person unlawfully assuming the capacity of a person holding a public office;

(3) by a person making a public appeal with a view to issuing securities;

(4) by a person making a public appeal with a view to raisingfunds for humanitarian or social assistance;

(5) by an organised criminal enterprise.

Article 381: attempt

An attempt to commit the misdemeanours defined in this section shall be punishable by the same penalties.

Article 382: additional penalties (nature and duration)

The following additional penalties may be imposed in respect of the offences defined in this section:

(1) forfeiture of certain rights, either permanently or for a period not exceeding five years;

(2) prohibition from practising a profession in the practice of or in connection with which the offence was committed, either permanently or for a period not exceeding five years;

(3) local exclusion for a period not exceeding five years for a misdemeanour;

(4) prohibition of a convicted alien from entering and remaining in the territory of the Kingdom of Cambodia, either

permanently or for a period not exceeding five years;

(5) confiscation of any instruments, materials or items which were used or intended to be used to commit the offence;

(6) confiscation of the items or funds which were the subject of the offence;

(7) confiscation of the proceeds or property arising out of the offence;

(8) confiscation of the utensils, materials and furnishings in the premises in which the offence was committed;

(9) confiscation of one or more vehicles belonging to the convicted person;

(10) prohibition from possessing or carrying any weapon, explosive or ammunition of any kind, either permanently or for a period not exceeding five years;

(11) publication of sentencing decision for a period not exceeding two months;

(12) publication of sentencing decision in the print media;

(13) broadcasting of sentencing decision by any audio-visual communication for a period not exceeding eight days.

Section 2   Offences Similar to Fraud

Sub-Section 1   Exploitation of Weakness

Article 383: taking advantage of ignorance or weakness

Knowingly taking advantage of the ignorance or weakness of a person who is particularly vulnerable by reason of his or her age, pregnancy, or disability by compelling him or her to commit an act or not to commit an act to his or her grave prejudice shall be punishable by imprisonment from one month to one year and a fine from one hundred thousand to two million riels.

Sub-Section 2   Dishonesty

Article 384: definition of dishonesty

"Dishonesty" is where a person, knowing himself or herself to be wholly unable to meet payment or being determined not to pay:

(1) orders food or drink in a bar, restaurant or other establishment open to the public;

(2) books and effectively occupies a room in a hotel or other establishment open to the public;

(3) causes himself to be transported by a tricycle, taxi or other means of transport.

Dishonesty shall be punishable by imprisonment from six days to three months and a fine from one hundred thousand to five hundred thousand riels.

Article 385: attempt

An attempt to commit the misdeneanours defined in this sub-section shall be punishable by the same penalties.

Article 386: additional penalties (nature and duration)

The following additional penalties may be imposed in respect of the offences defined in this sub-section:

(1) forfeiture of certain rights, either permanently or for a period not exceeding five years;

(2) prohibition from practising a profession in the practice of or in connection with which the offence was committed, either permanently or for a period not exceeding five years;

(3) confiscation of the proceeds or property arising out of the offence;

(4) confiscation of one or more vehicles belonging to the convicted person;

(5) publication of sentencing decision for a period not exceeding two months;

(6) publication of sentencing decision in the print media;

(7) broadcasting of sentencing decision by any audio-visual communication for a period not exceeding eight days.

Sub-Section 3 Interference with Auctions

Article 387: improper bidding

In a public auction, the rejection of a bid or tampering with bids by gifts, promises, understandings or any other fraudulent means shall be punishable by imprisonment from six months to two years and a fine from one million to four million riels.

Article 388: hindering the freedom of biddings

Hindering the freedom to make bids during a public sale by bidding, by violence or threats shall be punishable by imprisonment from one to three years and a fine from two million to six million riels.

Article 389: attempt

An attempt to commit the misdemeanours defined in this section shall be punishable by the same penalties.

Article 390: additional penalties (nature and duration)

The following additional penalties may be imposed in respect of the offence defined in this section:

(1) forfeiture of certain rights, either permanently or for a period not exceeding five years;

(2) prohibition from practising a profession in the practice of or in connection with which the offence was committed, either permanently or for a period not exceeding five years;

(3) confiscation of the proceeds or property arising out of the offence;

(4) confiscation of one or more, vehicles belonging to the convicted person;

(5) publication of sentencing decision for a period not exceeding two months;

(6) publication of sentencing decision in the print media;

(7) broadcasting of sentencing decision by any audio-visual communication for a period not exceeding eight days.

Chapter 3　Breach of Trust and Related Offences

Section 1　Breach of Trust

Article 391: definition of breach of trust

"Breach of trust" is committed when a person, to the prejudice of other persons, misappropriates funds, valuables or any property that were handed over to him or her and that he or she accepted subject to the condition of returning, redelivering, presenting or using them in a specified way.

Article 392: applicable penalty

Breach of trust shall be punishable by imprisonment from six months to three years and a fine from one million to six million riels.

Article 393: breach of special trust by administrators or other persons

Breach of trust shall be punishable by imprisonment from two to five years and a fine from four million to ten million riels if it is committed by a director or manager of a limited liability or a joint stock corporation or a judicially appointed official or a person who is authorized by a legal entity with the intention to make a personal gain or a profit for a third party or with the intention to causing damage to a legal entity and damages have been made to the property.

The provisions of paragraph 1 shall also be applicable where a liquidator of a limited liability or a joint stock corporation or a judicially appointed official acting on behalf of the liquidator committed an offence within the meaning of paragraph 1 and caused damage to the property of the legal entity.

An attempt to commit the offences provided for in article 393 (1) and (2) shall be punishable by the same penalties.

Article 394: aggravating circumstances (status of the perpetrator)

Breach of trust shall be punishable by imprisonment from two to five years and a fine from four million to ten million riels, if it is committed:

(1) by a person who made a public offering in order to receive funds or assets for his or her own behalf or on behalf of a commercial or industrial enterprise;

(2) by a judicially appointed official or officer of the court in the performance of his or her duties or in connection therewith;

(3) by a civilian or military public official in the performance of his or her duties or in connection therewith.

Article 395: attempt

An attempt to commit the misdemeanours defined in this section shall be punishable by the same penalties.

Article 396: additional penalties (nature and duration)

The following additional penalties may be imposed in respect of the offences defined in this section:

(1) forfeiture of certain rights, either permanently or for a period not exceeding five years;

(2) prohibition from practising a profession in the practice of or in connection with which the offence was committed, either permanently or for a period not exceeding five years;

(3) confiscation of any instruments, materials or items which were used or intended to be used to commit the offence;

(4) confiscation of the items or funds which were the subject of the offence;

(5) confiscation of the proceeds or property arising out of the offence;

(6) confiscation of the utensils, materials and furnishings in the premises in which the offence was committed;

(7) confiscation of one or more vehicles belonging to the convicted person;

(8) publication of sentencing decision, for a period not exceeding two months;

(9) publication of sentencing decision in the print media;

(10) broadcasting of sentencing decision by any audio-visual communication for a period not exceeding eight days.

Section 2 Embezzlement of Items Seized or Pledged

Article 397: embezzlement of items seized or pledged

The destruction or misappropriation, by a debtor of an item

seized by a competent authority or pledged as security shall be punishable by imprisonment from one month to one year and a fine from one hundred thousand to two million riels.

Article 398: attempt

An attempt to commit the misdemeanours shall be punishable by the same penalties.

Chapter 4 Additional Offences

Section 1 Receiving Stolen Goods

Article 399: definition of receiving stolen goods

"Receiving stolen goods" is the receiving, concealment, retention or transfer of an item, knowing that that item was obtained by a felony or misdemeanour.

"Receiving stolen goods" shall also mean:

(1) serving as intermediary in order to transfer an item, knowing that that item was obtained by a felony or misdemeanour;

(2) knowingly benefiting from the proceeds of a felony or misdeneanour.

Article 400: applicable penalty

Receiving stolen goods shall be punishable by imprisonment from two to five years and a fine from four million to ten million riels.

Article 401: aggravating circumstances

Receiving stolen goods shall be punishable by imprisonment from five to ten years if it is committed:

(1) habitually;

(2) by using the facilities conferred by the exercise of a profession;

(3) by an organised criminal enterprise.

Article 402: maximum fines

The maximum fine incurred may be raised to the value of the goods handled.

Article 403: additional penalties (nature and duration)

The following additional penalties may be imposed in respect of the offences defined in this section:

(1) forfeiture of certain rights, either permanently or for a period not exceeding five years;

(2) prohibition from practising a profession in the practice of or in connection with which the offence was committed, either permanently or for period not exceeding five years;

(3) prohibition from driving any motor vehicle permanently or for a period not exceeding five years;

(4) local exclusion for a period not exceeding ten years for a felony or not exceeding five years for a misdemeanour;

(5) prohibition from entering and residing in the territory of the Kingdom of Cambodia for a convicted foreigner, either

permanently or for a period not exceeding five years;

(6) confiscation of any instruments, materials or items which were used or intended to be used to commit the offence;

(7) confiscation of the items or funds which were the subject of the offence;

(8) confiscation of the proceeds or property arising out of the offence;

(9) confiscation of the utensils, materials and furnishings in the premises in which the offence was committed;

(10) confiscation of one or more vehicles belonging to the convicted person;

(11) prohibition from possessing or carrying any weapon, explosive or ammunition of any kinds;

(12) closure of an establishment used to plan or to commit the offence, either permanently or for a period not exceeding five years;

(13) prohibition from operating an establishment that is open to or used by the public, either permanently or for a period not exceeding five years;

(14) publication of sentencing decision for a period not exceeding two months;

(15) publication of sentencing decision in the print media;

(16) broadcasting of sentencing decision by any audio-visual communication for a period not exceeding eight days.

Section 2　Money Laundering

Article 404: definition of money laundering

"Money laundering" is the act of facilitating by any means the false justification of the origin of the direct or indirect proceeds of a felony or misdemeanour.

"Money laundering" shall also include providing assistance in investing, concealing or converting the direct or indirect proceeds of a felony or misdemeanour.

Article 405: applicable penalty

Money laundering shall be punishable by imprisonment from two to five years and a fine of four million riels. The maximum fine may be raised to amount to the value of the funds or property which was the subject of the money laundering.

Where the offence which produced the property or funds which was the subject of the money laundering is punishable by imprisonment sentence higher than that imposed in paragraph 1 above, the offence of money laundering shall be punishable by the penalties applicable to the offence known to the perpetrator, and if the offence was accompanied by aggravating circumstances, by such penalties known to him or her.

Article 406: aggravating circumstances

Money laundering shall be punishable by imprisonment from five to ten years if it is committed:

(1) habitually;

(2) by using the facilities conferred by the exercise of a profession;

(3) by an organised criminal enterprise.

Article 407: attempt

An attempt to commit the misdemeanours defined in this section shall be punishable by the same penalties.

Article 408: additional penalties (nature and duration)

The following additional penalties may be imposed in respect of the offences defined in this section:

(1) forfeiture of certain rights, either permanently or for a period not exceeding five years;

(2) prohibition from practising a profession in the practice of or in connection with which the offence was committed, either permanently or for a period not exceeding five years;

(3) confiscation of any instruments, materials or items which were used or intended to be used to commit the offence;

(4) confiscation of the items or funds which were the subject of the offence;

(5) confiscation of the proceeds or property arising out of the offence;

(6) confiscation of the utensils, materials and furnishings in the premises in which the offence was committed;

(7) confiscation of one or more vehicles belonging to the

convicted person;

(8) publication of sentencing decision for a period not exceeding two months;

(9) publication of sentencing decision in the print media;

(10) broadcasting of sentencing decision by any audio-visual communication for a period not exceeding eight days.

Article 409: criminal responsibility of legal entities

Legal entities may be found criminally responsible under article 42 (criminal responsibility of legal entities) of this code for the offences defined in article 404 (definition of money laundering) of this code.

Legal entities shall be punishable by a fine from one hundred million to five hundred million riels and by one or more of the following additional penalties:

(1) dissolution pursuant to article 170 (dissolution and liquidation of legal entities) of this code;

(2) placement under judicial supervision pursuant to article 171 (placement under judicial supervision) of this code;

(3) prohibition from carrying on one or more activities pursuant to article 172 (prohibition from carrying on activities) of this code;

(4) disqualification from public tenders pursuant to article 173 (disqualification from public tenders) of this code;

(5) prohibition from making a public offering pursuant to

article 174 (prohibition from making a public offering) of this code;

(6) confiscation of any instruments, materials or items which were used or intended to be used to commit the offence pursuant to article 178 (ownership, sale and destruction of items confiscated) and article 179 (confiscation and rights of third parties) of this code;

(7) confiscation of the proceeds or property arising out of the offence according article 178 (ownership, sale and destruction of items confiscated) and article 179 (confiscation and rights of third parties) of this code;

(8) publication of sentencing decision pursuant to article 180 (publication of decisions) of this code;

(9) publication of sentencing decision in the print media or broadcasting of sentencing decision by any audio-visual communication pursuant to article 181 (broadcasting of decision by audio-visual communication) of this code.

Title 2 Infringements on Property

Chapter 1 Destruction, Defacement and Damage

Section 1 Destruction, Defacement and Damage

Article 410: intentionally causing damage

Intentionally destroying, defacing or damaging property belonging to another person shall be punishable by imprisonment from six months to two years and a fine from one million to four million riels, except where only minor damage has ensued.

Article 411: aggravating circumstances

The offence defined in article 410 (intentionally causing damage) shall be punishable by imprisonment from two to five years and a fine from four million to ten million riels:

(1) if it is committed by several persons acting as perpetrators, co-perpetrators, instigators or accomplices;

(2) if it is committed within dwelling premises;

(3) if it is committed on the premises used for the safekeeping of funds, securities, goods or equipment;

(4) if it results in damages to a public building or road;

(5) if it is committed and causes damages to farm products or crops;

(6) if it results in damages to international border markers of the Kingdom of Cambodia.

Article 412: aggravating circumstances (status of the victim)

The offence defined in article 410 (intentionally causing damage) shall be punishable by imprisonment from two to five years and a fine from four million to ten million riels if it is committed to the prejudice of:

(1) a judge, a public official or a lawyer, with a view to influencing his or her conduct in the discharge of his or her duties;

(2) a victim or a civil party, either to prevent him or her from reporting the offence or seeking reparations for the damages;

(3) a witness, either to prevent him or her from making a statement during a judicial investigation, an enquiry, a trial or during other court proceedings, or to influence his or her testimony;

(4) a victim or a civil party after he or she filed a complaint or sought reparations for the damages;

(5) a witness on account of his or her testimony given during a judicial investigation, an enquiry, a trial or during other court proceedings.

Article 413: aggravating circumstances (employing means dangerous to persons)

Intentionally destroying, defacing or damaging property

belonging to another person by the use of an explosion, fire or other means likely to endanger persons shall be punishable by imprisonment from two to five years and a fine from four million to ten million riels.

Article 414: aggravating circumstances (causing injury to others)

The offence defined in article 413 aggravating circumstances (employing means dangerous to persons) of this code shall be punishable by imprisonment from five to ten years if it results in injury to others.

Article 415: aggravating circumstances (mutilation or disability)

The offence defined in article 413 aggravating circumstances (employing means dangerous to persons) of this code shall be punishable by imprisonment from seven to fifteen years if it results in the mutilation or permanent disability of a person.

Article 416: aggravating circumstances (commission of offences by an organized criminal enterprise)

The offence defined in article 413 aggravating circumstances (employing means dangerous to persons) of this code shall be punishable by imprisonment from seven to fifteen years if it is committed by an organised criminal enterprise.

Article 417: aggravating circumstances (death of another person)

The offence defined in article 413 aggravating circumstances (employing means dangerous to persons) of this code shall be punishable by imprisonment from ten to twenty years if it unintentionally results in the death of another person.

Article 418: minor damage

Intentionally destroying, defacing or damaging property belonging to another person shall be punishable by imprisonment from one day to six days and a fine from one thousand to one hundred thousand riels, if only minor damage ensued.

The provisions of this article are not applicable to public or private cultural properties which are part of the national patrimony of the Kingdom of Cambodia.

Article 419: other damage due to recklessness or breach of regulations

Destroying, defacing or damaging property belonging to another person by the use of an explosive or fire shall be punishable by imprisonment from one month to one year and a fine from one hundred thousand to two million riels if it is caused by:

(1) negligence, recklessness or carelessness;

(2) failure to observe the safety requirement or due diligence imposed by law.

Article 420: damaging official poster or notice

Unintentionally destroying, defacing or damaging an official poster or official notice posted by the administration shall be punishable by imprisonment from one day to six days and a fine from one thousand to one hundred thousand riels.

Article 421: attempt

Except for the offences defined in article 419 (other damage due to recklessness or breach of regulations) of this code, an attempt to commit the misdemeanours defined in this section shall be punishable by the same penalties.

Article 422: additional penalties (nature and duration)

The following additional penalties may be imposed in respect of the offences defined in this section:

(1) forfeiture of certain rights, either permanently or for a period not exceeding five years;

(2) prohibition from practising a profession in the practice of or in connection with which the offence was committed, either permanently or for a period not exceeding five years;

(3) prohibition from driving any motor vehicle permanently or for a period not exceeding five years;

(4) local exclusion for a period not exceeding ten years for a felony or not exceeding five years for a misdemeanour;

(5) prohibition of a convicted alien from entering and remaining in the territory of the Kingdom of Cambodia, either

permanently or for a period not exceeding five years;

(6) confiscation of any instruments, materials or items which were used or intended to be used to commit the offence;

(7) confiscation of the items or funds which were the subject of the offence;

(8) confiscation of the proceeds or property arising out of the offence;

(9) confiscation of the utensils, materials and furnishings in the premises in which the offence was committed;

(10) confiscation of one or more vehicles belonging to the convicted person;

(11) prohibition from possessing or carrying any weapon, explosive or ammunition of any kind;

(12) closure of an establishment used to plan or to commit the offence, either permanently or for a period not exceeding five years;

(13) prohibition from operating an establishment that is open to or used by the public, either permanently or for a period not exceeding five years;

(14) publication of sentencing decision for a period not exceeding two months;

(15) publication of sentencing decision in the print media;

(16) broadcasting of sentencing decision by any audio-visual communication for a period not exceeding eight days.

Section 2　Threats to Destroy, Deface or Damage

Article 423：threats to cause damage

The threat to cause any destruction, defacement or damage shall be punishable by imprisonment from one month to six months and a fine from one hundred thousand to one million riels if it is repeated, or if it is put in material form by writing, pictures or other objects.

Where the value of the property which is the subject of the threat to cause destruction, defacement or damage is little, the offence shall be punishable by a fine from five thousand to one hundred thousand riels.

Article 424：threats to destroy followed by an order

The threat to cause any destruction, defacement or damage shall be punishable by imprisonment from one to two years and a fine from two million to four million riels if it is accompanied by an order to perform or not to perform an act.

Article 425：false information

The communication or disclosure of any false information with a view to inducing a belief that a destruction, defacement or damage dangerous to other persons will be carried out shall be punishable by imprisonment from one to two years and a fine from two million to four million riels.

Article 426：additional penalties (nature and duration)

The following additional penalties may be imposed in respect of

the offences defined in this section:

(1) forfeiture of certain rights, either permanently or for a period not exceeding five years;

(2) prohibition from practising a profession in the practice of or in connection with which the offence was committed, either permanently or for a period not exceeding five years;

(3) prohibition from driving any motor vehicle permanently or for a period not exceeding five years;

(4) local exclusion for a period not exceeding ten years for a felony or not exceeding five years for a misdemeanour;

(5) prohibition of a convicted alien from entering and remaining in the territory of the Kingdom of Cambodia, either permanently or for a period not exceeding five years;

(6) confiscation of any instruments, materials or items which were used or intended to be used to commit the offence;

(7) confiscation of the items or funds which were the subject of the offence;

(8) confiscation of the proceeds or property arising out of the offence;

(9) confiscation of the utensils, materials and furnishings in the premises in which the offence was committed;

(10) confiscation of one or more vehicles belonging to the convicted person;

(11) prohibition from possessing or carrying any weapon, explosive or ammunition of any kind;

(12) closure of an establishment used to plan or to commit the offence, either permanently or for a period not exceeding five years;

(13) prohibition from operating an establishment that is open to or used by the public, either permanently or for a period not exceeding five years;

(14) publication of sentencing decision for a period not exceeding two months;

(15) publication of sentencing decision in the print media;

(16) broadcasting of sentencing decision by any audio-visual communication for a period not exceeding eight days.

Chapter 2   Offences Related to Information Technology

Article 427: unauthorized access to or remaining in automated data processing system

Fraudulently accessing or remaining within an automated data processing system shall be punishable by imprisonment from one month to one year and a fine from one hundred thousand to two million riels.

Where the act causes the destruction or modification of data contained in that system, or any alteration of the functioning of that system, the sentence is imprisonment from one to two years and a fine from two million to four million riels.

Article 428: obstructing the functioning of automated data processing system

Obstructing the functioning of an automated data processing system shall be punishable by imprisonment from one to two years and a fine from two million to four million riels.

Article 429: fraudulent introduction, deletion or modification of data

The fraudulent introduction of data into an automated data processing system or the fraudulent deletion or modification of the data that it contains shall be punishable by imprisonment from one to two years and a fine from two million to four million riels.

Article 430: participation in a group or conspiracy to commit offences

Participating in a group or a conspiracy established with a view to the planning of one or more offences defined in this section shall be punishable by imprisonment from one to two years and a fine from two million to four million riels.

Article 431: attempt

An attempt to commit the misdemeanours defined in this section shall be punishable by the same penalties.

Article 432: additional penalties (nature and duration)

The following additional penalties may be imposed in respect of the misdemeanours defined in this section:

(1) forfeiture of certain rights, either permanently or for a period not exceeding five years;

(2) prohibition from practising a profession in the practice of or in connection with which the offence was committed, either permanently or for a period not exceeding five years;

(3) confiscation of any instruments, materials or items which were used or intended to be used to commit the offence;

(4) confiscation of the items or funds which were the subject of the offence;

(5) confiscation of the proceeds or property arising out of the offence;

(6) confiscation of the utensils, materials and furnishings in the premises in which the offence was committed;

(7) confiscation of one or more vehicles belonging to the convicted person;

(8) publication of sentencing decision for a period not exceeding two months;

(9) publication of sentencing decision in the print media;

(10) broadcasting of sentencing decision by any audio-visual communication for a period not exceeding eight days.

BOOK 4

Offences Against the Nation

Title 1 Infringements Against Major Institutions of State

Chapter 1 Offences Against the King

Article 433: regicide

Regicide is the assassination of the king.

Regicide shall be punishable by life imprisonment.

Article 434: acts of torture or cruelty against the king

Acts of torture or cruelty committed against the king shall be punishable by imprisonment from ten to twenty years.

Article 435: violence against the king

Intentionally committing violence against the king shall be punishable by imprisonment from seven to fifteen years.

Article 436: aggravating circumstances (mutilation or disability)

Intentional violence committed against the king shall be punishable by imprisonment from ten to twenty years if it results in the mutilation or permanent disability of the king.

Article 437: aggravating circumstances (death of the king)

Intentional violence committed against the king shall be punishable by imprisonment from twenty to thirty years if it unintentionally caused the death of the king.

Article 438: additional penalties (nature und duration)

The following additional penalties may be imposed in respect of the offences defined in this chapter:

(1) forfeiture of certain rights, either permanently or for a period not exceeding five years;

(2) prohibition from practising a profession in the practice of or in connection with which the offence was committed, either permanently or for a period not exceeding five years;

(3) local exclusion for a period not exceeding ten years for a felony or not exceeding five years for a misdemeanour;

(4) prohibition from leaving the territory of the Kingdom of Cambodia for a period not exceeding five years;

(5) prohibition of a convicted alien from entering and remaining in the territory of the Kingdom of Cambodia, either permanently or for a period not exceeding five years:

(6) confiscation of any instruments, materials or items which were used or intended to be used to commit the offence;

(7) prohibition from possessing or carrying any weapon, explosive or ammunition of any kind, either permanently or for a period not exceeding five years;

(8) publication of sentencing decision for a period not exceeding two months;

(9) publication of sentencing decision in the print media;

(10) broadcasting of sentencing decision by any audio-visual communication for a period not exceeding eight days.

Chapter 2   Breach of State Security

Section 1   Treason and Espionage

Article 439: treason and espionage

The offences defined in this section constitute treason where they are committed by a cambodian national or a soldier in the service of Cambodia, and constitute espionage where they are committed by any other person.

Article 440: handing over to foreign state all or part of the national territory

Handing over all or part of the national territory to a foreign state or to its agents shall be punishable by life imprisonment.

Article 441: handing over to foreign state national armed forces

Handing over troops belonging to the national armed forces to a foreign state or its agents shall be punishable by life imprisonment.

Article 442: handing over to foreign state equipment assigned to national defence

Handing over food, equipment, constructions, installations or mechanical apparatus assigned to the national defence to a foreignstate or its agents shall be punishable by imprisonment from fifteen to thirty years.

Article 443: conspiracy with foreign power

Conspiracy with a foreign power is the act of having secret agreement with a foreign state or its agents, with a view to fomenting hostilities or acts of aggression against the Kingdom of Cambodia.

It shall be punishable by imprisonment from fifteen to thirty years.

Article 444: furnishing foreign state with means to foment hostilities or acts of aggression

Furnishing a foreign state or its agents with the means to foment hostilities or commit acts of aggression against the Kingdom of Cambodia shall be punishable by imprisonment from fifteen to thirty years.

Article 445: supplying foreign state with information prejudicial to national defence

Supplying or making accessible to a foreign state or its agents information, processes, objects, documents, computerised data or files which are liable to prejudice the national defence shall be punishable by imprisonment from seven to fifteen years.

Article 446: collecting information prejudicial to national defence

Receiving or collecting information, processes, objects,

documents, computerised data or files, with a view to supplying them to a foreign state or its agents which are liable to prejudice the national defence shall be punishable by imprisonment from five to ten years.

Article 447: destruction of equipment prejudicial to national defence

Destroying, defacing or misappropriating any food, document, equipment, construction, installation, mechanical apparatus, technical device, weaponry, technical spare parts or other technical support apparatus or computerised system, or rendering them defective, where this is liable to prejudice the national defence shall be punishable by imprisonment from seven to fifteen years.

Article 448: supplying false information

Supplying the Cambodian civilian or military authority with false information liable to damage the national defence in order to serve the interests of a foreign state shall be punishable by imprisonment from two to five years and a fine from four million to ten million riels.

Article 449: attempt

An attempt to commit the misdemeanours defined in article 448 (supplying false information) shall be punishable by the same penalties.

Article 450: additional penalties (nature and duration)

The following additional penalties, may be imposed in respect of the offences defined in this section:

(1) forfeiture of certain rights, either permanently or for a period not exceeding five years;

(2) prohibition from practising a profession in the practice of or in connection with which the offence was committed, either permanently or for a period not exceeding five years;

(3) local exclusion for a period not exceeding ten years for a felony or not exceeding five years for a misdemeanour;

(4) prohibition from leaving the territory of the Kingdom of Cambodia for a period not exceeding five years;

(5) prohibition of a convicted alien from entering and remaining in the territory of the Kingdom of Cambodia, either permanently or for a period not exceeding five years;

(6) confiscation of any instruments, materials or items which were used or intended to be used to commit the offence;

(7) confiscation of one or more vehicles belonging to the convicted person;

(8) prohibition from possessing or carrying any weapon, explosive or ammunition of any kind, either permanently or for a period not exceeding five years;

(9) publication of sentencing decision for a period not exceeding two months;

(10) publication of sentencing decision in the print media;

(11) broadcasting of sentencing decision by any audio-visual communication for a period not exceeding eight days.

Section 2   Attack and Plotting

Article 451 : attack

An attack consists of the commission of one or more acts of violence liable to endanger the institutions of the Kingdom of Cambodia or violate the integrity of the national territory.

It shall be punishable by imprisonment from fifteen to thirty years.

Article 452 : aggravating circumstances (status of the perpetrator)

The attack shall be punishable by life imprisonment where it was committed by a person holding public authority.

Article 453 : plotting

Plotting consists of a resolution agreed upon by two or more persons to commit an attack where the resolution was put into effect by one or more material actions.

Plotting shall be punishable by imprisonment from five to ten years.

The imprisonment penalty is increased from ten to twenty years where the offence was committed by a person holding public authority.

Article 454 : exemption from penalty

Any person who has participated in the plotting is exempted

from penalty where, before being prosecuted, he or she has informed the competent authorities of the existence of the plotting and the identification of other participants.

Article 455: additional penalties (nature and duration)

The following additional penalties may be imposed in respect of the felonies defined in this section:

(1) forfeiture of certain rights, either permanently or for a period not exceeding five years;

(2) prohibition from practising a profession in the practice of or in connection with which the offence was committed, either permanently or for a period not exceeding five years;

(3) local exclusion for a period not exceeding ten years;

(4) prohibition from leaving the territory of the Kingdom of Cambodia for a period not exceeding five years;

(5) prohibition of a convicted alien from entering and remaining in the territory of the Kingdom of Cambodia, either permanently or for a period not exceeding five years;

(6) confiscation of any instruments, materials or items which were used or intended to be used to commit the offence;

(7) confiscation of one or more vehicles belonging to the convicted person;

(8) prohibition from possessing or carrying any weapon, explosive or ammunition of any kind, either permanently or for a period not exceeding five years;

(9) publication of sentencing decision for a period not exceeding two months;

(10) publication of sentencing decision in the print media;

(11) broadcasting of sentencing decision by any audio-visual communication for a period not exceeding eight days.

Section 3   Insurrectionary Movement

Article 456: definition of insurrectionary movement

An insurrectionary movement consists of any collective violence liable to endanger the institutions of the Kingdom of Cambodia or violate the integrity of the national territory.

Article 457: applicable penalty

Participating in an insurrectionary movement:

(1) by building barricades, fortifications or by any construction whose objective is to prevent or obstruct the action of the public forces;

(2) by occupying with force or by deceit any building or installation;

(3) by destroying any building or installation;

(4) by assuring the transport or logistics supplies of the insurgents;

(5) by directly inciting the insurgents to gather;

(6) by personally holding or carrying a weapon, explosive or ammunition;

(7) by usurping a lawful authority;

Shall be punishable by imprisonment from seven to fifteen years.

Article 458: aggravating circumstances (insurrectionary movement)

Participating in an insurrectional movement:

(1) by securing weapons, ammunitions explosive or dangerous substances liable to endanger persons;

(2) by providing the insurgents with weapons, ammunitions, or explosive or dangerous substances liable to endanger persons;

Shall be punishable by imprisonment from ten to twenty years.

Article 459: leading insurrectional movement

Leading an insurrectional movement shall be punishable by imprisonment from twenty to thirty years.

Article 460: additional penalties (nature and duration)

The following additional penalties may be imposed in respect of the offences defined in this section:

(1) forfeiture of certain rights, either permanently or for a period not exceeding five years;

(2) prohibition from practising a profession in the practice of or in connection with which the offence was committed, either permanently or for a period not exceeding five years;

(3) local exclusion for a period not exceeding ten years;

(4) prohibition from leaving the territory of the Kingdom of Cambodia for a period not exceeding five years;

(5) prohibition of a convicted alien from entering and remaining in the territory of the Kingdom of Cambodia, either permanently or for a period not exceeding five years;

(6) confiscation of any instruments, materials or items which were used or intended to be used to commit the offence;

(7) confiscation of one or more vehicles belonging to the convicted person;

(8) prohibition from possessing or carrying any weapon, explosive or ammunition, either permanently or for a period not exceeding five years;

(9) publication of sentencing decision for a period not exceeding two months;

(10) publication of sentencing decision in the print media;

(11) broadcasting of sentencing decision by any audio-visual communication for a period not exceeding eight days.

Section 4 Usurpation of Command and Raising Armed Forces

Article 461: usurpation of military command

The unlawful or unauthorised assumption of any military command against orders by the lawful authorities shall be punishable by imprisonment from fifteen to thirty years.

Article 462: unlawful holding of military command

The holding of any military command against orders by the

lawful authorities shall be punishable by imprisonment from fifteen to thirty years.

Article 463: unlawful raising of armed forces

The raising of armed forces without the order or authorisation of the lawful authorities shall be punishable by imprisonment from fifteen to thirty years.

Article 464: inciting people to arms against state authority

The direct incitement of people to arms against the authority of the state shall be punishable by imprisonment from two to five years and a fine from four million to ten million riels.

Where the incitement was effective, the penalty is imprisonment from fifteen to thirty years.

Article 465: inciting people to arms against part of population

The direct incitement of people to arms against a part of the population shall be punishable by imprisonment from two to five years and a fine from four million to ten million riels.

Where the incitement was effective, the penalty is imprisonment from fifteen to thirty years.

Article 466: attempt

An attempt to commit the misdemeanours defined in this section shall be punishable by the same penalties.

Article 467: additional penalties (nature and duration)

The following additional penalties may be imposed in respect of the offences defined in this section:

(1) forfeiture of certain rights, either permanently or for a period not exceeding five years;

(2) prohibition from practising a profession in the practice of or in connection with which the offence was committed, either permanently or for a period not exceeding five years;

(3) local exclusion for a period not exceeding ten years for a felony and not exceeding five years for a misdemeanour;

(4) prohibition from leaving the territory of the Kingdom of Cambodia for a period not exceeding five years;

(5) prohibition of a convicted alien from entering and remaining in the territory of the Kingdom of Cambodia, either permanently or for a period not exceeding five years;

(6) confiscation of any instruments, materials or items which were used or intended to be used to commit the offence;

(7) confiscation of one or more vehicles belonging to the convicted person;

(8) prohibition from possessing or carrying any weapon, explosives or ammunition, either permanently or for a period not exceeding five years;

(9) publication of sentencing decision for a period not exceeding two months;

(10) publication of sentencing decision in the print media;

(11) broadcasting of sentencing decision by any audio-visual communication for a period not exceeding eight days.

Section 5 Offences Against the Security of Armed Forces

Article 468: inciting soldiers to serve foreign power

The direct incitement of soldiers belonging to the Cambodian armed forces to enter the service of a foreign power or its agents, designed to harm national defence, shall be punishable by imprisonment from five to ten years.

Article 469: obstructing normal operation of military equipment

Obstructing the normal operation of military equipment, designed to harm national defence, shall be punishable by imprisonment from two to five years and a fine from four million to ten million riels.

Article 470: obstructing the movement of military personnel or equipment

Obstructing the movement of military personnel or equipment, designed to harm national defence, shall be punishable by imprisonment from two to five years and a fine from four million to ten million riels.

Article 471: inciting military personnel to disobedience

The direct incitement to disobedience of soldiers, designed to harm national defence, shall be punishable by imprisonment from two to five years and a fine from four million to ten million riels.

Article 472: demoralization of the army

Participating in an operation to demoralise the army, designed to harm national defence, shall be punishable by imprisonment from two to five years and a fine from four million to ten million riels.

Article 473: fraudulently gaining access to military bases

Fraudulently gaining access, without the authorisation of the competent authority, to any land or building, or any facility assigned to the military authority or placed under its control shall be punishable by imprisonment from six months to one year and a fine from one million to two million riels.

Article 474: obstructing services to national defence

Any obstruction to the normal operation of the establishments or enterprises, public or private services of importance to the national defence, designed to harm national defence, shall be punishable by imprisonment from one to three years and a fine from two million to six million riels.

Article 475: attempt

An attempt to commit the misdemeanours defined in this section shall be punishable by the same penalties.

Article 476: additional penalties (nature and duration)

The following additional penalties may be imposed in respect of the offences defined in this section:

(1) forfeiture of certain rights, either permanently or for a period not exceeding five years;

(2) prohibition from practising a profession in the practice of or in connection with which the offence was committed, either permanently or for a period not exceeding five years;

(3) local exclusion for a period not exceeding ten years for a felony and not exceeding five years for a misdemeanour;

(4) prohibition from leaving the territory of the Kingdom of Cambodia for a period not exceeding five years;

(5) prohibition of a convicted alien from entering and remaining in the territory of the Kingdom of Cambodia, either permanently or for a period not exceeding five years;

(6) confiscation of any instruments, materials or items which were used or intended to be used to commit the offence;

(7) confiscation of one or more vehicles belonging to the convicted person;

(8) prohibition from possessing or carrying any weapon, explosive or ammunition, either permanently or for a period not exceeding five years;

(9) publication of sentencing decision for a period not exceeding two months;

(10) publication of sentencing decision in the print media;

(11) broadcasting of sentencing decision by any audio-visual communication for a period not exceeding eight days.

Section 6 Violation of National Defence Secrets

Article 477: principle of protection of national defence secret

Information, processes, objects, documents, and computerised data or files the disclosure of which is liable to prejudice national defence are subject to protective orders intended to restrict their circulation.

The royal government shall provide the procedure for these protective measures.

Article 478: definition of national defence secrets

The quality of national defence secrets attaches to information, processes, objects, documents, and computerised data or files the circulation of which is restricted.

Article 479: intentional or unintentional revealing of national defence secrets

A penalty of imprisonment from two to five years and a fine from four million to ten million riels shall be applicable to any person holding such a confidential information due to his or her position. Occupation or mission, who communicates to an unauthorized person any information, process, object, document, or computerised data or file which is a national defence secret.

It shall be punishable by imprisonment from six months to two years and a fine from one million to four million riels where the violation of a national defence secret occurred due to recklessness, carelessness, negligence or disobedience.

Article 480: unauthorised possession of national defence secrets

Intentionally acquiring possession of any information, process, object, document, computerised data or file which is a national defence secret by an unauthorized person shall be punishable by imprisonment from two to five years and a fine from four million to ten million riels.

Article 481: destruction or duplication of national defence secrets

Destruction or duplication of any information, process, object, document, computerised data or file which is a national defence secret shall be punishable by imprisonment from two to five years and a fine from four million to ten million riels.

Article 482: attempt

An attempt to commit the misdemeanours defined in this section shall be punishable by the same penalties.

Article 483: additional penalties (nature and duration)

The following additional penalties may be imposed in respect of the offences defined in this section:

(1) forfeiture of certain rights, either permanently or for a period not exceeding five years;

(2) prohibition from practising a profession in the practice of or in connection with which the offence was committed, either permanently or for a period not exceeding five years;

(3) publication of sentencing decision for a period not exceeding two months;

(4) publication of sentencing decision in the print media;

(5) broadcasting of sentencing decision by any audio-visual communication for a period not exceeding eight days.

Chapter 3   Violation of Public Security

Section 1   Combat Groups

Article 484: definition of combat group

"A combat group" is any group of persons having access to weapons, which has an organised hierarchy and is liable to disturb public order.

Article 485: participation in combat group

Participating in a combat group shall be punishable by imprisonment from one to three years and a fine from two million to six million riels.

Article 486: organising combat group

Organising a combat group shall be punishable by imprisonment from two to five years and a fine from four million to ten million riels.

Article 487: additional penalties (nature and duration)

The following additional penalties may be imposed in respect of the misdemeanours defined in this section:

(1) forfeiture of certain rights, either permanently or for a

period not exceeding five years;

(2) prohibition from practising a profession in the practice of or in connection with which the offence was committed, either permanently or for a period not exceeding five years;

(3) local exclusion for a period not exceeding five years;

(4) confiscation of any instruments, materials or items which were used or intended to be used to commit the offence;

(5) prohibition from possessing or carrying any weapon, explosive or ammunition, either permanently or for a period not exceeding five years;

(6) publication of sentencing decision for a period not exceeding two months;

(7) publication of sentencing decision in the print media;

(8) broadcasting of sentencing decision by any audio-visual communication for a period not exceeding eight days.

Section 2   Offences Relating to Weapons, Explosives and Ammunitions

Article 488: production or trafficking of weapons, explosives and ammunitions

The production, import or export and stocking of weapons, explosives and ammunitions of any kind without the authorization of the competent authorities shall be punishable by imprisonment from five to ten years.

Weapon refers to any gun that is produced or modified which can be used to kill or injure persons or damage property.

Ammunition and explosive refer to any equipment or material that is produced or modified which can be used to kill or injure persons or damage property.

Chemical weapon, biological weapon on other ammunitions containing chemical or biological substance refer to any substance that is produced or modified which can be used to endanger health, life or property and environment.

Article 489: production or trafficking of other assault weapons

The production, import or export and stocking of other assault weapons such as bayonets, swords, brass knuckles for killing or injuring persons, without the authorization of the competent authorities shall be punishable by imprisonment from two to five years and a fine from four million to ten million riels.

Article 490: unauthorized holding or transporting weapons

Any person, outside of his or her residence, carries or transports, without the authorization of the competent authorities, a weapon, an explosive or ammunition shall be punishable by imprisonment from six months to three years and a fine from one million to six million riels.

The same penalty shall be applicable to any person who, outside of his or her residence, carries or transports a weapon defined in article 489 (production or trafficking of other assault weapons).

Article 491: abandonment of weapon in public place

The abandonment in a public place or a place accessible to the public of a weapon or any other object that can endanger persons shall be punishable by imprisonment from six months to three years and a fine from one million to six million riels.

Article 492: additional penalties (nature and duration)

The following additional penalties may be imposed in respect of the offences defined in this section:

(1) forfeiture of certain rights, either permanently or for a period not exceeding five years;

(2) prohibition from practising a profession in the practice of or in connection with which the offence was committed, either permanently or for a period not exceeding five years;

(3) local exclusion for a period not exceeding ten years for a felony and not exceeding five years for a misdemeanour;

(4) prohibition from leaving the territory of the Kingdom of Cambodia for a period not exceeding five years;

(5) prohibition of a convicted alien from entering and remaining in the territory of the Kingdom of Cambodia, either permanently or for a period not exceeding five years;

(6) confiscation of any instruments, materials or items which were used or intended to be used to commit the offence;

(7) confiscation of one or more vehicles belonging to the convicted person;

(8) prohibition from possessing or carrying any weapon, explosive or ammunition, either permanently or for a period not exceeding five years;

(9) publication of sentencing decision for a period not exceeding two months;

(10) publication of sentencing decision in the print media;

(11) broadcasting of sentencing decision by any audio-visual communication for a period not exceeding eight days.

Article 493: confiscation of weapon abandoned in public place

For the offences defined in article 491 (abandonment of weapon in public place) of this code, a court may order confiscation of such weapon or object that can endanger persons.

Section 3   Incitement to Commit Offences

Article 494: existence of incitement

For the enforcement of this section, the incitement is punishable when it is committed:

(1) by speech of any kind, made in a public place or meeting;

(2) by writing or picture of any kind, either displayed or distributed to the public;

(3) by any audio-visual communication to the public.

Article 495: incitement to commit felony

The direct incitement to commit a felony or to disturb social security by employing one of the means defined in article 494 (existence of incitement) of this code shall be punishable by imprisonment from six months to two years and a fine from one million to four million riels, where the incitement was ineffective.

Article 496: incitement to discriminate

The direct incitement, by one of the means defined in article 494 (existence of incitement) of this code, to discriminate, to be malicious or violent against a person or a group of persons because of their membership or non-membership of a particular ethnicity, nationality, race or religion, shall be punishable by imprisonment from one to three years and a fine from two million to six million riels, where the incitement was ineffective.

Article 497: incitement through the print media

The offences defined in this section when committed through the print media are subject to the provisions of the press law.

Article 498: additional penalties (nature and duration)

The following additional penalties may be imposed in respect of the offences defined in this section:

(1) forfeiture of certain rights, either permanently or for a period not exceeding five years;

(2) prohibition from possessing or carrying any weapon, explosive or ammunition either permanently or for a period not

exceeding five years;

(3) publication of sentencing decision for a period not exceeding two months;

(4) publication of sentencing decision in the print media;

(5) broadcasting of sentencing decision by any audio-visual communication for a period not exceeding eight days.

Section 4   Criminal Association

Article 499: participation in criminal association

The participation in a group on conspiracy which is formed:

(1) to commit one or more felonies against the persons defined from Chapter 1 (homicide) to Chapter 6 (violations of personal liberty) in Title 2 (offences against the person) of Book 2 (crime against persons) of this code;

(2) to commit one or more felonies against property defined in Book 3 of this code;

Shall be punishable by imprisonment from two to five years and a fine from four million to ten million riels.

Article 500: exemption from penalty

Any person who has participated in the group or conspiracy is exempted from penalty if before any prosecution is initiated, he or she discloses the existence of the group or conspiracy to the competent authorities and enables the other participants to be identified.

Any person who has participated in the plotting is exempted from penalty where, before being prosecuted, he or she has informed the competent authorities of the existence of the plotting and the identification of other participants.

Article 501: additional penalties (nature and duration)

The following additional penalties may be imposed in respect of the misdemeanours defined in this section:

(1) forfeiture of certain rights, either permanently or for a period not exceeding five years;

(2) prohibition from practising a profession in the practice of or in connection with which the offence was committed, either permanently or for a period not exceeding five years;

(3) local exclusion for a period not exceeding five years;

(4) confiscation of any instruments, materials or items which were used or intended to be used to commit the offence;

(5) prohibition from possessing or carrying any weapon, explosive or ammunition, either permanently or for a period not exceeding five years;

(6) publication of sentencing decision for a period not exceeding two months;

(7) publication of sentencing decision in the print media;

(8) broadcasting of sentencing decision by any audio-visual communication for a period not exceeding eight days.

Chapter 4   Offences Against State Authorities

Single Section   Insult and Obstruction of Public Officials

Article 502: insult

Insult consists of words, gestures, written documents, pictures or objects liable to undermine the dignity of a person.

An insult addressed to a public official or holder of public elected office, acting in the discharge or on the occasion of his or her office shall be punishable by imprisonment from one day to six days and a fine from one thousand to one hundred thousand riels.

Article 503: obstruction of public official

Obstruction consists of violent resistance against a public official acting in the discharge of his or her office for the enforcement of laws, orders from a public authority or judicial decisions.

Obstruction of public officials shall be punishable by imprisonment from one month to three months and a fine from one hundred thousand to five hundred thousand riels.

Article 504: aggravating circumstances (obstruction of public official)

Obstruction of public officials shall be punishable by

imprisonment from six months to one year and a fine from one million to two million riels where it was committed:

(1) by several perpetrators, co-perpetrators, instigators or accomplices;

(2) by armed perpetrator.

Article 505: incitement to obstruct a public official

Direct incitement to obstruction of public officials shall be punishable by imprisonment from one day to one month and a fine from one thousand to one hundred thousand riels.

Article 506: obstruction of public works

Obstructing, by acts of violence, the execution of public works or works of public utility shall be punishable by imprisonment from one month to three months and a fine from one hundred thousand to five hundred thousand riels.

Article 507: additional penalties (nature and duration)

The following additional penalties may be imposed in respect of the offences defined in this section:

(1) prohibition from possessing or carrying any weapon, explosive or ammunition for a period not exceeding five years;

(2) publication of sentencing decision for a period not exceeding two months;

(3) publication of sentencing decision in the print media;

(4) broadcasting of sentencing decision by any audio-visual communication for a period not exceeding eight days.

Chapter 5 Offences Against State Religion

Section 1 Offences Against Buddhism

Article 508: unauthorized wearing of Buddhist robes

The unauthorized wearing of Buddhist monks' robes in public shall be punishable by imprisonment from six days to three months and a fine from one hundred thousand to five hundred thousand riels.

Article 509: theft of Buddhist sacred object

Without prejudice to the most severe penalties stipulated in this code, the theft of a Buddhist sacred object committed in a religious premise shall be punishable by imprisonment from two to five years and a fine from four million to ten million riels.

Article 510: damaging Buddhist religious premises or sacred objects

Without prejudice to the most severe penalties stipulated in this code, the intentional destruction, defacement or damage of a religious premise dedicated to Buddhism or a sacred object of this religion shall be punishable by imprisonment from two to five years and a fine from four million to ten million riels.

Article 511: attempt

An attempt to commit the misdemeanours defined in this

section shall be punishable by the same penalties.

Article 512: additional penalties (nature and duration)

The following additional penalties may be imposed in respect of the misdemeanours defined in this section:

(1) forfeiture of certain rights, either permanently or for a period not exceeding five years;

(2) prohibition from practising a profession in the practice of or in connection with which the offence was committed, either permanently or for a period not exceeding five years;

(3) prohibition from possessing or carrying any weapon, explosive or ammunition, either permanently or for a period not exceeding five years;

(4) publication of sentencing decision for a period not exceeding two months;

(5) publication of sentencing decision in the print media;

(6) broadcasting of sentencing decision by any audio-visual communication for a period not exceeding eight days.

Section 2   Offences Against Buddhist Monks, Nuns and Laymen

Sub-Section 1   Violence

Article 513: intentional violence

Intentional violence against Buddhist monks, nuns or laymen shall be punishable by imprisonment from two to five years and a fine from four million to ten million riels.

Article 514: aggravating circumstances (mutilation or disability)

Intentional violence against Buddhist monks, nuns or laymen shall be punishable by imprisonment from seven to fifteen years where it causes mutilation or permanent disability.

Article 515: aggravating circumstances (death of the victim)

Intentional violence against Buddhist monks, nuns or laymen shall be punishable by imprisonment from ten to twenty years when it unintentionally causes the death of a victim.

Sub-Section 2   Insult

Article 516: insult of Buddhist monks, nuns and laymen

When insult as defined in paragraph 1 of article 502 (insult) of this code is committed against a Buddhist monk. Nun or layman in the exercise or on the occasion of the exercise of the functions, it shall be punishable by imprisonment from one day to six days and a fine from one thousand to one hundred thousand riels.

Title 2 Infringement of Justice

Chapter 1 Offences Against Judicial Institution

Section 1 Corruption of Judges

Article 517: bribery by judges

The direct or indirect request or unlawful acceptance of a gift, offer, promise or interest by a judge:

(1) to perform an act pertaining to his or her function;

(2) to refrain from performing an act pertaining to his or her function.

Shall be punishable by imprisonment from seven to fifteen years.

Article 518: bribery of judges

The direct, indirect or unlawful giving of a gif, offer, promise or benefit to a judge with a view to obtaining from such a judge:

(1) the performance of an act pertaining to his or her function;

(2) the non-performance of an act pertaining to his or her function.

Shall be punishable by imprisonment from five to ten years.

Article 519: criminal responsibility of legal entities

Legal entities may be found criminally responsible under article 42 (criminal responsibility of legal entities) of this code for the offences defined in article 518 (bribery of judges) of this code.

Legal entities shall be punishable by a fine from ten million to fifty million riels and by one or more of the following additional penalties:

(1) dissolution pursuant to article 170 (dissolution and liquidation of legal entities) of this code;

(2) placement under judicial supervision pursuant to article 171 (placement under judicial supervision) of this code;

(3) prohibition from exercising one or more activities pursuant to article 172 (prohibition from carrying on activities) of this code;

(4) disqualification from public tenders pursuant to article 173 (disqualification from public tenders) of this code;

(5) prohibition from making a public offering pursuant to article 174 (prohibition from making a public offering) of this code;

(6) confiscation of the items or funds which were the subject of the offence pursuant to article 178 (ownership, sale and destruction of items confiscated) and article 179 (confiscation and

rights of third parties) of this code;

(7) confiscation of the proceeds or property arising out of the offence pursuant to article 178 (ownership, sale and destruction of items confiscated) and article 179 (confiscation and rights of third parties) of this code;

(8) publication of sentencing decision pursuant to article 180 (publication of decisions) of this code;

(9) publication of sentencing decision in the print media or broadcasting of sentencing decision by any audio-visual communication pursuant to article 181 (broadcasting of decision by audio-visual communication) of this code.

Section 2   Infringement of Judicial Decisions

Article 520: refusal to enforce judicial decisions

Refusal by a public official to enforce judgement, decision or order of the judicial authority in the exercise of his or her function shall be punishable by imprisonment from two to five years and a fine from four million to ten million riels.

Article 521: issuing unlawful order to detain or release

Unlawful issuance, in any form, of an order to detain or release a detainee by a public official or a holder of public elected office shall be punishable by imprisonment from two to five years and a fine from four million to ten million riels.

Article 522: publication of commentaries intended to

unlawfully coerce judicial authorities

The publication, prior to the pronouncement of a final judicial decision, of commentaries intending to put pressure on the court seised of the complaint, in order to influence its judicial decision shall be punishable by imprisonment from one month to six months and a fine from one hundred thousand to one million riels.

Article 523: discrediting judicial decisions

Criticizing a judicial letter or decision aiming at disturbing public order or endangering an institution of the Kingdom of Cambodia shall be punishable by imprisonment from one month to six months and a fine from one hundred thousand to one million riels.

Failure to enforce a judicial decision shall be punishable by the same penalties defined in paragraph 523(1) above.

Article 524: false denunciation to judicial authorities

False denunciation made to a judicial or administrative authority of a fact constituting an offence, where such denunciation leads to a frivolous investigation shall be punishable by imprisonment from one month to six months, and a fine from one hundred thousand to one million riels.

Article 525: attempt

An attempt to commit the misdemeanours defined from article 520 (refusal to enforce judicial decisions) to article 524 (false denunciation to judicial authorities) of this code shall be punishable by the same penalties.

Article 526: additional penalties (nature and duration)

The following additional penalties may be imposed in respect of the misdemeanours defined in this section:

(1) forfeiture of certain rights, either permanently or for a period not exceeding five years;

(2) prohibition from practising a profession in the practice of or in connection with which the offence was committed, either permanently or for a period not exceeding five years;

(3) confiscation of any instruments, materials or items which were used or intended to be used to commit the offence;

(4) prohibition from possessing or carrying any weapon, explosive or ammunition, either permanently or for a period not exceeding five years;

(5) publication of sentencing decision for a period not exceeding two months;

(6) publication of sentencing decision in the print media;

(7) broadcasting of sentencing decision by any audio-visual communication for a period not exceeding eight days.

Chapter 2   Offences Against Judicial Processes

Section 1   Filing of Complaints Before Courts

Article 527: intimidation in order to prevent filing of complaint

Any threat or intimidation made against a victim with a view to persuading him or her not to file a complaint or to withdraw it shall be punishable by imprisonment from one to three years, and a fine from two million to six million riels.

It shall be punishable by imprisonment from two to five years and a fine from four million to ten million riels if the act was effective.

Article 528: omission to file complaint against a felony or misdemeanour by public official

Any public official or holder of public elected office who, having knowledge of a felony or a misdemeanour through the exercise or on the occasion of his or her function, omits to inform the judicial authority or other competent authorities, shall be punishable by imprisonment from one to three years and a fine from two million to six million riels.

Article 529: omission to file complaint against a felony and exceptions

Any person who, having knowledge of a felony the consequences of which is still possible prevent or limit, omits to inform the judicial authority or other competent authorities shall be punishable by imprisonment from one month to one year and a fine from one hundred thousand to two million riels.

However, the following persons are exempted from penalty:

(1) the ascendant and descendant, and the brothers and sisters of the perpetrator, co-perpetrator, instigator or accomplice to

the felony;

(2) the spouse of the perpetrator, co-perpetrator, instigator or accomplice to the felony;

(3) persons bound by a legal obligation of professional secrecy.

Article 530: omission to file complaint against mistreatment of minor

Any person who, having knowledge of maltreatment or sexual assaults inflicted upon a minor under fifteen years of age, omits to inform the judicial authority or other competent authorities shall be punishable by imprisonment from one to three years and a fine from two million to six million riels.

Section 2 Gathering of Evidence

Article 531: concealment of corpse

The concealment or hiding of the corpse of a victim of a homicide or of a person who has died as a result of acts of violence shall be punishable by imprisonment from six months to two years and a fine from one million to four million riels.

Article 532: concealment of evidence

Modifying the scene of a felony or a misdemeanour either by the alteration, concealment or destruction of clues or marks where it is done in order to obstruct the discovery of the truth. Shall be punishable by imprisonment from one to three years and a fine from two million to six million riels.

Article 533: destruction of exhibit

Destroying, displacing or removing any given object from the scene of a felony or a misdemeanour, where it is done in order to obstruct the discovery of the truth, shall be punishable by imprisonment from one to three years and a fine from two million to six million riels.

Article 534: destruction of document

Intentionally destroying, purloining, or altering a document or an object liable to facilitate the discovery of a felony or a misdemeanour, the identification of perpetrator or his or her arrest shall be punishable by imprisonment from one to three years and a fine from two million to six million riels.

Article 535: breaking of seal

The breaking of seal affixed by the competent authority shall be punishable by imprisonment from six months to two years and a fine from one million to four million riels.

Article 536: destruction or misappropriation of object placed under seal

The destruction or misappropriation of an object placed under seal affixed by the competent authority shall be punishable by imprisonment from six months to two years and a fine from one million to four million riels.

Article 537: refusal to respond to questions

A person who, having publicly declared that he or she knows the perpetrator, co-perpetrator, instigator or accomplice of a felony or a misdemeanour, refuses to respond to questions put to him or her in this respect by a judge shall be punishable by imprisonment from one month to one year and a fine from one hundred thousand to two million riels.

Article 538: refusal to appear

Any person summoned to be heard as a witness before a prosecuting authority, an investigating judge or a criminal court, refuses to appear without proper justification shall be punishable by imprisonment from one month to six months and a fine from one hundred thousand to one million riels.

Article 539: failure to provide exculpatory evidence and exceptions

Any person who, having evidence that a charged person, an accused or a convicted person is innocent, abstains from presenting the evidence before the judicial authority or other competent authorities shall be punishable by imprisonment from one to three years and a fine from two million to six million riels

However, the following persons are exempted from penalty:

(1) the perpetrator, co-perpetrator, instigator or accomplice to the offence that led to the prosecution;

(2) the ascendant and descendant, and the brothers and

sisters of the perpetrator, co-perpetrator, instigator or accomplice;

(3) the spouse of the perpetrator, co-perpetrators, instigator or accomplice;

(4) persons bound by an obligation of professional secrecy.

Article 540: using identity of another person

Assuming the name of another person in circumstances that lead or could have led to the initiation of a criminal prosecution against such a person shall be punishable by imprisonment from one to three years and a fine from two million to six million riels.

Article 541: refusal to follow official orders

The driver of a vehicle who refuses to follow the order to stop issued by a police officer or a military police officer who, wearing a clearly visible police or military police uniform or emblem, is in search for evidence shall be punishable by imprisonment from six days to three months and a fine from ten thousand to five hundred thousand riels.

Article 542: refusal by driver to be examined

The driver of a vehicle who refuses to have himself or herself or his or her vehicle examined by a police officer or a military police officer who, wearing a clearly visible police or military police uniform or emblem, is in search for evidence shall be punishable by imprisonment from six days to three months and a fine from ten thousand to five hundred thousand riels.

Article 543: evasion

The driver of a terrestrial vehicle, or a maritime craft who, knowing that he or she has just caused an accident or damage, fails to stop and thereby attempts to evade any civil or criminal liability, shall be punishable by imprisonment from six months to two years and a fine from one million to four million riels.

Article 544: providing assistance to perpetrator and exceptions

Providing the perpetrator, co-perpetrator, instigator or accomplice to a felony with:

(1) accommodation;

(2) a hiding-place;

(3) the means of existence; or

(4) any other means of evading a search or an arrest.

Shall be punishable by imprisonment from one to three years and a fine from two million to six million riels.

However, the following persons are exempted from penalty:

(1) the ascendant and descendant, and the brothers and sisters of the perpetrator co-perpetrator, instigator or accomplice to the felony;

(2) the spouse of the perpetrator, co-perpetrator, instigator or accomplice to the felony.

Article 545: providing false testimony and exceptions

False testimony made under oath before any court of law or before a judicial police officer acting under the authority of a rogatory letter shall be punishable by imprisonment from two to five years and a fine from four million to ten million riels.

However, such witness is exempted from penalty where he or she retracts his or her testimony spontaneously and only speaks the truth before the decision terminating the investigating or trial procedure has been made.

Article 546: intimidating witness

Any act of intimidation committed by a perpetrator alone or in concert with a third party to persuade a witness not to make a statement or to provide a false oral or written testimony shall be punishable by imprisonment from two to five years and a fine from four million to ten million riels.

It shall be punishable by imprisonment from five to ten years where the act was effective.

Article 547: bribery by witness to provide false testimony

The direct or indirect request or acceptance of a gift, offer, promise or interest by a witness in order:

(1) not to testify;

(2) to provide a false testimony;

Shall be punishable by imprisonment from five to ten years.

Article 548: bribery of witness

The direct or indirect giving of a gift, offer, promise or interest by a person to a witness in order:

(1) not to testify;

(2) to provide a false testimony;

Shall be punishable by imprisonment from five to ten years.

Article 549: coerced publication intended to influence witness

The coerced publication, prior to the pronouncement of the final judicial decision, of commentaries intended to influence the statement of a witness shall be punishable by imprisonment from six days to one month and a fine from ten thousand to one hundred thousand riels.

Section 3 Interpretation/Translation and Expert Reports

Article 550: misrepresentation by interpreter

The intentional misrepresentation of the substance of the translated words or documents committed by an interpreter/translator shall be punishable by imprisonment from two to five years and a fine from four million to ten million riels.

Article 551: falsification by expert

The falsification of any data or findings by an expert in his or her written report or oral presentation shall be punishable by imprisonment from two to five years and a fine from four million to ten million riels.

Article 552: intimidating expert or interpreter/translator

Intimidating an expert or an interpreter/translator in order to influence his or her conduct in exercising his or her function shall be punishable by imprisonment from two to five years and a fine from four million to ten million riels.

It shall be punishable by imprisonment from five to ten years where the act was effective.

Article 553: bribery by interpreter/translator

The direct or indirect request or acceptance of a gift, offer, promise or interest by an interpreter/translator in order to misrepresent the substance of the translated words or documents shall be punishable by imprisonment from five to ten years.

Article 554: bribery of interpreter/translator

The direct or indirect giving of a gift, offer, promise or interest by a person to an interpreter/translator in order to misrepresent the substance of the translated words or documents shall be punishable by imprisonment from five to ten years.

Article 555: bribery by expert

The direct or indirect request or acceptance of a gift, offer, promise or interest by an expert in order to falsify any data or findings in his or her written report or oral presentation shall be punishable by imprisonment from five to ten years.

Article 556: bribery of expert

The direct or indirect giving of a gift, offer, promise or interest by a person to an expert in order to falsify any data or findings in his or her written report or oral presentation shall be punishable by imprisonment from five to ten years.

Section 4 Attempt and Additional Penalties

Article 557: attempt

An attempt to commit the misdemeanours defined in article 527 (intimidation in order to prevent filing of complaint), article 531 (concealment of corpse), article 536 (destruction or misappropriation of object placed under seal), article 540 (using identity of another person) and article 544 (providing assistance to perpetrator and exceptions) of this code shall be punishable by the same penalties.

Article 558: additional penalties (nature and duration)

The following additional penalties may be imposed in respect of the offences defined in this chapter:

(1) forfeiture of certain rights, either permanently or for a period not exceeding five years;

(2) prohibition from practising a profession in the practice of or in connection with which the offence was committed, either permanently or for a period not exceeding five years;

(3) local exclusion for a period not exceeding ten years for a felony and not exceeding five years for a misdemeanour;

(4) confiscation of any instruments, materials or items which were used or intended to be used to commit the offence;

(5) confiscation of the objects or funds which is the subject of the offence;

(6) confiscation of the proceeds or property arising out of the offence;

(7) confiscation of one or more vehicles belonging to the convicted person;

(8) prohibition from possessing or carrying any weapon, explosive or ammunition, either permanently or for a period not exceeding five years;

(9) publication of sentencing decision for a period not exceeding two months;

(10) publication of sentencing decision in the print media;

(11) broadcasting of sentencing decision by any audio-visual communication for a period not exceeding eight days.

Article 559: criminal responsibility of legal entities

Legal entities may be found criminally responsible under article 42 (criminal responsibility of legal entities) for offences defined in article 548 (bribery of witness) article 554 (bribery of interpreter/translator) and article 556 (bribery of expert) of this code.

Legal entities shall be punishable by a fine from twenty million to two hundred million riels and by one or more of the following additional penalties:

(1) dissolution pursuant to article 170 (dissolution and liquidation of legal entities) of this code;

(2) placement under judicial supervision pursuant to article 171 (placement under judicial supervision) of this code;

(3) prohibition from exercising one or more activities pursuant to article 172 (prohibition from carrying on activities) of this code;

(4) disqualification from public tenders pursuant to article 173 (disqualification from public tenders) of this code;

(5) prohibition from making a public offering pursuant to article 174 (prohibition from making a public offering) of this code;

(6) confiscation of the items or funds which were the subject of the offence pursuant to article 178 (ownership, sale and destruction of items confiscated) and article 179 (confiscation and rights of third parties) of this code;

(7) confiscation of the proceeds or property arising out of the offence pursuant to article 178 (ownership, sale and destruction of items confiscated) and article 179 (confiscation and rights of third parties) of this code;

(8) publication of sentencing decision pursuant to article 180 (publication of decisions) of this code;

(9) publication of sentencing decision in the print media or broadcasting of sentencing decision by any audio-visual communication pursuant to article 181 (broadcasting of decision by audio-visual communication) of this code.

Chapter 3   Offences Related to Detention

Section 1   Escape

Article 560: definition of escape

"Escape" occurs when a detainee absconds from custody by any means.

It also constitutes an escape when the above means is committed by a third party.

A person is considered a detainee when he or she:

(1) is in custody;

(2) is about to be or is being brought before a judicial authority at the end of the custody or pursuant to an order to bring or an arrest warrant;

(3) has been served a detention order or an arrest warrant;

(4) is serving a prison sentence or who has been arrested to serve that sentence;

(5) is placed in custody pending extradition;

(6) is placed on day release under article 127 (a vailability of day release) of this code.

Article 561: applicable penalty

Escape shall be punishable by imprisonment from one to three years and a fine from two million to six million riels.

Article 562: acts amounting to escape

The following are deemed to be an escape and shall be punishable by the same penalties:

(1) a detainee placed in a hospital or health institution, or other places such as a court, police or military police office, absconds from supervision;

(2) a convicted person fails to return to the penitentiary at the end of a period of day release, suspended sentence or instalment arrangement, or permission to leave the penitentiary.

Section 2 Aggravating Circumstances in Connection with Escape and Facilitation of Escape

Article 563: intimidation by weapon or by concerted activity

Escape shall be punishable by imprisonment from two to five years and a fine from four million to ten million riels, if it is committed under any of the following circumstances:

(1) with the threat to use a weapon or an explosive; or

(2) by several detainees in a concerted activity.

Article 564: use of weapon

Escape shall be punishable by imprisonment from five to ten years where a weapon or an explosive was used.

Article 565: procuring means of escape

Any person who facilitates or procures a detainee with any means of absconding from custody shall be punishable by imprisonment from one to three years and a fine from two million to six million riels.

Article 566: aggravating circumstances (procuring means of escape)

Supplying a detainee with a weapon, an explosive, incendiary substance, toxic substance or acid to be used as means of escape or to facilitate an escape shall be punishable by imprisonment from two to five years and a fine from four million to ten million riels.

Article 567: facilitation of escape by supervisor

Any person exercising the supervision of a detainee who facilitates or plans his or her escape, even by deliberate omission, shall be punishable by imprisonment from five to ten years.

Article 568: aggravating circumstances (facilitation of escape by supervisor)

Any person exercising the supervision of a detainee who supplies him or her with a weapon, an explosive, incendiary substance, toxic substance or acid to be used as means of escape or to facilitate an escape shall be punishable by imprisonment from seven to fifteen years.

Article 569: facilitation of escape (persons authorized to enter prison)

Any person authorized by his or her position to enter a prison who facilitates or plans a detainee to escape, even by deliberate omission, shall be punishable by imprisonment from five to ten years.

Article 570: aggravating circumstances (facilitation of escape by persons authorized to enter prison)

Any person authorized by his or her position to enter a prison who supplies a detainee with a weapon, an explosive, incendiary substance, toxic substance or acid to be used as means of escape or to facilitate an escape shall be punishable by imprisonment from seven to fifteen years.

Section 3　Unlawful Delivery of Money and Items to Detainees

Article 571: unlawful delivery and aggravating circumstances

Any person who delivers or sends to a detainee any money, correspondence, item or substance other than those permitted by the regulations shall be punishable by imprisonment from one month to one year and a fine from one hundred thousand to two million riels.

The offences above shall be punishable by imprisonment from one to two years and a fine from two million to four million riels if they are committed:

(1) by a person exercising the supervision of a detainee;

(2) by a person authorized by his or her position to enter a prison.

Article 572: unlawful receiving and aggravating circumstances

Any person who receives from a detainee any money, correspondence, item or substance other than those permitted by the regulations shall be punishable by imprisonment from one month to one year and a fine from one hundred thousand to two million riels.

The offences above shall be punishable by imprisonment from one to two years and a fine from two million to four million riels if they are committed:

(1) by a person exercising the supervision of a detainee;

(2) by a person authorized by his or her position to enter a prison.

Section 4 Attempt and Penalties

Article 573: attempt

An attempt to commit the misdemeanours defined in this chapter shall be punishable by the same penalties.

Article 574: exemption from penalty

Any person who has attempted to commit, either as perpetrator, co-perpetrator, instigator or accomplice, any of the offences defined in article 561 (applicable penalty) and from article 563 (intimidation by weapon or by concerted activity) to article 570 aggravating circumstances (facilitation of escape by persons authorized to enter prison) of this code shall be exempted from penalty if, after informing the judicial or administrative authorities, the escape was prevented.

Article 575: additional penalties (nature and duration)

The following additional penalties may be imposed in respect of the offences defined in this chapter:

(1) forfeiture of certain rights, either permanently or for a period not exceeding five years;

(2) prohibition from practising a profession in the practice of or in connection with which the offence was committed, either permanently or for a period not exceeding five years;

(3) local exclusion for a period not exceeding ten years for a felony and not exceeding five years for a misdemeanor;

(4) confiscation of any instruments, materials or items which were used or intended to be used to commit the offence;

(5) confiscation of the objects or funds which is the subject of the offence;

(6) confiscation of the proceeds or property arising out of the offence;

(7) confiscation of one or more vehicles belonging to the convicted person;

(8) prohibition from possessing or carrying any weapon, explosive or ammunition, either permanently or for a period not exceeding five years;

(9) publication of sentencing decision for a period not exceeding two months;

(10) publication of sentencing decision in the print media;

(11) broadcasting of sentencing decision by any audio-visual communication for a period not exceeding eight days.

Chapter 4   Breach of Certain Judicial Decisions

Article 576: breach of local exclusion

The appearance in a prohibited place prescribed by a judicial authority by any person subject to local exclusion shall be punishable by imprisonment from one to two years and a fine from two million to four million riels.

Article 577: failure to respect supervision measures

Any person subject to local exclusion who evades any supervision measure prescribed by a judicial authority shall be punishable by imprisonment from one to two years and a fine from two million to four million riels.

Article 578: violation of publication of sentencing decision

Where a judgement has ordered as a penalty the publication of sentencing decision, the destruction, concealing or tearing of such publication shall be punishable by imprisonment from one month to six months and a fine from one hundred thousand to one million riels.

Article 579: violation of prohibition to practice profession

Where a prohibition to practice a profession has been ordered as a penalty by a judicial authority, any violation of the prohibition shall be punishable by imprisonment from one to two years and a fine from two million to four million riels.

Article 580: violation of penalty to forfeit certain rights

Any breach by the convicted person of any obligations or prohibitions arising from suspension of a driving license, the prohibition to possess or to carry a weapon, explosive or ammunition, the prohibition to issue cheques, the closure of premises or the disqualification from public tenders shall be punishable by imprisonment from one to two years and a fine from two million to four million riels.

Article 581: failure to adhere to confiscation orders

The destruction, concealment or misappropriation of confiscated items shall be punishable by imprisonment from one to two years and a fine from two million to four million riels.

Article 582: refusal to surrender driving license

Refusal to surrender to the competent authorities a suspended driving license or a confiscated item by failing to comply with a judicial decision in force shall be punishable by imprisonment from one to two years and a fine from two million to four million riels.

Article 583: breach of community service obligation

Breach by the convicted person of the obligations derived from community service imposed shall be punishable by imprisonment from one to two years and a fine from two million to four million riels.

Article 584: breach of obligations imposed upon legal entity

Where obligations or prohibitions have been imposed upon a

legal person, breach by a natural person of such obligations or prohibitions shall be punishable by imprisonment from one to two years and a fine from two million to four million riels.

Article 585: additional penalties (nature and duration)

The following additional penalties may be imposed in respect of the misdemeanours defined in this chapter:

(1) forfeiture of certain rights, either permanently or for a period not exceeding five years;

(2) publication of sentencing decision for a period not exceeding two months;

(3) publication of sentencing decision in the print media;

(4) broadcasting of sentencing decision by any audio-visual communication for a period not exceeding eight days.

Title 3 Infringement of The Functioning of Public Administration

Chapter 1 Infringement of Public Administration by Representative of Public Authorities

Section 1 Dereliction of Duties

Sub-Section 1 Abuse of Power

Article 586: measures to obstruct law enforcement and aggravating circumstances

The taking of measures designed to obstruct law enforcement, committed by a public official or a holder of public elected office, in the discharge or on the occasion of his or her function, shall be punishable by imprisonment from two to five years and a fine from four million to ten million riels.

It shall be punishable by imprisonment from five to ten years where the act was effective.

Article 587: unlawful continuation of functions

The continued exercise of an office by a public official or a holder of public elected office, after having been officially informed of the decision terminating his or her functions, shall be punishable by imprisonment from six months to two years and a fine from one million to four million riels.

Sub-Section 2 Abuse of Power Against Individuals

Article 588: infringement of personal freedom

The arbitrary act of violation of personal freedom committed by a public official or a holder of public elected office, acting in the exercise or on the occasion of his or her function, shall be punishable by imprisonment from two to five years and a fine from four million to ten million riels.

Article 589: refusal to release unlawfully detained person

The unlawful deprivation of liberty, the wilful failure either to put an end to such deprivation when he or she has the power, or the wilful failure to bring about the intervention of a competent authority, by a public official or a holder of public elected office who has knowledge of such deprivation in the course of or on the occasion of his or her function, shall be punishable by imprisonment from one to three years and a fine from two million to six million riels.

Article 590: unlawful detention or release

The reception or retention of a person by an agent of the prison administration, without a warrant, a judgement, a detention order or a release order drafted in conformity with the law shall be punishable by imprisonment from two to five years and a fine from four million to ten million riels.

Article 591: prolongation of unlawful detention

The unlawful prolongation of detention of a person by an agent of the prison administration shall be punishable by imprisonment from two to five years and a fine from four million to ten million riels.

Section 2   Corruption and Related Offences

Sub-Section 1   Misappropriation of Public Funds

Article 592: definition of misappropriation of public funds

The misappropriation of public funds is an act committed by a public official or a holder of public elected office:

(1) to demand or receive as entitlements duties or taxes of any sum known not to be due, or known to exceed the due amount;

(2) to grant, in any form and for any reason, any exoneration or exemption from duties or taxes in breach of law.

Article 593: applicable penalty

Misappropriation of public funds shall be punishable by imprisonment from two to five years and a fine from four million to ten million riels.

Sub-Section 2   Acceptance of Bribery

Article 594: acceptance of bribery

The direct or indirect request for or acceptance of gifts, offers, promises or interests, without authorization, by a public official or a holder of public elected office shall be punishable by imprisonment from seven to fifteen years where it is committed:

(1) perform an act related to or facilitated by his or her function;

(2) to refrain from performing an act related to or facilitated by his or her function.

Sub-Section 3 Passive Trading in Influence

Article 595: definition of passive trading in influence

"Passive trading in influence" is the act committed by a public official or a holder of public elected office to directly or indirectly request or accept, without authorization, gifts, offers, promises or interests so that such a person may unlawfully use his or her real or supposed influence with a view to obtaining public tenders emblem or any other favourable decision from a state institution.

Article 596: applicable penalty

Passive trading in influence shall be punishable by imprisonment from five to ten years.

Sub-Section 4 Unlawful Exploitation

Article 597: definition of unlawful exploitation

"Unlawful exploitation" is the act committed, either directly or indirectly, by a public official or a holder of public elected office to take, receive or keep any interest in:

(1) an enterprise by such a public official or a holder of public elected office who has the duty of ensuring, in whole or in part, its supervision, management or liquidation;

(2) an operation by such a public official or a holder of public elected office who has the duty of ensuring, in whole or in part, its supervision or liquidation.

Article 598: applicable penalty

Unlawful exploitation shall be punishable by imprisonment from two to five years and a fine from four million to ten million riels.

Sub-section 5 Favouritism

Article 599: definition of favouritism

"Favouritism" is the act committed by a public official or a holder of public elected office to obtain for others an unlawful advantage in respect of public tenders.

Article 600: applicable penalty

Favouritism shall be punishable by imprisonment from six months to two years and a fine from one million to four million riels.

Section 3 Destruction and Embezzlement

Article 601: intentional destruction and embezzlement

The intentional destruction or embezzlement of a document or security, of private or public funds, or of any other item entrusted to him or her, committed by a public official or a holder of public elected office shall be punishable by imprisonment from five to ten years.

Article 602: unintentional destruction or loss

The unintentional destruction or loss of a document or security, of private or public funds, or of any other item entrusted to him or her, committed by a public official or a holder of public elected office shall be punishable by imprisonment from one month to six months and a fine from one hundred thousand to one million riels.

Section 4   Attempt and Penalties

Article 603: attempt

An attempt to commit the misdemeanours defined in this chapter shall be punishable by the same penalties, except for the misdemeanours defined in article 589 (refusal to release unlawfully detained person) and article 602 (unintentional destruction or loss) of this code.

Article 604: additional penalties (nature and duration)

The following additional penalties may be imposed in respect of the offences defined in this chapter:

(1) forfeiture of certain rights, either permanently or for a period not exceeding five years;

(2) prohibition from practising a profession in the practice of or in connection with which the offence was committed, either permanently or for a period not exceeding five years;

(3) confiscation of any instruments, materials or items which were used or intended to be used to commit the offence;

(4) confiscation of the objects or funds which is the subject of the offence;

(5) confiscation of the proceeds or property arising out of the offence;

(6) confiscation of one or more vehicles belonging to the convicted person;

(7) prohibition from possessing or carrying any weapon, explosive or ammunition, either permanently or for a period not exceeding five years;

(8) publication of sentencing decision for a period not exceeding two months;

(9) publication of sentencing decision in the print media;

(10) broadcasting of sentencing decision by any audio-visual communication for a period not exceeding eight days.

Chapter 2 Offences Against Public Administration by Individuals

Section 1 Corruption and Related Offences

Sub-Section 1 Proffering of Bribes

Article 605: proffering of bribes

Unlawfully proffering, directly or indirectly, any gift, offer, promise or interest, in order to induce a public official or a holder of public elected office:

(1) to perform an act pertaining to or facilitated by his or her function;

(2) to refrain from performing an act pertaining to or facilitated by his or her function.

Shall be punishable by imprisonment from five to ten years.

Sub-Section 2   Active Trading in Influence

Article 606: active trading in influence

Unlawfully proffering, directly or indirectly, any gift, offer, promise or interest, in order to induce a public official or a holder of public elected office so that such a person may unlawfully use his or her real or supposed influence with a view to obtaining public tenders, emblem or any other favourable decision from a state institution shall be punishable by imprisonment from two to five years and a fine from four million to ten million riels.

Sub-Section 3   Intimidation

Article 607: intimidation

Intimidating a public official or a holder of public elected office:

(1) to perform an act pertaining to his or her function;

(2) to refrain from performing an act pertaining to his or her function;

(3) to use his or her real or supposed influence with a view to

obtaining public tenders, emblem or any other favourable decision.

Shall be punishable by imprisonment from two to five years and a fine from four million to ten million riels.

Section 2 Destruction and Embezzlement

Article 608: destruction and embezzlement

The destruction, embezzlement or purloining of a document or security, of private or public funds, or of any other item entrusted to a public official or a holder of public elected office, by reason of his or her function, shall be punishable by imprisonment from two to five years and a fine from four million to ten million riels.

Section 3 Interference in Public Functions and Official

Article 609: unlawful interference in the discharge of public functions

Any person acting without authority who interferes in the discharge of a public function by performing an act reserved for the holder of this office shall be punishable by imprisonment from one to three years and a fine from two million to six million riels.

Article 610: activities causing misapprehension with the discharge of public functions

Any person who conducts an activity in conditions liable to cause in the mind of the public a misapprehension with the discharge of a public function shall be punishable by imprisonment from one month to one year and a fine from one hundred thousand to two million riels.

Article 611: use of letter or document causing misapprehension

Any person who uses letters or written documents presenting a similarity to judicial documents or to administrative documents, liable to cause misapprehension in the mind of the public shall be punishable by imprisonment from one month to one year and a fine from one hundred thousand to two million riels.

Article 612: unlawful use of costume designated for public authority

Any person who, without authorization, wears in public a costume, uniform or decoration designated for a public authority shall be punishable by imprisonment from one month to one year and a fine from one hundred thousand to two million riels.

Article 613: unlawful use of certificate of profession

Any person who, without authorization, publicly uses a document certifying a profession regulated by the public authority shall be punishable by imprisonment from one month to one year and a fine from one hundred thousand to two million riels.

Article 614: unauthorized use of emblem regulated by public authority

Any person who, without authorization, publicly uses an emblem regulated by the public authority shall be punishable by imprisonment from one month to one year and a fine from one hundred thousand to two million riels.

Article 615: unauthorized use of vehicle with emblem used by police or military

Any person who, without authorization, uses a vehicle displaying an outwardly visible emblem used by the police or the military shall be punishable by imprisonment from one month to one year and a fine from one hundred thousand to two million riels.

Article 616: use of uniform similar to police or military uniform

Any person who, without authorization, wears in public a costume, uniform, identity card, badge or vehicle which bears a resemblance to the costumes, uniforms, identity cards, badges or vehicles reserved for the police or the military, thus liable to cause misapprehension in the mind of the public shall be punishable by imprisonment from one month to six months and a fine from one hundred thousand to one million riels.

Article 617: aggravating circumstances (planning of felony or misdemeanour)

The offences defined in article 611 (use of letter or document causing misapprehension) to article 616 (use of uniform similar to police or military uniform) shall be punishable by imprisonment from one to three years and a fine from two million to six million riels where their intent is to plan or facilitate the commission of a felony or a misdemeanour.

Article 618: unauthorized use of official certificate of

profession regulated by public authority

The unauthorized use of an official certificate of a profession regulated by the public authority shall be punishable by imprisonment from one month to one year and a fine from one hundred thousand to two million riels.

Article 619: unauthorized use of diploma

The unauthorized use of a diploma or qualification of which the conditions of attribution are fixed by the public authority shall be punishable by imprisonment from one month to one year and a fine from one hundred thousand to two million riels.

Article 620: irregular use of title

A penalty of imprisonment from one month to one year and a fine from one hundred thousand to two million riels shall be imposed on the manager of an enterprise, who makes available or maintains in an enterprise's public advertisement in the interest of that enterprise, the name and title of a member or a former member of the royal government, the assembly, the senate, or of a judge or a former judge.

Article 621: use of identity different from official identity in public affairs

The use of an identity other than the official identity in a public document or in a document to be submitted to the public authority shall be punishable by imprisonment from one month to six months and a fine from one hundred thousand to one million riels.

Section 4   Shifting Boundary Posts

Article 622: shifting boundary post

Removing or shifting a boundary post erected by the public authority shall be punishable by imprisonment from one month to one year and a fine from one hundred thousand to two million riels.

Section 5   Attempt and Penalties

Article 623: attempt

An attempt to commit the misdemeanours defined in this chapter shall be punishable by the same penalties.

Article 624: additional penalties (nature and duration)

The following additional penalties may be imposed in respect of the offences defined in this chapter:

(1) forfeiture of certain rights either permanently or for a period not exceeding five years;

(2) prohibition from practising a profession in the practice of or in connection with which the offence was committed, either permanently or for a period not exceeding five years;

(3) confiscation of any instruments, materials or items which were used or intended to be used to commit the offence;

(4) confiscation of the objects or funds which is the subject of the offence;

(5) confiscation of the proceeds or property arising out of the

offence;

(6) confiscation of one or more vehicles belonging to the convicted person;

(7) prohibition from possessing or carrying any weapon, explosive or ammunition, either permanently or for a period not exceeding five years;

(8) publication of sentencing decision for a period not exceeding two months;

(9) publication of sentencing decision in the print media;

(10) broadcasting of sentencing decision by any audio-visual communication for a period not exceeding eight days.

Article 625: criminal responsibility of legal entities

Legal entities may be found criminally responsible under article 42 (criminal responsibility of legal entities) of this code for the offences defined in article 605 (proffering of bribes), article 606 (active trading in influence) and article 607 (intimidation) of this code.

Legal entities shall be punishable by a fine from ten million to fifty million riels and by one or more of the following additional penalties:

(1) dissolution pursuant to article 170 (dissolution and liquidation of legal entities) of this code;

(2) placement under judicial supervision pursuant to article 171 (placement under judicial supervision) of this code;

(3) prohibition from exercising one or mor activities pursuant to article 172 (prohibition from carrying on activities) of this code;

(4) disqualification from public tenders pursuant to article 173 (disqualification from public tenders) of this code;

(5) prohibition from making a public offering pursuant to article 174 (prohibition from making a public offering) of this code;

(6) confiscation of the items or funds which were the subject of the offence pursuant to article 178 (ownership, sale and destruction of items confiscated) and article 179 (confiscation and rights of third parties) of this code;

(7) confiscation of the proceeds or property arising out of the offence pursuant to article 178 (ownership, sale and destruction of items confiscated) and article 179 (confiscation and rights of third parties) of this code;

(8) publication of sentencing decision pursuant to article 180 (publication of decisions) of this code;

(9) publication of sentencing decision in the print media or broadcasting of sentencing decision by any audio-visual communication pursuant to article 181 (broadcasting of decision by audio-visual communication) of this code.

Title 4   Infringement of Public Confidence

Chapter 1   Forgery

Section 1   Forgery of Documents

Article 626: definition of forgery

Forgery consists of any fraudulent alteration of the truth, liable to cause harm and made by any means in a document or other medium of expression when all the following conditions are satisfied:

(1) where the forgery is intended or its effect is to provide evidence of a right or of an act carrying legal consequences;

(2) where the harm may cause damage.

Article 627: applicable penalty

Forgery shall be punishable by imprisonment from one to three years and a fine from two million to six million riels.

Article 628: use of forged document

The use of forged documents shall be punishable by imprisonment from one to three years and a fine from two million to six million riels.

Article 629: forgery of public document

Forgery committed in an authenticated document or a document issued by a public body for the purpose of establishing a right, an identity or a capacity, or to grant an authorisation shall be punishable by imprisonment from five to ten years.

Article 630: use of forged public document

The use of a forgery defined in article 629 (forgery of public document) of this code shall be punishable by imprisonment from two to five years and a fine from four million to ten million riels.

Article 631: fraudulent delivery of document

Fraudulently procuring for another person a document issued by a public body for the purpose of establishing a right, an identity or a capacity, or the grant of an authorisation shall be punishable by imprisonment from two to five years and a fine from four million to ten million riels.

Article 632: fraudulent request for document

Fraudulently obtaining from a public body any document intended to establish a right an identity or a capacity, or to grant an authorisation shall be punishable by imprisonment from six months to two years and a fine from one million to four million riels.

Article 633: false declaration

Providing a false declaration to a public body for the purpose of obtaining an allowance, a payment or any unlawful advantage shall be punishable by imprisonment from six months to two years and a fine from one million to four million riels.

Article 634: delivery of forged document

Except for the provisions defined in this section, making an attestation or a certificate stating facts that are materially inaccurate shall be punishable by imprisonment from one month to one year and a fine from one hundred thousand to two million riels.

Article 635: forging attestation

Forging an attestation or a certificate shall be punishable by imprisonment from one month to one year and a fine from one hundred thousand to two million riels.

Article 636: use of falsified or forged attestation

The use of a falsified or forged attestation or certificate shall be punishable by imprisonment from one month to one year and a fine from one hundred thousand to two million riels.

Article 637: bribery by authorized person to issue falsified attestation

Any person who, acting in the exercise of his or her profession, requests or accepts offers, gifts, promises or interests of any kind to produce an attestation or a certificate stating facts that are materially inaccurate shall be punishable by imprisonment from two to five years and a fine from four million to ten million riels.

Article 638: bribery of authorized person to issue falsified attestation

Any person who makes offers, gifts, promises or interests of any kind to another person to produce an attestation or a certificate stating facts that are materially inaccurate shall be punishable by imprisonment from one to three years and a fine from two million to six million riels.

Article 639: bribery by member of board of medical practitioners to issue falsified attestation

Any medical practitioner or member of the board of medical

practitioners who requests or accepts offers, gifts, promises or interests of any kind to produce an attestation or a certificate stating facts that are materially inaccurate shall be punishable by imprisonment from two to five years and a fine from four million to ten million riels.

Article 640: bribery of member of board of medical practitioners to issue falsified attestation

Any person who makes offers, gifts, promises or interests of any kind to a medical practitioner or member of the board of medical practitioners to produce an attestation or a certificate stating facts that are materially inaccurate shall be punishable by imprisonment from one to three years and a fine from two million to six million riels.

Article 641: application of misdemeanour in article 639 and article 640 for all medical professions

The provisions of article 639 (bribery by member of board of medical practitioners to issue falsified attestation) and article 640 (bribery of member of board of medical practitioners to issue falsified attestation) of this code are applicable to all medical practitioners.

Article 642: attempt

An attempt to commit the misdemeanours defined in article 632 (fraudulent request for document), article 638 (bribery of authorized person to issue falsified attestation) and article 640 (bribery of member of board of medical practitioners to issue falsified attestation) of this code shall be punishable by the same penalties.

Article 643: additional penalties (nature and duration)

The following additional penalties may be imposed in respect of the offences defined in this section:

(1) forfeiture of certain rights, either permanently or for a period not exceeding five years;

(2) prohibition from practising a professor in the practice of or in connection with which the offence was committed, either permanently or for a period not exceeding five years;

(3) local exclusion for a period not exceeding ten years for a felony and not exceeding five years for a misdemeanour;

(4) confiscation of any instruments, materials or items which were used or intended to be used to commit the offence;

(5) confiscation of the objects or funds which is the subject of the offence;

(6) confiscation of the proceeds or property arising out of the offence;

(7) confiscation of one or more vehicles belonging to the convicted person;

(8) publication of sentencing decision for a period not exceeding two months;

(9) publication of sentencing decision in the print media;

(10) broadcasting of sentencing decision by any audio-visual communication for a period not exceeding eight days.

Article 644: criminal responsibility of legal entities

Legal entities may be found criminally responsible under article 42 (criminal responsibility of legal entities) for the offences defined in article 638 (bribery of authorized person to issue falsified attestation) and article 640 (bribery of member of board of medical practitioners to issue falsified attestation) of this code.

Legal entities shall be punishable by a fine from ten million to one hundred million riels and by one or more of the following additional penalties:

(1) dissolution pursuant to article 170 (dissolution and liquidation of legal entities) of this code;

(2) placement under judicial supervision pursuant to article 171 (placement under judicial supervision) of this code;

(3) prohibition from exercising one or more activities pursuant to article 172 (prohibition from carrying on activities) of this code;

(4) disqualification from public tenders pursuant to article 173 (disqualification from public tenders) of this code;

(5) prohibition from making a public offering pursuant to article 174 (prohibition from making a public offering) of this code;

(6) confiscation of the items or funds which were the subject of the offence pursuant to article 178 (ownership, sale and destruction of items confiscated) and article 179 (confiscation and rights of third parties) of this code;

(7) confiscation of the proceeds or property arising out of the offence pursuant to article 178 (ownership, sale and destruction of items confiscated) and article 179 (confiscation and rights of third parties) of this code;

(8) publication of sentencing decision pursuant to article 180

(publication of decisions) of this code;

(9) publication of sentencing decision in the print media or broadcasting of sentencing decision by any audio-visual communication pursuant to article 181 (broadcasting of decision by audio-visual communication) of this code.

Section 2 Counterfeit Currency and Banknotes

Article 645: counterfeiting currency being legal tender

The counterfeiting of banknotes or coins being legal tender in the Kingdom of Cambodia shall be punishable by imprisonment from fifteen to thirty years or by life imprisonment.

Article 646: counterfeiting banknotes being legal tender

The counterfeiting of banknotes being legal tender issued by authorized international or foreign institutions shall be punishable by imprisonment from ten to twenty years.

Article 647: circulating counterfeit currency and banknotes

Circulation of counterfeit currency or banknotes as defined in article 645 (counterfeiting currency being legal tender) and article 646 (counterfeiting banknotes being legal tender) shall be punishable by imprisonment from five to ten years.

Where the offence was committed by an organised criminal enterprise, it shall be punishable by imprisonment from ten to twenty years.

Article 648: stockpiling counterfeit currency and banknotes

Transporting or stockpiling with a view to putting into

circulation any counterfeit currency or banknotes defined in article 645 (counterfeiting currency being legal tender) and article 646 (counterfeiting banknotes being legal tender) of this code shall be punishable by imprisonment from five to ten years.

Where the offence was committed by an organised criminal enterprise, it shall be punishable by imprisonment from ten to twenty years.

Article 649: counterfeiting currency and banknotes no longer being legal tender

The counterfeiting of currency or banknotes which are no longer legal tender shall be punishable by imprisonment from one to three years and a fine from two million to six million riels.

Article 650: unlawful possession of equipment for manufacturing currency and banknotes

The unauthorised possession of equipment or any other object specially-designed for the manufacture of currency or banknotes shall be punishable by imprisonment from five to ten years.

Article 651: recirculation of counterfeit currency and banknote

Any person who receives counterfeit currency or banknotes defined in article 645 (counterfeiting currency being legal tender) and article 646 (counterfeiting banknotes being legal tender) of this code and thinks they are authentic, puts them into circulation again knowing the same to be counterfeit shall be punishable by imprisonment from one day to six days and a fine from one hundred thousand to ten million riels.

Article 652: exemption from penalty

Any person who has attempted to commit one of the offences defined this section is exempted from penalty if, having informed the judicial or administrative authorities, he or she has made it possible to prevent the offence and to identify the other offenders.

Article 653: additional penalties (nature and duration)

The following additional penalties may be imposed in respect of the offences defined in this section:

(1) forfeiture of certain rights, either permanently or for a period not exceeding five years;

(2) prohibition from practising a profession in the practice of or in connection with which the offence was committed, either permanently or for a period not exceeding five years;

(3) local exclusion for a period not exceeding ten years for a felony and not exceeding five years for a misdemeanour;

(4) confiscation of any instruments, materials or items which were used or intended to be used to commit the offence;

(5) confiscation of the objects or funds which is the subject of the offence;

(6) confiscation of the proceeds or property arising out of the offence;

(7) confiscation of one or more vehicles belonging to the convicted person;

(8) prohibition from possessing or carrying any weapon,

explosive or ammunition, either permanently or for a period not exceeding five years;

(9) publication of sentencing decision for a period not exceeding two months;

(10) publication of sentencing decision in the print media;

(11) broadcasting of sentencing decision by any audio-visual communication for a period not exceeding eight days.

Chapter 2   Forging Documents of Public Authorities

Section 1   Forging Bonds and Postal Stamps

Article 654: forging bonds of the Kingdom of Cambodia

The forgery of bonds issued by the Kingdom of Cambodia shall be punishable by imprisonment from ten to twenty years.

Article 655: forging foreign bonds

The forgery of bonds issued by foreign states shall be punishable by imprisonment from five to ten years.

Article 656: use of forged bonds

The use of forged bonds shall be punishable by imprisonment from two to five years and a fine from four million to ten million riels.

Article 657: forging postal stamps

The forgery of postal stamps or other postal fiduciary products issued by the Kingdom of Cambodia shall be punishable by imprisonment from one to five years and a fine from five million to twenty million riels.

Article 658: use of forged postal stamps

The use of forged postal stamps or other postal fiduciary products shall be punishable by imprisonment from one month to one year and a fine from one million to five million riels.

Article 659: attempt

An attempt to commit the misdemeanours defined in this section shall be punishable by the same penalties.

Article 660: additional penalties (nature and duration)

The following additional penalties may be imposed in respect of the offences defined in this section:

(1) forfeiture of certain rights, either permanently or for a period not exceeding five years;

(2) prohibition from practising a profession in the practice of or in connection with which the offence was committed, either permanently or for a period not exceeding five years;

(3) local exclusion for a period not exceeding five years;

(4) confiscation of any instruments, materials or items which were used or intended to be used to commit the offence;

(5) confiscation of the objects or funds which is the subject of the offence;

(6) confiscation of the proceeds or property arising out of the offence;

(7) confiscation of one, or more vehicles belonging to the convicted person;

(8) prohibition from possessing or carrying any weapon, explosive or ammunition, either permanently or for a period not exceeding five years;

(9) publication of sentencing decision fora period not exceeding two months;

(10) publication of sentencing decision in the print media;

(11) broadcasting of sentencing decision by any audio-visual communication for a period not exceeding eight days.

Section 2 Forging Emblems of Authorities

Article 661: forging official seal of the Kingdom of Cambodia

The forgery of the official seal of the Kingdom of Cambodia shall be punishable by imprisonment from two to five years and a fine from four million to ten million riels.

Article 662: use of forged seal

The use of forged seal of the Kingdom of Cambodia shall be punishable by imprisonment from two to five years and a fine from four million to ten million riels.

Article 663: forging official letterhead

The forgery of official letterhead used by the public authorities shall be punishable by imprisonment from one month to one year and a fine from one hundred thousand to two million riels.

Article 664: use of forged official letterhead

The use of forged official letterhead used by public authorities shall be punishable by imprisonment from one month to one year and a fine from one hundred thousand to two million riels.

Article 665: manufacture of printed paper causing misapprehension

The manufacture, sale, distribution or use of printed papers which so closely resemble papers carrying a heading used by the public authorities, liable to cause misapprehension in the mind of the public shall be punishable by imprisonment from one month to one year and a fine from one hundred thousand to two million riels.

Article 666: attempt

An attempt to commit the misdemeanours defined in this section shall be punishable by the same penalties.

Article 667: additional penalties (nature and duration)

The following additional penalties may be imposed in respect of the offences defined in this section:

(1) forfeiture of certain rights, either permanently or for a period not exceeding five years;

(2) prohibition from practising a profession in the practice of or in connection with which the offence was committed, either permanently or for a period not exceeding five years;

(3) local exclusion for a period not exceeding ten years for a felony and not exceeding five years for a misdemeanour;

(4) confiscation of any instruments, materials or items which

were used or intended to be used to commit the offence;

(5) confiscation of the objects or funds which is the subject of the offence;

(6) confiscation of the proceeds or property arising out of the offence;

(7) confiscation of one or more vehicles belonging to the convicted person;

(8) prohibition from possessing or carrying any weapon, explosive or ammunition, either permanently or for a period not exceeding five years;

(9) publication of sentencing decision for a period not exceeding two months;

(10) publication of sentencing decision in the print media;

(11) broadcasting of sentencing decision by any audio-visual communication for a period not exceeding eight days.

BOOK 5

Transitional Provisions

BOOK 5
Transitional Provisions

Single Chapter Transitional Provisions

Article 668: application of other criminal legislation

Other criminal legislation and criminal provisions in force shall be applicable to the offences defined and punished under such legislation and provisions.

In the event of conflict between other criminal legislation and criminal provisions and the provisions of this code, the provisions of Book 1 (general provisions) of this code shall prevail.

The provision of paragraph 668 (2) above shall not be applicable to special criminal legislation.

Article 669: time limit for statute of limitations of sentence

The statute of limitations of a sentence for offences pronounced after the entry into force of the code of criminal procedure shall be governed by the provisions of this code.

Article 670: extension of application of Book 1 (general provisions) of this code

All criminal provisions shall be governed by the provisions of Book 1 (general provisions) of this code, except where otherwise provided for by other provisions.

BOOK 6

Final Provision

Single Chapter   Final Provision

Article 671: abrogation and effect of previous criminal provisions

The following criminal law and provisions shall have no effect from the date of the application of this code:

(1) all criminal provisions before 1992;

(2) criminal provisions of the provisions concerning judicial system, criminal law and criminal procedure applicable in the Kingdom of Cambodia during the transitional period adopted on 10 September 1992;

(3) the law on aggravating circumstances of felonies promulgated by *kram* No. 0102/004 dated 7 January 2002.

During the application of this code, only the incompatible parts of the provisions of other laws in force shall have no effect from the date of the application of this code.

However, the previous criminal provisions as defined in paragraphs 671(1) and 671(2) above shall continue to have effect on offences committed before the application of this code except for the provision in paragraph 668(2) (application of other criminal legislation) of this code.

Article 672: application of this code

Except for the general provisions of Book 1 (general provisions) of this code which shall immediately be applicable after the entry into force of this code, other provisions shall be applicable one year after its entry into force.

刑法典修正案

第一条　对 2009 年 11 月 30 日根据敕令第 NS/RD/1109/022 号发布的刑法典进行修正,增加第四百三十七条之一。

第四百三十七条之一　侮辱国王罪

侮辱系指通过演说、动作、文书、图画或者物件损坏他人名誉的行为。

犯侮辱国王罪,应当处以一年至五年监禁,并处二百万瑞尔至一千万瑞尔的罚金。

根据本法典第四十二条(法人的刑事责任),可以确定法人对侮辱国王罪承担刑事责任。

应当对法人处以一千万瑞尔至五千万瑞尔的罚金,在特定的犯罪被加重的情形下,并处下列附加刑中的一项或者多项:

(一)依照本法典第一百七十条(法人的解散和清算)予以解散;

(二)依照本法典第一百七十一条(置于司法监视)予以司法监视;

(三)依照本法典第一百七十二条(禁止活动的开展),禁止进行一项或者多项活动;

(四)依照本法典第一百七十六条(关闭场所)关闭场所;

（五）依照本法典第一百七十八条（没收物品的所有权、出售和销毁）和第一百七十九条（没收与第三方权利）没收用于或者打算用于实施罪行的任何工具、材料或者物品；

（六）依照本法典第一百七十八条（没收物品的所有权、出售和销毁）和第一百七十九条（没收与第三方权利）没收涉及犯罪的物品或者资金；

（七）依照本法典第一百七十八条（没收物品的所有权、出售和销毁）和第一百七十九条（没收与第三方权利）没收犯罪产生的收益或者财产；

（八）依照本法典第一百八十条（公布判决），公布量刑结果；

（九）依照本法典第一百八十一条（以视听传媒播放判决），以印刷媒体公布量刑结果，或者以任何视听传媒播放量刑结果。

第二条 本修正案即日公布。

代理国家元首 赛冲亲王
2018 年 2 月 27 日金边